The Fretboard

VOLUME 1
Scales, Modes, & Arpeggios

By David DeLoach

www.MasterGuitarists.com

This book is available in eBook format.
Also, a video lesson of the material in this book
will be available in 2017
at
www.MasterGuitarists.com
or at
amazon.com

Front cover drawing by Nashville artist *Michael Lax*
freakily.net

Back cover drawing by guitarist Jay Pilkington
(Jay has been unable to see since the mid-1970s)
JayPilkington.com

Final page artwork by Karin Dreyer
KarinDreyerCreative.com

Art direction and design by Wendell McGuirk
Edited by Stephanie McGuirk
thecreativeperch.com

Music proof reading by Lindsey Miller
allmusic.com/artist/lindsey-miller-MN0003448649

COPYRIGHT © 2016 BY DAVID DELOACH
All Rights Reserved. No part of this publication may be reproduced or distributed in any form or by any means, or stored in a database or retrieval system, without the prior written permission by the copyright owner.

ISBN 978-0-692-80186-4

Dedicated to Tina.
On our first date in 1982 a band asked me to sit in for a song.
We played "Listen to the Music" by The Doobie Brothers.

*"Ohhhh, listen to the music,
Ohhhh, listen to the music,
Ohhhh, listen to the music,
all the time...."*

And thus our lives have been.

Acknowledgements

Many thanks to the amazing Jack Petersen who opened the door which allowed me to experience unlimited fretboard freedom. Simultaneously intimidating and inspiring, Jack has to be one of the best guitar teachers to have ever walked this planet.

Much gratitude to Dan Haerle and Rich Matteson for not only teaching me, but for the example of how to undertake a journey which has no end.

Mike Harris, Kim Platko, Jim Wells, and Steve Kaufman, although you may not remember me, I certainly remember you and the great music you taught me.

I have learned something from literally every musician I have played with or taught. For this I remain truly grateful and humbled.

Introduction

Greetings fellow guitarists. Welcome to my latest effort to help guitarists enjoy their instrument to the utmost.

This is actually the second book I've written on this topic. My first book, *Play Skillfully*, was completed in 2007. At 386 pages, it was a handful. Yet as has been wisely said, "Inside every big book is a little book trying to get out." It is in that spirit which I have compiled this smaller book. While it covers the same content which my previous book covered (in approximately half the pages of the original book), I have presented the material in a new format and approach which hopefully will provide a more efficient path to finding true freedom of expression on the guitar.

Why on earth have I put the time and effort into writing first *Play Skillfully*, and now *The Fretboard, Volume 1*. I realize there is only a small percentage of guitarists with DNA which drives them to master their instruments to the level presented in these pages. If I were seeking sales and money, I would have written a beginner's book, or taught "50 Classic Rock Solos."

In all honesty, I have written the book I wish someone would have written for me all those decades ago when I was a young guitarist practicing six to eight hours a day, seven days a week, and gigging five or six nights a week. Like me, something in you compels you to learn and master every nook and cranny of the fretboard. It is for those kindred spirits that I have taken the time to create this book.

It is my hope that in the crazy mixed up world, that the music you will find and create will be used to make this world a better place. That you will experience those Spiritual encounters when the music flowing through you moves you deeply—as well as those who are listening to the sounds you create.

Table of Contents

THE PURPOSE OF THIS BOOK 2
HOW TO USE THIS BOOK 3
THE GOAL: COMPLETE FRETBOARD FREEDOM 6
DESCRIPTION OF NOTATION USED 7
PURPOSE OF THIS BOOK 7
THE 6 FRET CHROMATIC CONCEPT 8

SECTION 1 - SPELLING 9
    Why Are There 15 Major Keys 11
    Why Are There 15 Minor Keys 12
    Major, Natural Minor, Melodic Minor, and Harmonic Minor Relationships 13

PART 1 – THE MODES OF THE MAJOR SCALES 15
    Two Octave Major Scale Fingerings and Spellings 16
    Modes of the Major Scale Explained 22
    Mode 1: Ionian 24
    Mode 2: Dorian 26
    Mode 3: Phrygian 28
    Mode 4: Lydian 30
    Mode 5: Mixolydian 32
    Mode 6: Aeolian 34
    Mode 7: Locrian 36

PART 2 – THE MODES OF THE MELODIC MINOR SCALES 39
    Two Octave Major Scale Fingerings and Spellings 40
    Modes of the Melodic Minor Scale Explained 46
    Mode 1: Ionian ♭3 48
    Mode 2: Dorian ♭2 50
    Mode 3: Lydian Augmented 52
    Mode 4: Lydian Dominant 54
    Mode 5: Mixolydian ♭6 56
    Mode 6: Aeolian ♭5 58
    Mode 7: Super Locrian 60

PART 3 – THE MODES OF THE HARMONIC MINOR SCALES 63
    Two Octave Harmonic Minor Scale Fingerings and Spellings 64
    Modes of the Harmonic Minor Scale Explained 70
    Mode 1: Aeolian #7 72
    Mode 2: Locrian #6 74
    Mode 3: Ionian #5 76
    Mode 4: Dorian #4 78
    Mode 5: Phrygian Dominant 80
    Mode 6: Lydian #2 82
    Mode 7: Super Locrian ♭7 84

PART 4 – THE SYMMETRIC AND PENTATONIC SCALES 87
The Half Step/Whole Step Diminished Scale 88
The Whole Step/Half Step Diminished Scale 90
The Whole Tone Scale 92
The Major Pentatonic Scale 94
The Minor Pentatonic Scale 96

PART 5 – THE ARPEGGIOS 99
Diatonic 7th Chords of the Major Scales 100
Diatonic 6th Chords of the Major Scales 101
Diatonic 7th Chords of the Melodic Minor Scales 102
Diatonic 7th Chords of the Harmonic Minor Scales 103
Major 7th Arpeggios 104
Major 6th Arpeggios 106
Dominant 7th Arpeggios 108
Dominant 7th (♭5) Arpeggios 110
Dominant 7th (#5) Arpeggios 112
Minor 7th Arpeggios 114
Minor 7th (♭5) Arpeggios 116
Minor 6th Arpeggios 118
Minor ♭6th Arpeggios 120
Minor ♭6th (♭5) Arpeggios 122
Minor (Major 7th) Arpeggios 124
Major 7th (#5) Arpeggios 126
Diminished 7th Arpeggios 128
Review of the Arpeggios 130

SECTION 2 – LEARNING THE FINGERINGS 133

PART 6 – FINGERINGS FOR THE MODES OF THE MAJOR SCALES 136
Mode 1: Ionian 137
Mode 2: Dorian 138
Mode 3: Phrygian 139
Mode 4: Lydian 140
Mode 5: Mixolydian 141
Mode 6: Aeolian 142
Mode 7: Locrian 143

PART 7 – FINGERINGS FOR THE MELODIC MINOR SCALES 144
Mode 1: Ionian ♭3 145
Mode 2: Dorian ♭2 146
Mode 3: Lydian Augmented 147
Mode 4: Lydian Dominant 148
Mode 5: Mixolydian ♭6 149
Mode 6: Aeolian ♭5 150
Mode 7: Super Locrian/Altered Scale 151

PART 8 – FINGERINGS FOR THE HARMONIC MINOR SCALES ... 152
- Mode 1: Aeolian #7 ... 153
- Mode 2: Locrian #6 ... 154
- Mode 3: Ionian #5 ... 155
- Mode 4: Dorian #4 ... 156
- Mode 5: Phrygian Dominant ... 157
- Mode 6: Lydian #2 ... 158
- Mode 7: Super Locrian ♭♭7 ... 159

PART 9 – FINGERINGS FOR THE SYMMETRIC AND PENTATONIC SCALES ... 160
- The Half Step/Whole Step Diminished Scale ... 161
- The Whole Step/Half Step Diminished Scale ... 162
- The Whole Tone Scale ... 163
- The Major Pentatonic Scale ... 164
- The Minor Pentatonic Scale ... 165

PART 10 – FINGERINGS FOR THE ARPEGGIOS ... 166
- Major 7th Arpeggios ... 167
- Major 6th Arpeggios ... 168
- Dominant 7th Arpeggios ... 169
- Dominant 7th (♭5) Arpeggios ... 170
- Dominant 7th (#5) Arpeggios ... 171
- Minor 7th Arpeggios ... 172
- Minor 7th (♭5) Arpeggios ... 173
- Minor 6th Arpeggios ... 174
- Minor ♭6th Arpeggios ... 175
- Minor ♭6th(♭5) Arpeggios ... 176
- Minor (Major 7th) Arpeggios ... 177
- Major 7th (#5) Arpeggios ... 178
- Diminished 7th Arpeggios ... 179

SECTION 3 – FORGETTING THE FINGERINGS ... 180

PART 11 – BLENDING THE 12 PATTERNS INTO ONE COMPREHENSIVE ROADMAP ... 181
- Method for Patterns Which Begin With a Whole Step Interval ... 182
- Example for Patterns Which Begin With a Whole Step Interval ... 183
- Example for Patterns With an Arpeggio ... 186
- Method for Patterns Which Begin With a Half Step Interval ... 188
- Example for Patterns Which Begin With a Half Step Interval ... 189
- 3 Octave Scales ... 193
- 3 Octave Major Arpeggios ... 197
- 3 Octave Minor Arpeggios ... 200

APPENDIX ... 203
- Notes on the Fretboard ... 204
- Note on Each String ... 205
- Diatonic 7th Chords of the Major Scales ... 206
- Diatonic 6th Chords of the Major Scales ... 210
- Diatonic 7th Chords of the Melodic Minor Scales ... 214
- Diatonic 7th Chords of the Harmonic Minor Scales ... 218

Overview of this Book

SECTION 1

Learning to SPELL the Scales, Modes, and Arpeggios

SECTION 2

Learning the 12 FINGERINGS for each Scale, Mode, and Arpeggio

SECTION 3

FORGETTING the 12 Fingerings for Each Scale, Mode, and Arpeggio By Blending Them Into a Single Comprehensive Map of the Fretboard

The Purpose of This Book

This book was written to help you explore, navigate, and master every part of the fretboard—in every key. It's as simple as that.

Think of that area of the fretboard which currently feels a bit like "No Man's Land" where you have uncertainty about what is there. For me, it was the area on the 5th, 4th, and 3rd strings between the 8th and 11th frets. That area just stumped me for the longest time.

Now think of that "No Man's Land" area of the fretboard in your least favorite keys. I was bound to stumble if I found myself on those frets and strings, and therefore I tended to stay in the safer parts of the fingerboard.

Yet, after mastering the contents of this book, there are no more mysterious sections of the fingerboard. It is literally as if someone flips on a switch and all the notes in a G7 or a Bdim7, or the 7th mode of the Melodic Minor light up *all over the neck*. I'm able to SEE the notes, the patterns, the scales, and the arpeggios over the entire neck—from the open strings all the way up to the highest fret on every string.

The resulting freedom from this breakthrough has helped me immensely in arranging for guitar, soloing/improvising, and connecting my hands and ears into a guitar playing team.

This book focuses on learning the fretboard—inside out, upside down, front to back, east to west, north to south, and all points in between.

Take what you learn here and apply to SONGS you are learning, writing, or arranging. Use the knowledge you gain here to craft creative and meaningful solos.

How to Use This Book

This book is meant to supplement your other musical studies. Don't allow yourself to become a guitarist who focuses primarily on scales and arpeggios. Remember, the ultimate goal is to play SONGS!

While you may focus for a time exclusively on learning the fretboard, I would suggest you limit the time spent on this material to no more than 20% of your practice time. The other 80% of your time should be spent learning tunes, transcribing music that moves you, ear training, writing, arranging, listening, and jamming with other musicians and singers.

This book can be used in two ways:

1. Undertake the journey to learn the entire contents of this book

2. Use the book as a reference, pulling it off the shelf now and then when you find yourself in a rut and need to explore some new ground

If your goal is to master the contents of this book as quickly as possible, I'd suggest the following approach:

DON'T TRY TO MEMORIZE THE ENTIRE BOOK IN A DAY.
Take your time and keep at it. If you think it will be easy, it will tend to be easy. If you think it will be hard, it will tend to be difficult.

Everything in this book is simple. There are just a thousand simple things. Just learn one at a time and eventually you will get it as you follow the path laid out on the next page.

Know Your Fretboard:
- Learn the notes on the neck of the guitar (pages 204-205)
- If it's not fast and automatic, that's OK, but at least know how to figure out what note is being played on any string and any fret

Learn the Major Scales:
- Learn to spell the 15 major keys (pages 16-21)
- Memorize the 12 patterns for the major scale (page 137)
- Learn how to tie the 12 patterns together (page 182-191) and practice covering the entire fretboard for one key each day (e.g. on Monday tie the 12 patterns together for D major, on Tuesday, do it for A, on Wednesday, do it for E, etc.)

Learn the Melodic Minor Scales:
- Learn to spell the 15 melodic minor scales (pages 40-45)
- Memorize the 12 patterns for the melodic minor scale (page 145)
- Learn how to tie the 12 patterns together (page 182) and practice covering the entire fretboard for one key each day (e.g. on Monday tie the 12 patterns together for D Melodic Minor, on Tuesday, do it for A, on Wednesday, do it for E, etc.)

Learn the Harmonic Minor Scales:
- Learn to spell the 15 harmonic minor scales (pages 64-69)
- Memorize the 12 patterns for the harmonic minor scale (page 153)
- Learn how to tie the 12 patterns together (see page 182) and practice covering the entire fretboard for one key each day (e.g. on Monday tie the 12 patterns together for D harmonic minor, on Tuesday, do it for A, on Wednesday, do it for E, etc.)

Once the major, melodic minor, and harmonic minor scales and their fingering patterns have been memorized, apply the same learning approach for each of the modes of these three scales.

Remember, learning the root scales and fingerings first will make learning the modes significantly easier.

Learn the Arpeggios:
- Learn which chords are nested in the scales & modes (pages 100-103)
- Learn to spell the arpeggios (pages 104-131)
- Memorize the 12 patterns for each arpeggio (pages 166-179)
- Learn how to tie the 12 patterns together (see page 182) and practice covering the entire fingerboard
- Repeat the above three steps for each arpeggio
- Play all the arpeggios built on a particular note (e.g. Cmaj7, Cm7, C6, Cdim7, etc.) each day (e.g. for Monday play all arpeggios built on D, on Tuesday, arpeggios built on A, and Wednesday, arpeggios built on E, etc.)

Learn the Symmetric Scales and Pentatonic Scales:
- Use the system described above to burn the symmetric and pentatonic scales into your hands, ears, and mind:
    - Whole Step/Half Step
    - Half Step/Whole Step
    - Whole Tone
    - Minor Pentatonic
    - Major Pentatonic

The Goal – Complete Fretboard Freedom

OK friends, the goal of this book is not to memorize 12 patterns for each scale, mode, and arpeggio. Those are just steps towards the real goal of complete fretboard freedom.

The target you should be shooting for is to be able to SEE all the notes in a G major scale, an E7 chord, or the 4th mode of the C harmonic minor illuminated over the entire neck. As you improvise, arrange, solo, you want to be able to see all the options laid out there on the fretboard which allow you to take your fingers to any area on the neck and play easily in that location.

This freedom, these infinite options, will birth creativity and originality in your music. It may seem daunting and complex at the outset, but remember anything will become easy if you immerse yourself in it long enough.

Imagine this....

The time has passed, the effort has been expended, and you've mastered navigating the fretboard. You have put in the effort that few have the hunger and drive to expend. You have dug a very, very deep well and have found some really pure water way down there. Drink up. Enjoy! Make some awesome music!

Description of Notation Used in This Book

In Section 2 of the book, fingering patterns are taught using block diagrams which show what finger would be used on each fret of each string.

An example using a fingering pattern of the harmonic minor scale is shown below.

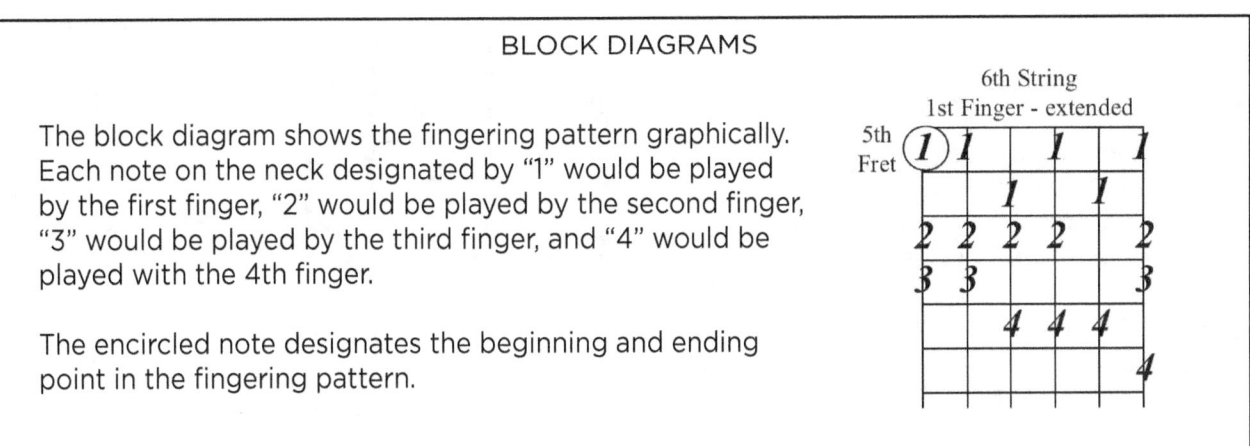

BLOCK DIAGRAMS

The block diagram shows the fingering pattern graphically. Each note on the neck designated by "1" would be played by the first finger, "2" would be played by the second finger, "3" would be played by the third finger, and "4" would be played with the 4th finger.

The encircled note designates the beginning and ending point in the fingering pattern.

The notation, tablature, and finger designations below show how this block diagram would be played.

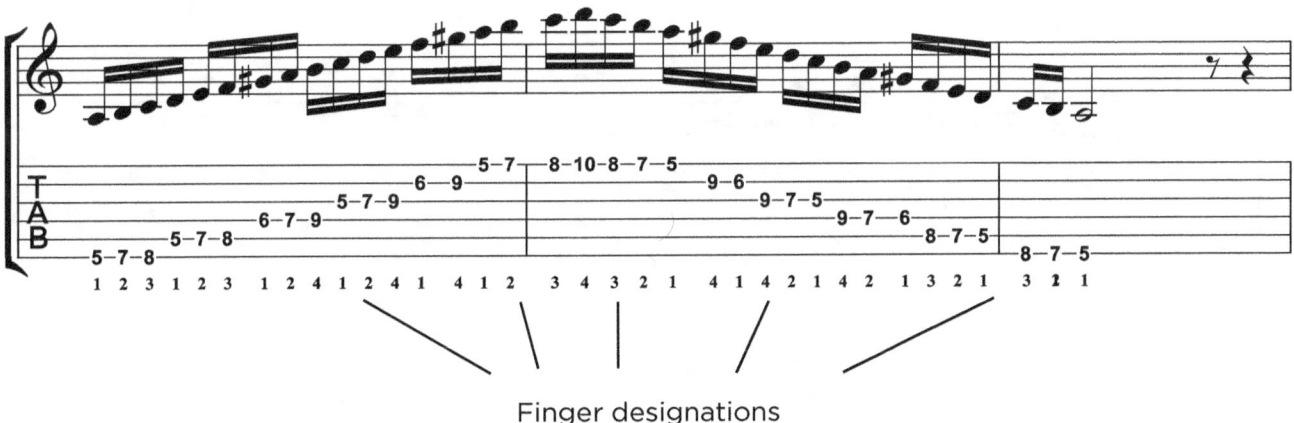

Finger designations

The 6 Fret Chromatic Concept

If you were to begin upon any fret of the 6th string, and play up 6 successive frets, then repeat that process on the same frets of the remaining 5 strings, you would play a little more than 2 octaves of the chromatic scale.

When playing the chromatic scale on 6 frets, use the index finger to fret the first 2 notes on the string and the little finger to fret the last 2 notes on the string.

By extending the 1st and 4th fingers, a chromatic scale can be played without shifting position on the neck of the guitar.

The fingering pattern shown at the right produces a chromatic scale which spans 2 octaves and an additional perfect 4th.

The TAB, notation, and fingerings are shown below.

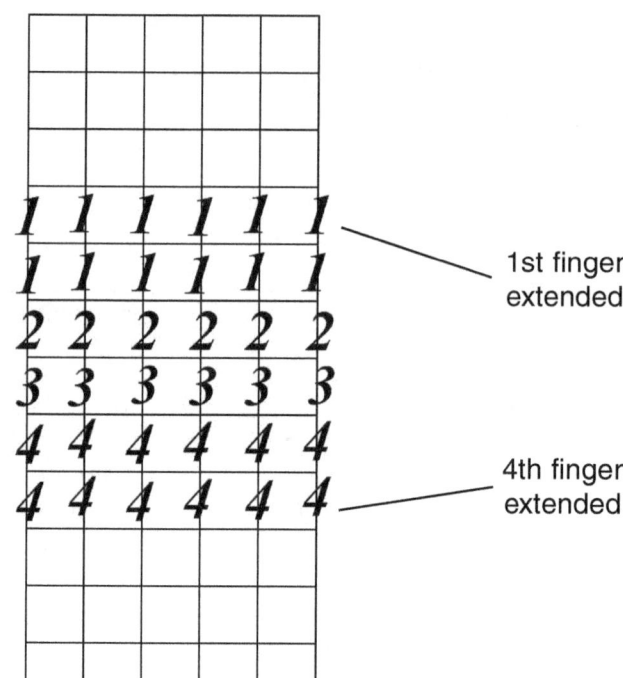

1st finger extended

4th finger extended

The value of this 2-plus octave chromatic fingering is that 2 octaves of every possible scale, mode, and arpeggio—in any key—are nested within this chromatic fingering—no matter what position the chromatic fingering is played on the neck! ★

The trick is to find all those 2 octave fingerings within the chromatic scale. The majority of what follows in this book shows how to extract hundreds of scale, mode, and arpeggio fingerings from the chromatic pattern shown above.

SECTION 1
Spelling

This section of the book is a dictionary which will assist you in learning how to spell the scales and the modes and arpeggios which are nested within those scales.

Learn to spell the scales first, THEN the modes and arpeggios—this will make learning to spell the modes and arpeggios much easier.

Why Are There 15 Major Keys

There are seven natural notes: A, B, C, D, E, F, and G. The keys are created by sharping or flatting certain natural notes.

C major has no sharped or flatted notes. G major has one note sharped, D major has two, etc., until C# has all seven notes sharped. At this point no additional sharp keys are possible (for example there is no key of A# major). F major has one note flatted, B♭ major has two, etc., until C♭ has all seven notes flatted. At this point no additional flat keys are possible.
See the 15 major scales below.

Why Are There 15 Minor Keys

A minor has no sharped or flatted notes. E minor has one note sharped, B minor has two, etc., until A# minor has all 7 notes sharped. At this point no additional sharp keys are possible (for example there is no key of E# minor). D minor has 1 note flatted, G minor has two, etc., until A♭ has all 7 notes flatted. At this point no additional flat keys are possible.

These are the 15 "natural minor" keys.

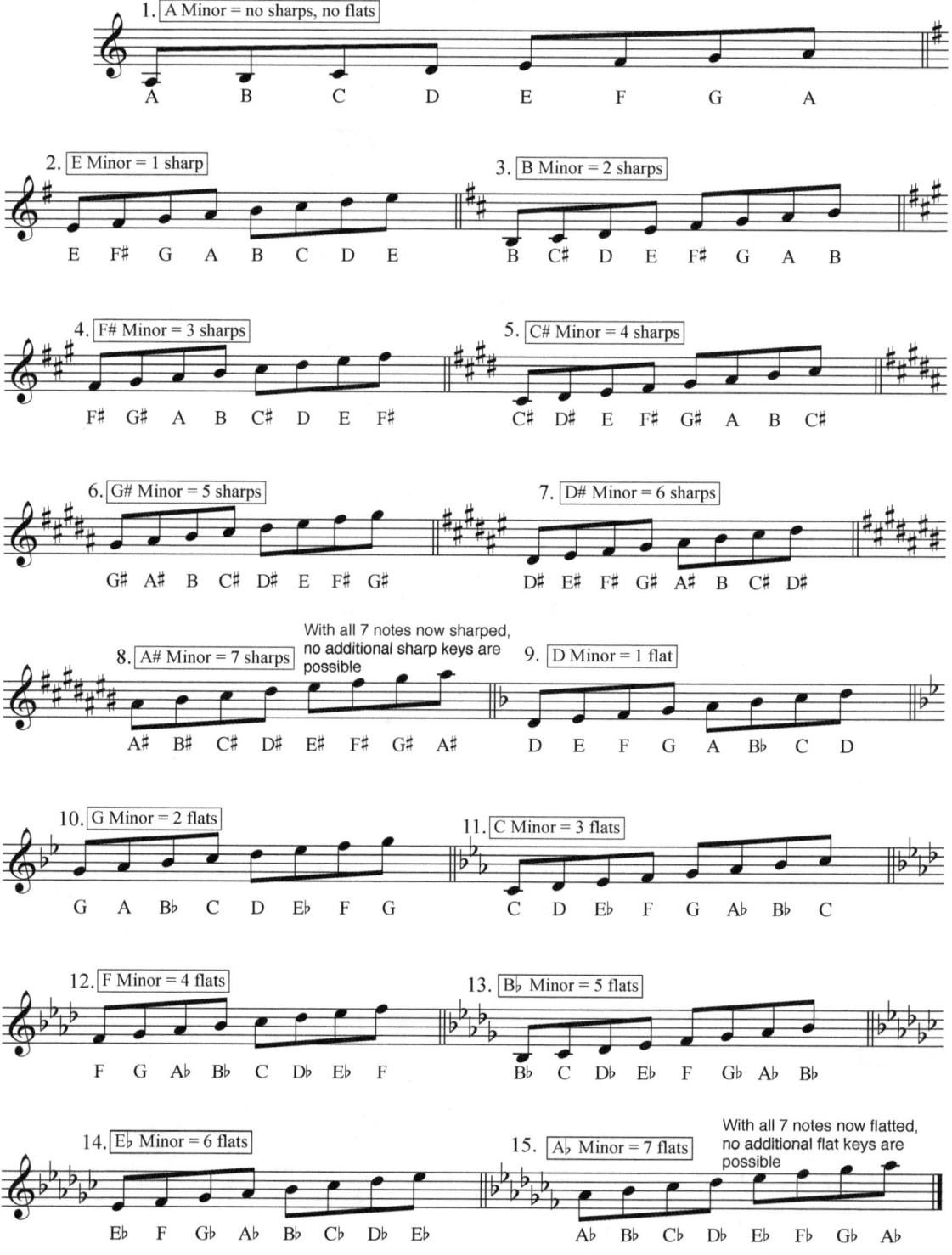

Scale Relationships

The relationship between the major scale, the natural minor scale, the melodic minor scale, and the harmonic minor scales

The 6th mode of the major scale is the aeolian mode; it can be called the natural minor scale (A aeolian = A natural minor).

If the 6th and 7th notes of the natural minor are sharped, the melodic minor scale is created.

If the 7th note of the natural minor is sharped, the harmonic minor scale is created.

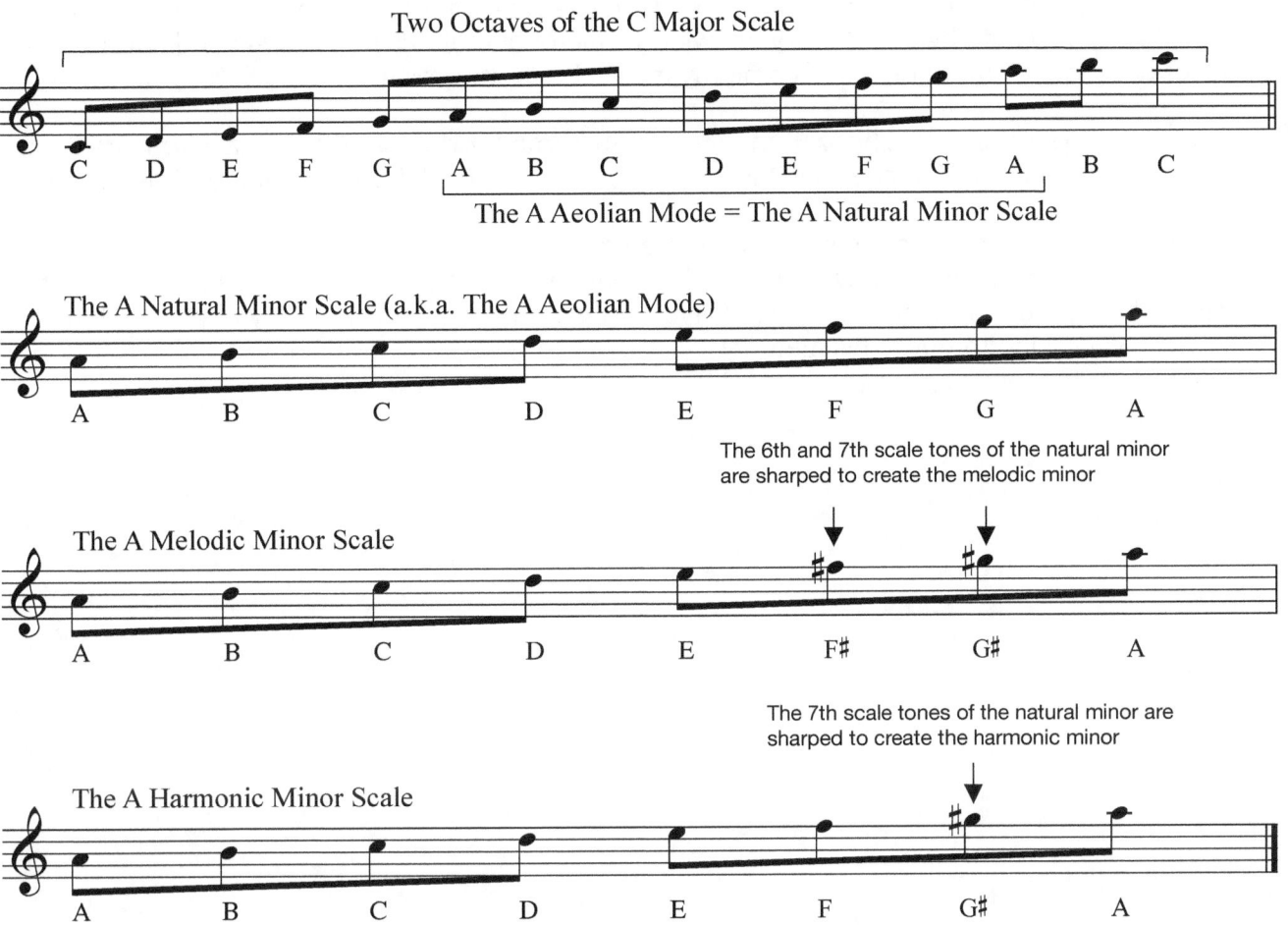

NOTE: In classical music theory, the melodic minor scale is played as shown above when ascending, but played as a natural minor scale when descending. In jazz music theory, the melodic minor scale is played ascending and descending.

Studying vs. Performing

This book contains a lot of material. Do not let that intimidate you. Even if you just learn a little bit at a time, every small advancement will have a good return.

There are two different states I tend to be in when I have a guitar in my hands: studying (practicing) or performing.

When studying, I spend time and energy learning music theory, learning to spell and play scales and chords, licks and songs. I am focused on mental academic thought processes such as memorization, how to apply some piece of music theory to a solo or arrangement, etc.

When performing, I tend to turn my brain off and just play from my heart. I try to play only those things which have become so easy that they require almost no thought at all. Material that I have to "remember" is just dry knowledge. Material that has become second nature and no longer requires thought has become my musical gift—my voice.

While working through this book, it may take some time for the material to transfer from being difficult or complex, to being easy. But it will happen over time! Just keep at it and persevere.

Try spending 30 minutes or an hour working on material in this book, and then go back and solo over a song that you know well—playing from your heart and not your head. Just play the things that come easy to you. You are likely to see some enhanced creativity in your soloing as a result of working through this material.

PART 1
The Modes of the Major Scales

Pages 16-21 spell the 15 major scales and provide 15 different finger patterns for playing 2 octaves of a major scale. (NOTE: Obviously the finger patterns are interchangeable between keys. For example the fingering pattern provided for C major can be used for D major by moving the pattern up 2 frets.)

Page 22 provides an overview of the modes of the major scale, how they are constructed, and the chord generally associated with the modes of the major scale.

Pages 24-37 spell the modes of the 15 major scales in each key.

To introduce the major scales, they are spelled here, and various 2 octave fingerings (which can be used for any key) are provided in the following six pages.

2 Octave Major Scales

C Major

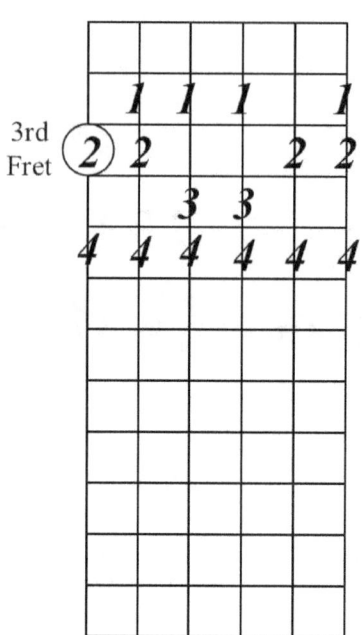

G Major

D Major

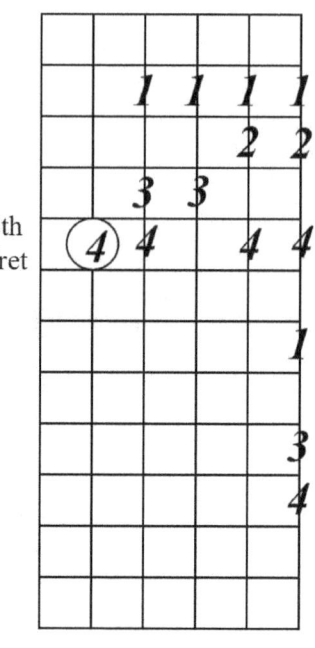

A Major

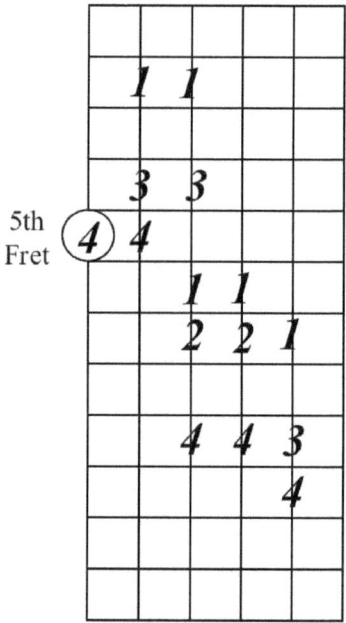

E Major

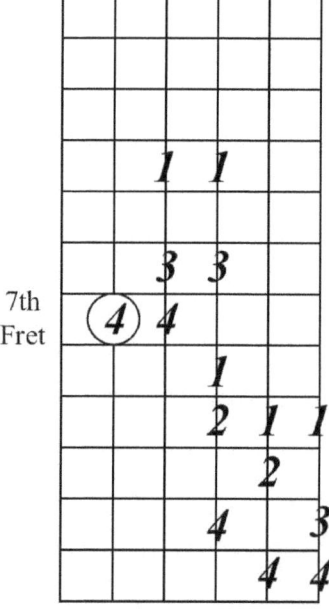

The 15 Major Scales Presented With 15 Fingerings

2 Octave Major Scales

B Major
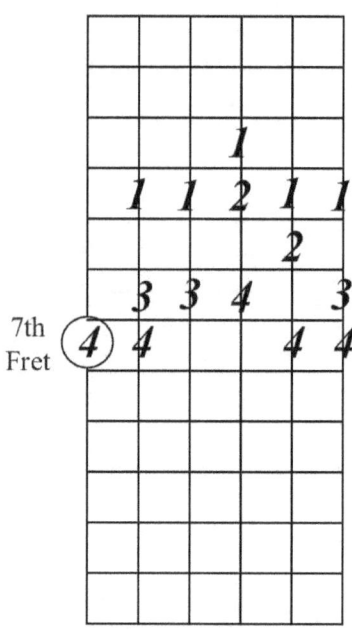

F# Major
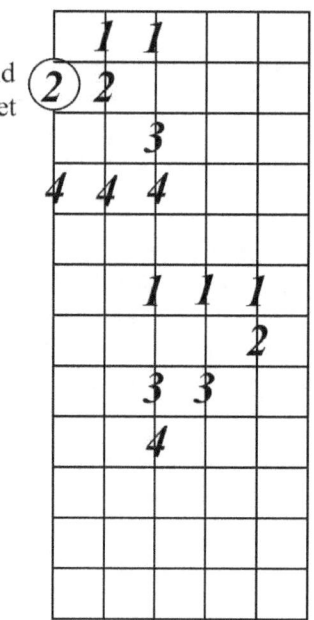

C# Major
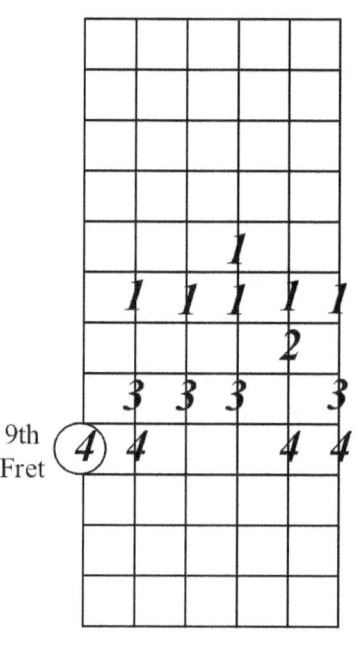

F Major
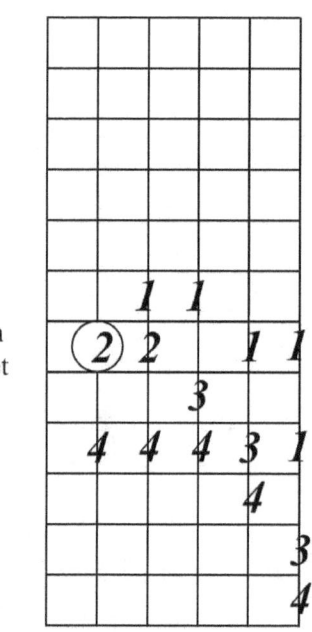

B♭ Major
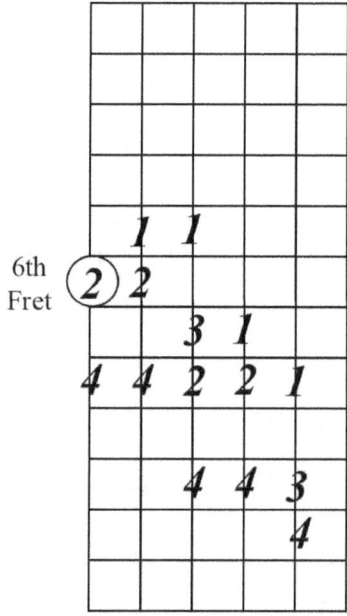

2 Octave Major Scales

E♭ Major
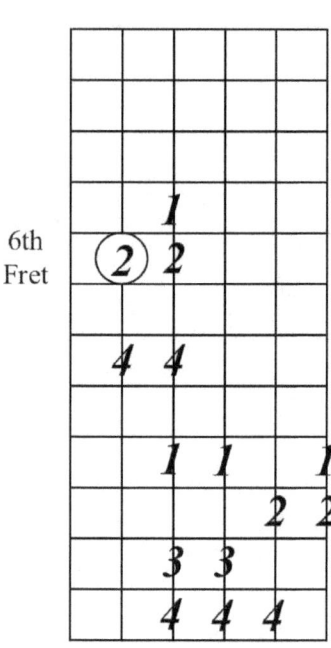

A♭ Major
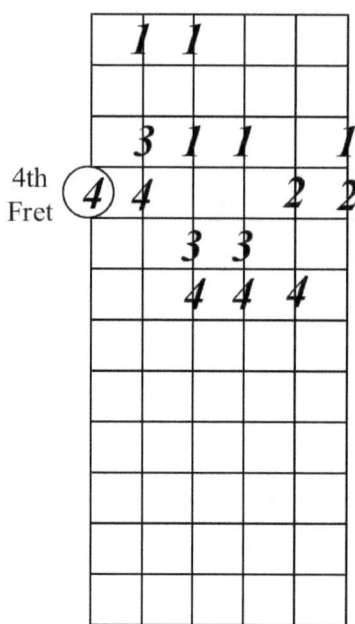

D♭ Major
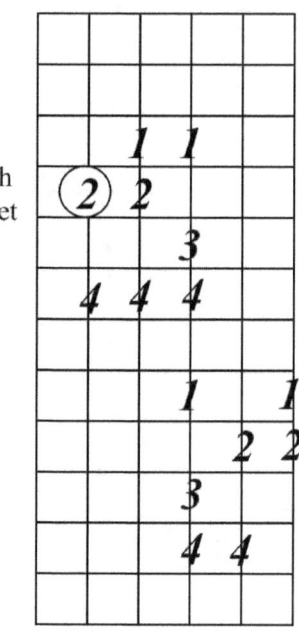

G♭ Major
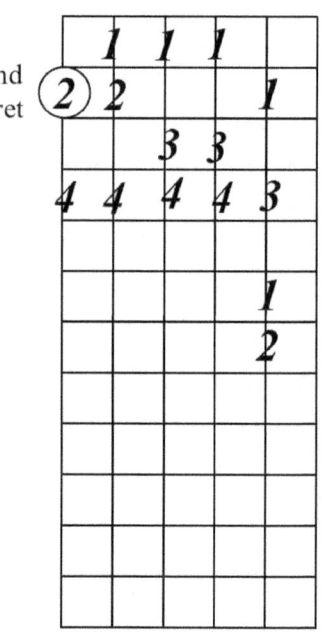

C♭ Major
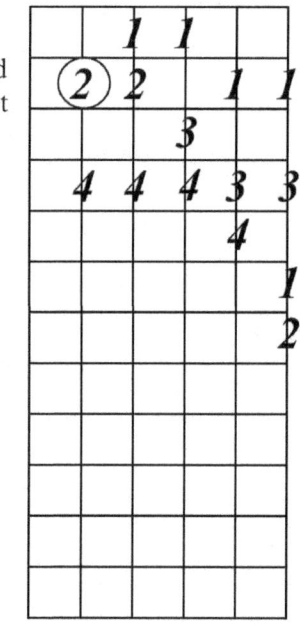

Modes of the Major Scale

The concept of modes is not complex. Once you have memorized a major scale, identifying the modes of the major scale is simply a matter of starting the scale at each of the seven scale notes.

For example, if you take the G major scale and play it starting at the 1st scale degree (G) and go up the scale 1 octave, you have just played the 1st mode of the major scale. If you take the G major scale and play it starting at the 2nd scale degree (A) and go up the scale 1 octave, you have just played the 2nd mode of the major scale. Continuing this concept with each of the 7 scale degrees of the major scale will result in the 7 modes of the major scale.

G Major Scale

Using the G major scale as an example, the 7 modes of the major scale are presented below. Note that the 1st mode is identical to the major scale.

Modes of the Major Scales

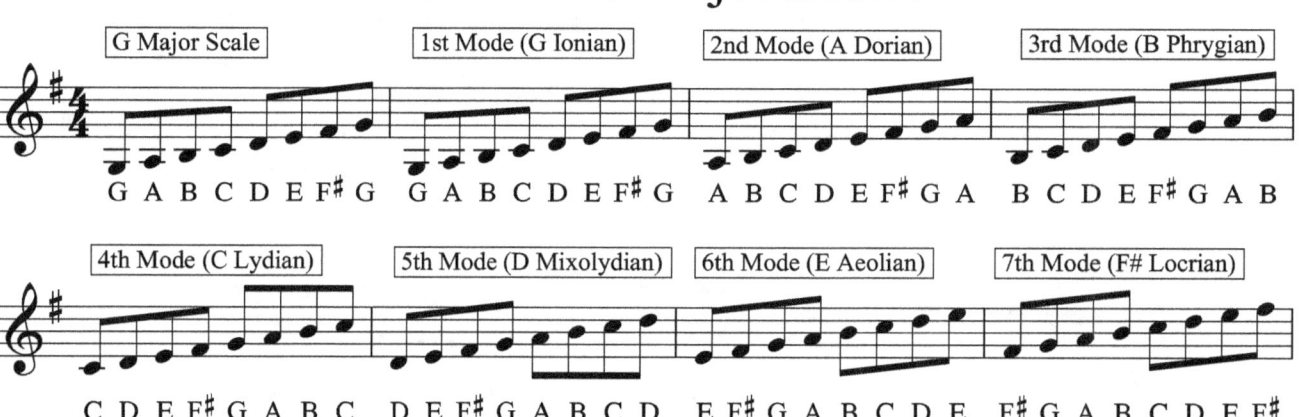

The 7 modes of the major scale correspond to the diatonic chords of the major scale. In other words, the modes can be used for improvisation over the diatonic chords. While the study of mode/chord relationships is a beneficial study, it should be viewed only as one of the many musical tools available to the improvising musician. However, building a solid knowledge base of mode/scale relationships on the guitar fretboard will reap an abundance of melodic ideas and fingering options to a guitarist who enjoys improvisation—in any style of music.

Major Scale Mode/Chord Relationships	4th mode: Major chords (w/ sharp 11th)
1st mode: Major chords	5th mode: Dominant chords
2nd mode: Minor chords (w/ natural 6th/13th)	6th mode: Minor chords (w/ flatted 6th/13th)
3rd mode: Minor chords (w/ flatted 6th/13th)	7th mode: Minor 7♭5 chords (half-diminished)

The following pages spell the major scales, and the modes nested within the major scales.

On the first row of each mode, the intervals between the notes of the mode are indicated by the following symbols found below the staff:

m2 = minor second interval

M2 = major second interval

m3 = minor third interval

M3 = major third interval

The notes making up each mode are bracketed above the staff, and suggested chords to use with each mode are shown above the brackets as seen in the example below.

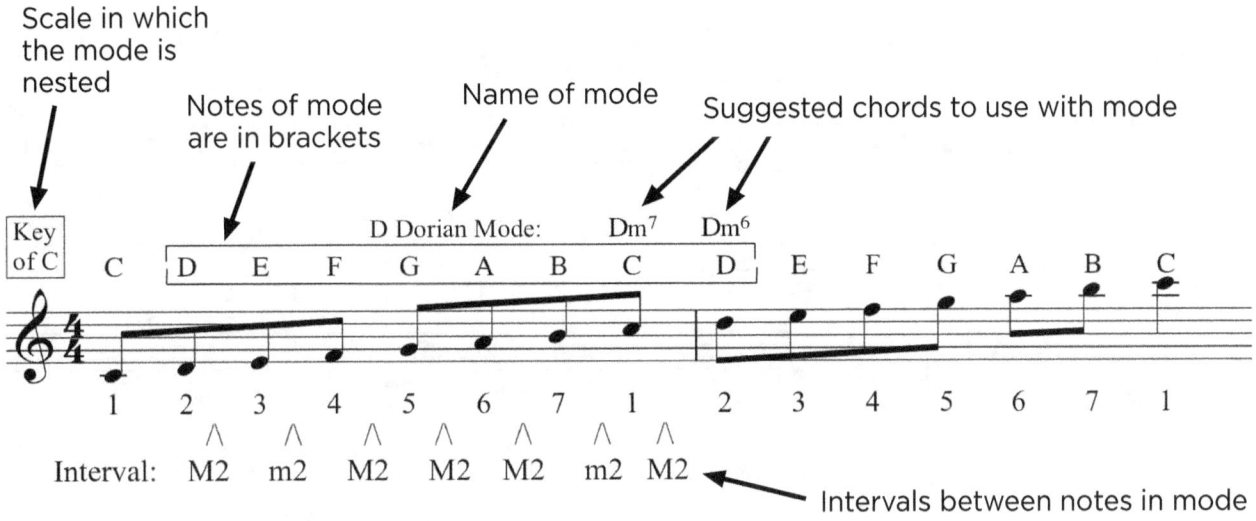

23

The 1st/ "Ionian" Mode of the Major Scale

The ionian mode basically is just another name for the major scale. C ionian = C major Scale. But now you can say "ionian," and sound like Dr. Technical on those old sci–fi movies.

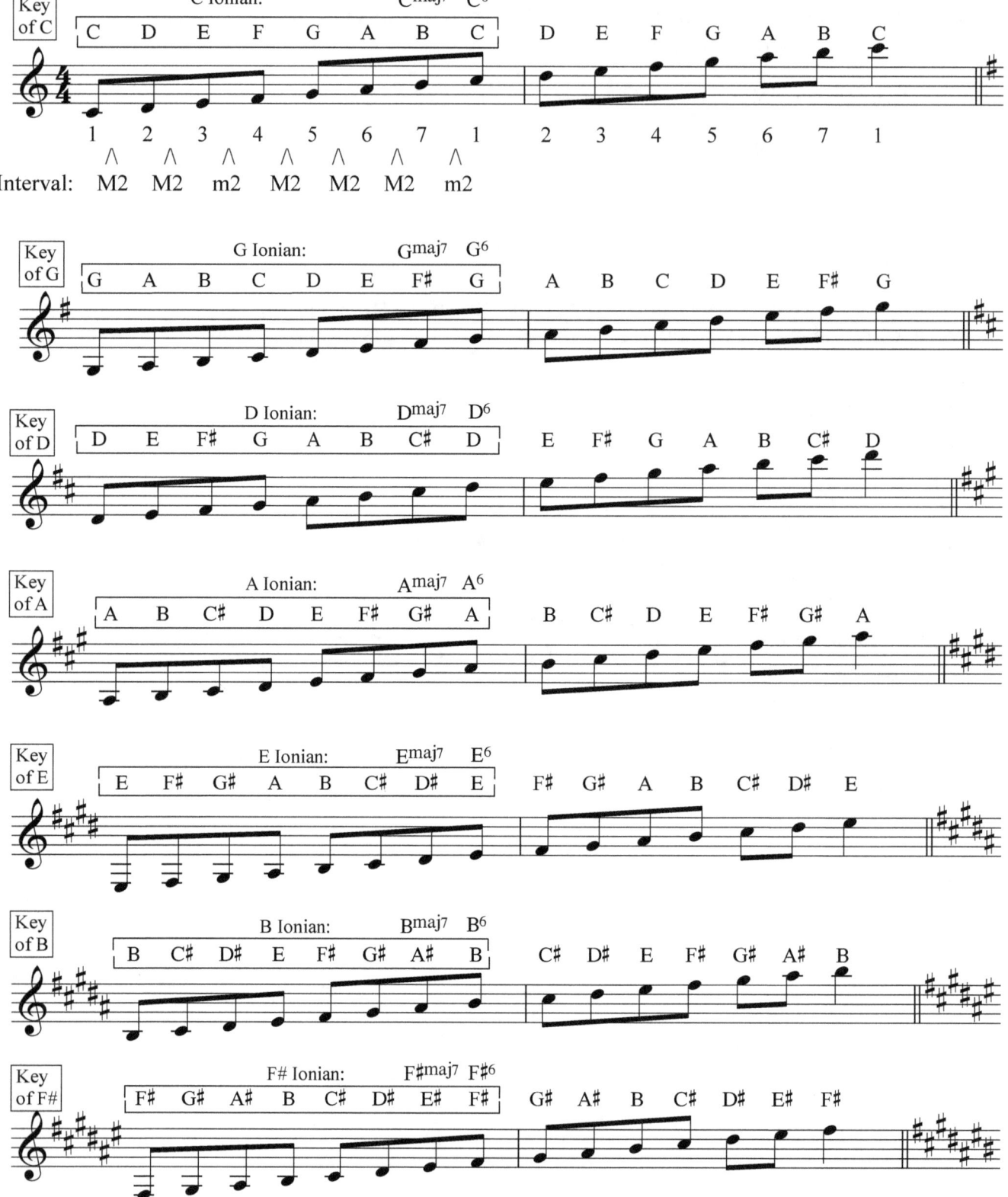

(See page 137 for fingering patterns for the ionian mode)

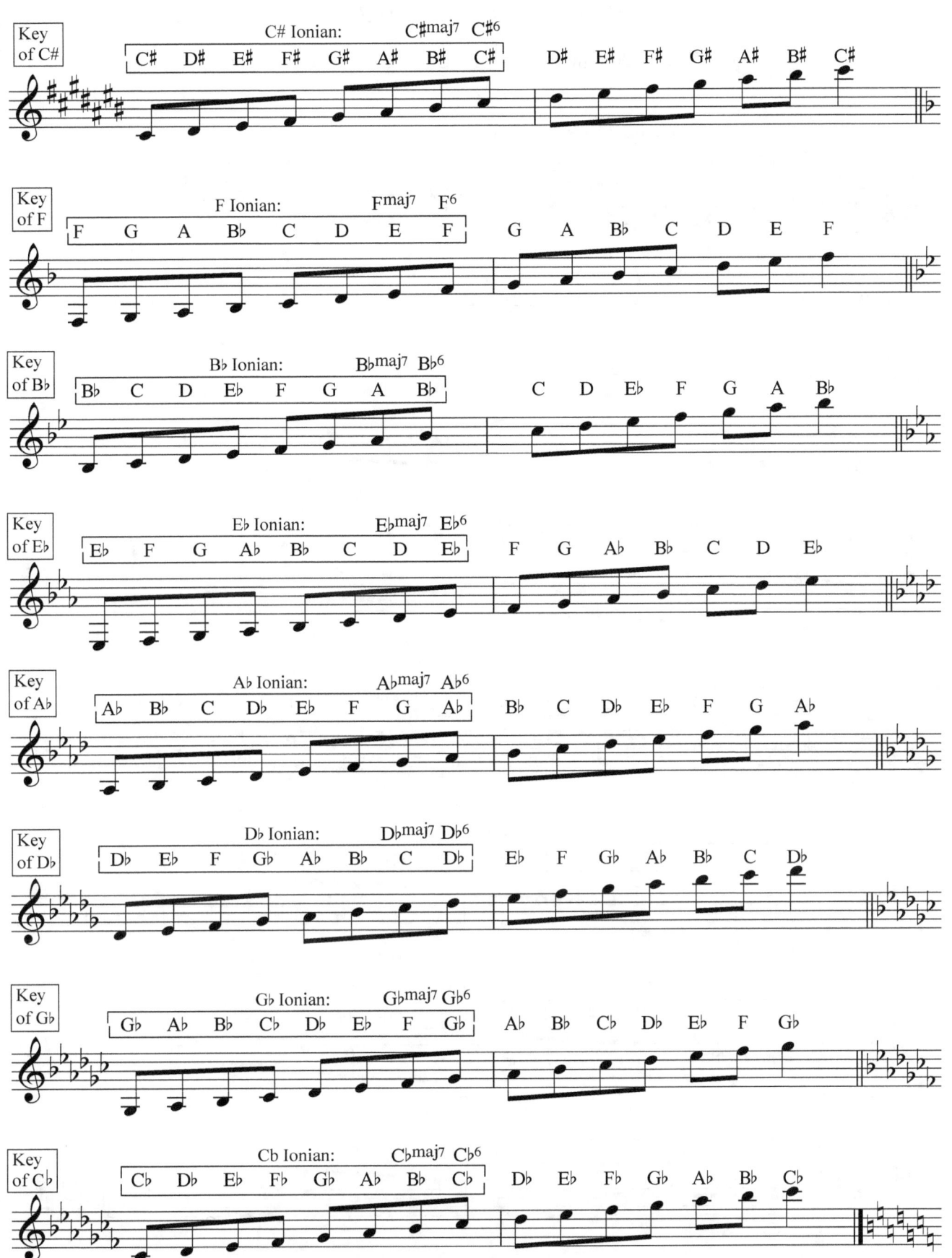

(See page 137 for fingering patterns for the ionian mode)

The 2nd/ "Dorian" Mode of the Major Scale

Many Celtic fiddle tunes are written based on the dorian mode.

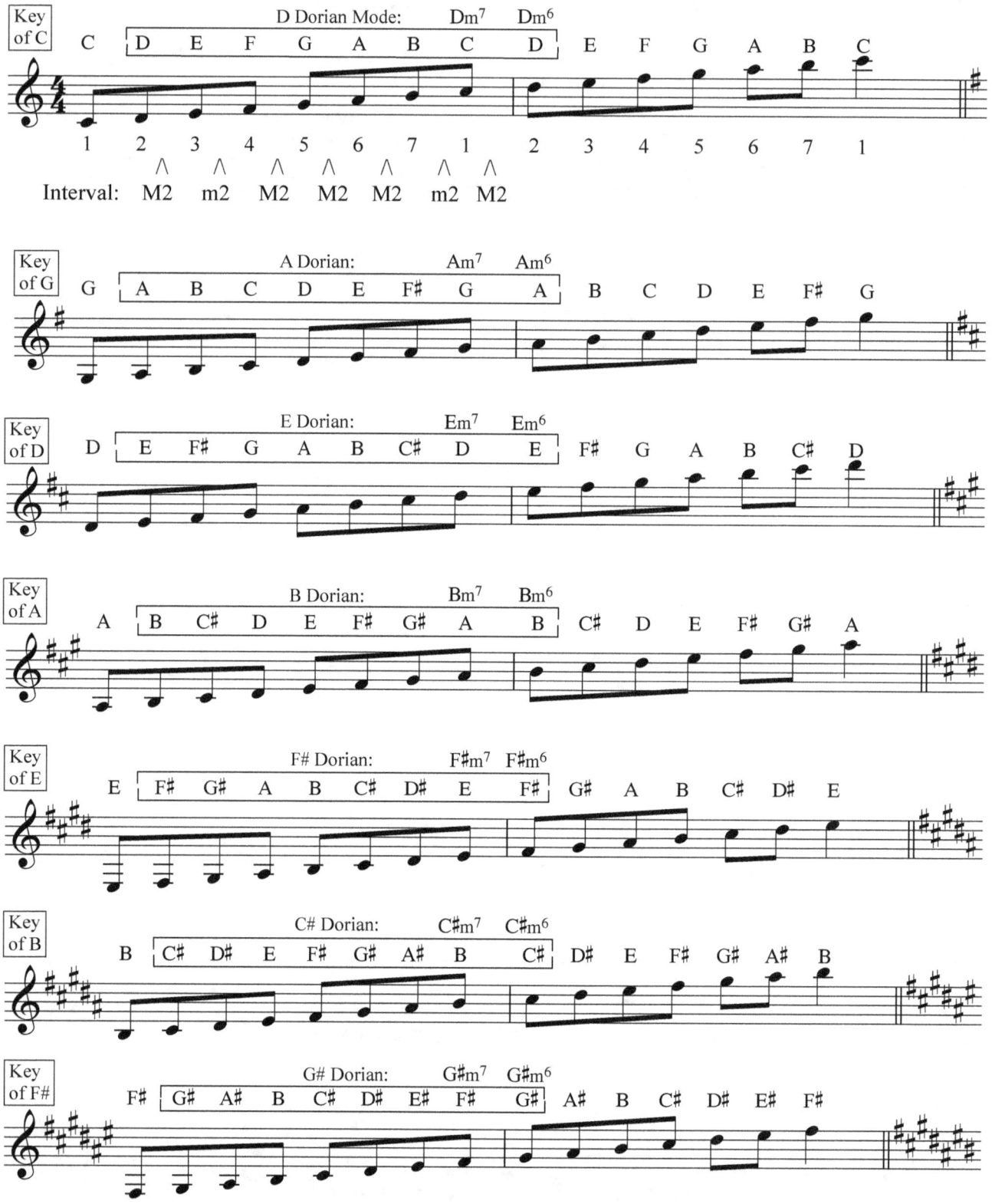

(See page 138 for fingering patterns for the dorian mode)

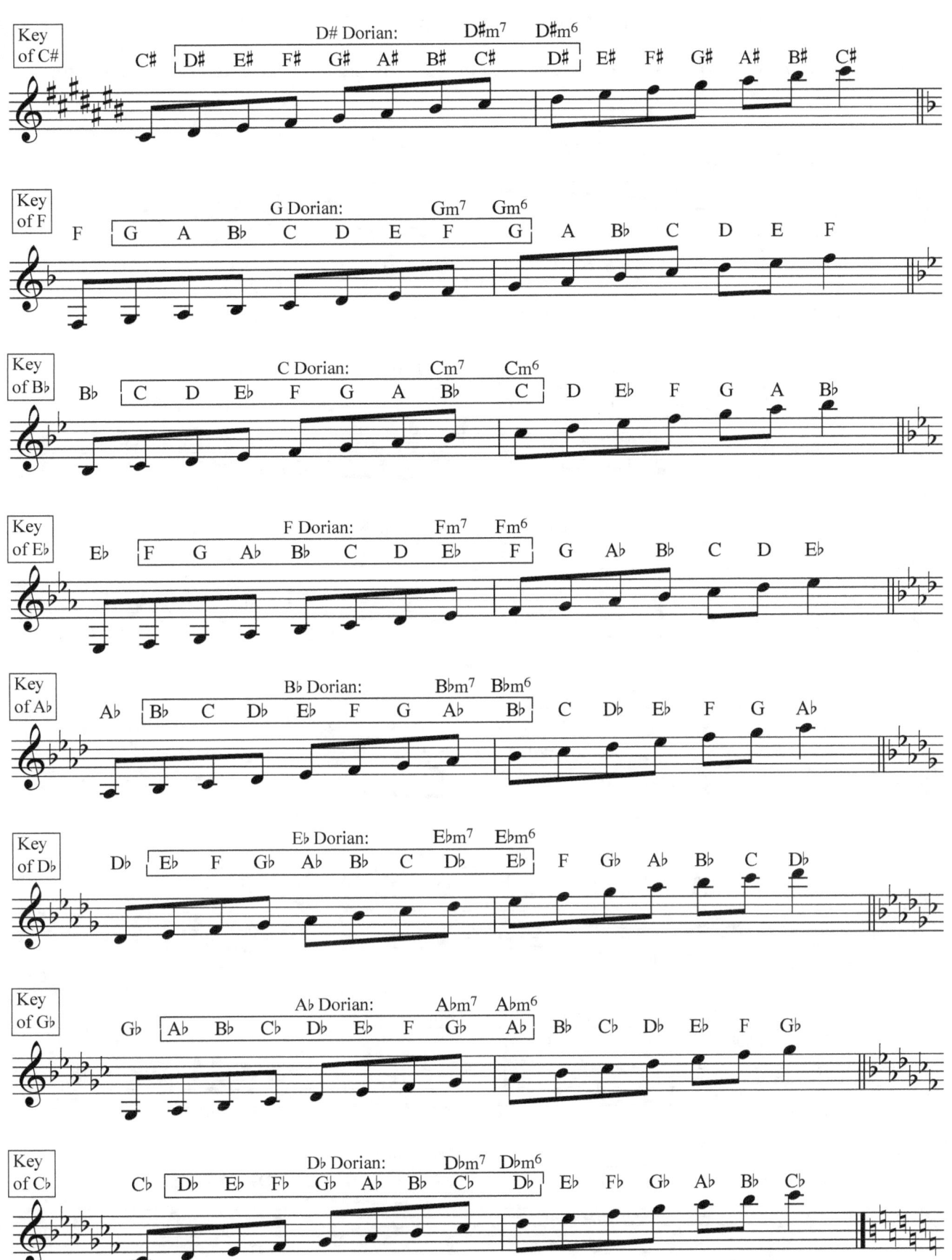

(See page 138 for fingering patterns for the dorian mode)

The 3rd/ "Phrygian" Mode of the Major Scale

Try playing E phrygian over Am - G - F, and then the A harmonic minor over an E7 to get a Latin vibe.

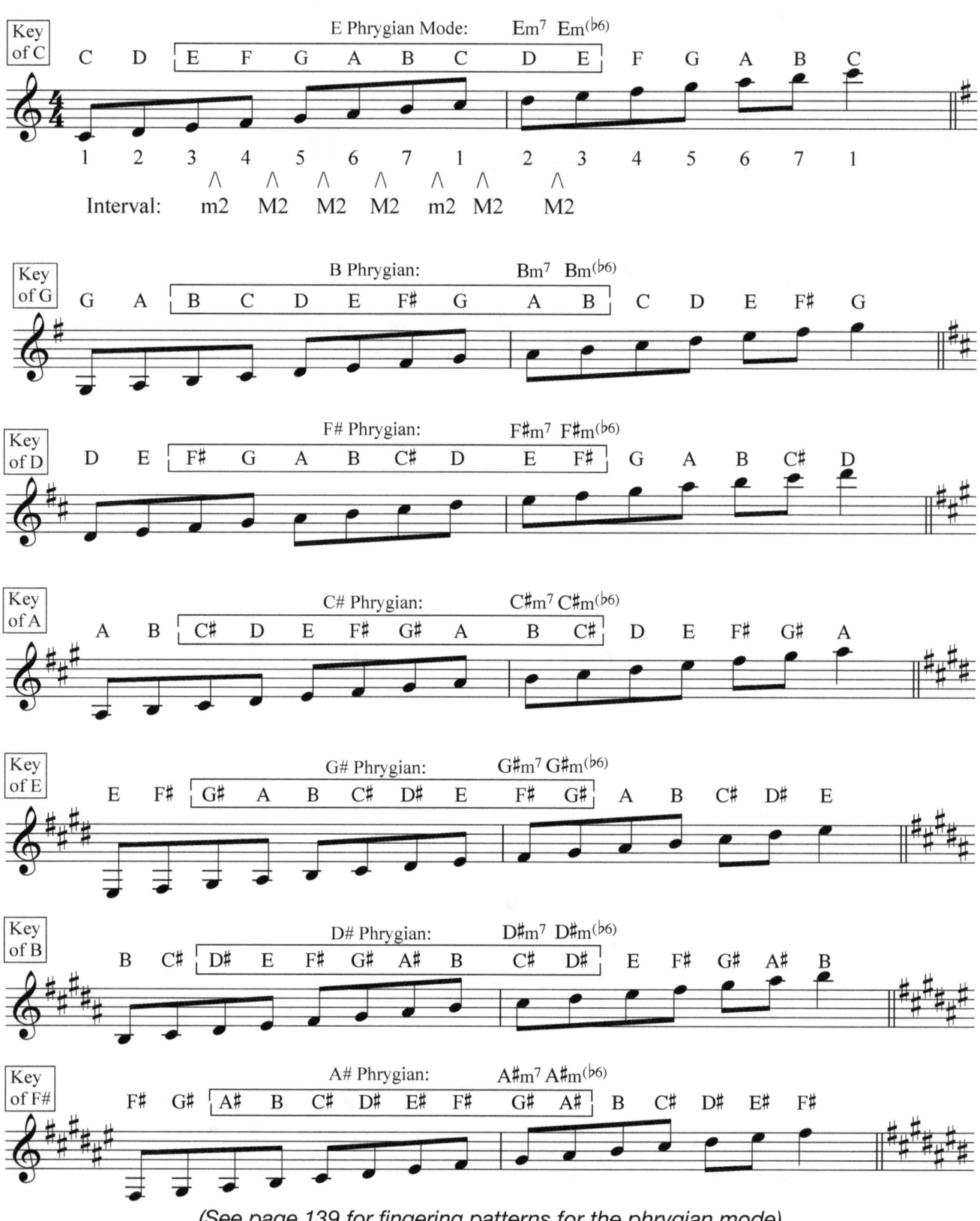

(See page 139 for fingering patterns for the phrygian mode)

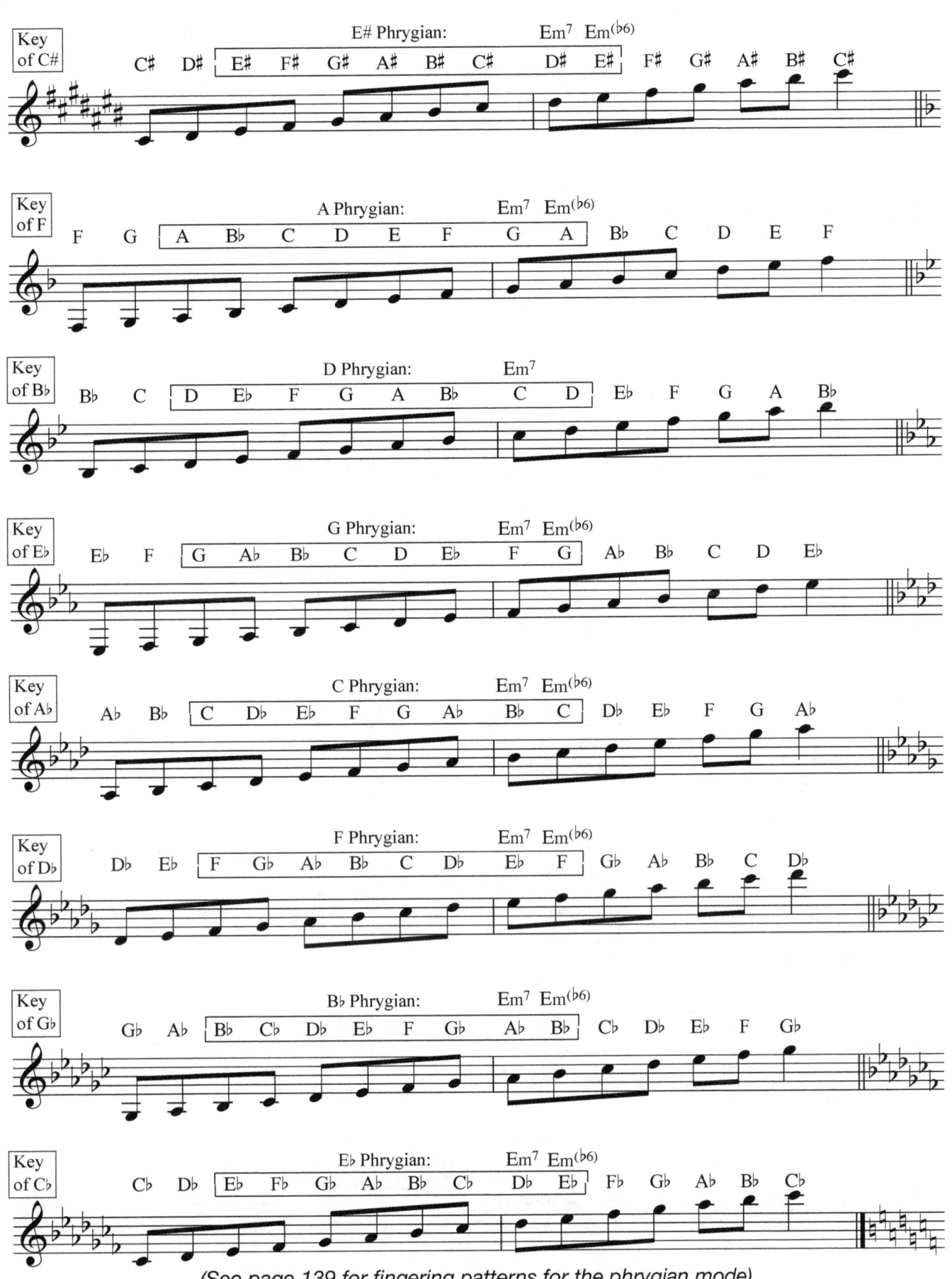

(See page 139 for fingering patterns for the phrygian mode)

The 4th/ "Lydian" Mode of the Major Scale

Have someone play a C chord on a synth pad while you improvise using the C lydian mode. The raised 4th scale degree of this mode gives you a totally different and cool vibe compared to using the C major scale.

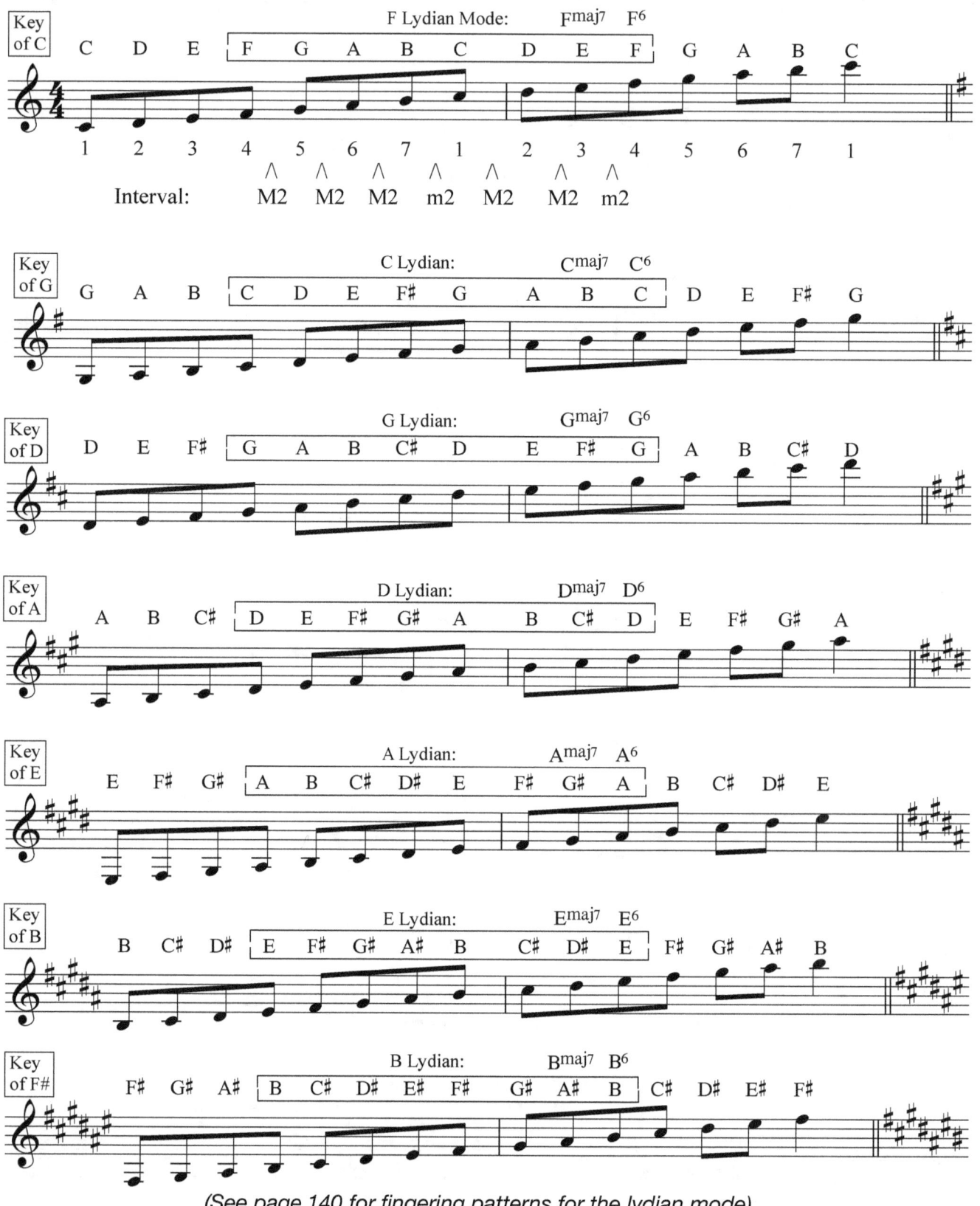

(See page 140 for fingering patterns for the lydian mode)

(See page 140 for fingering patterns for the lydian mode)

The 5th/ "Mixolydian" Mode of the Major Scale

You can find some great melodies playing the mixolydian mode over dominant 7th chords.

(See page 141 for fingering patterns for the mixolydian mode)

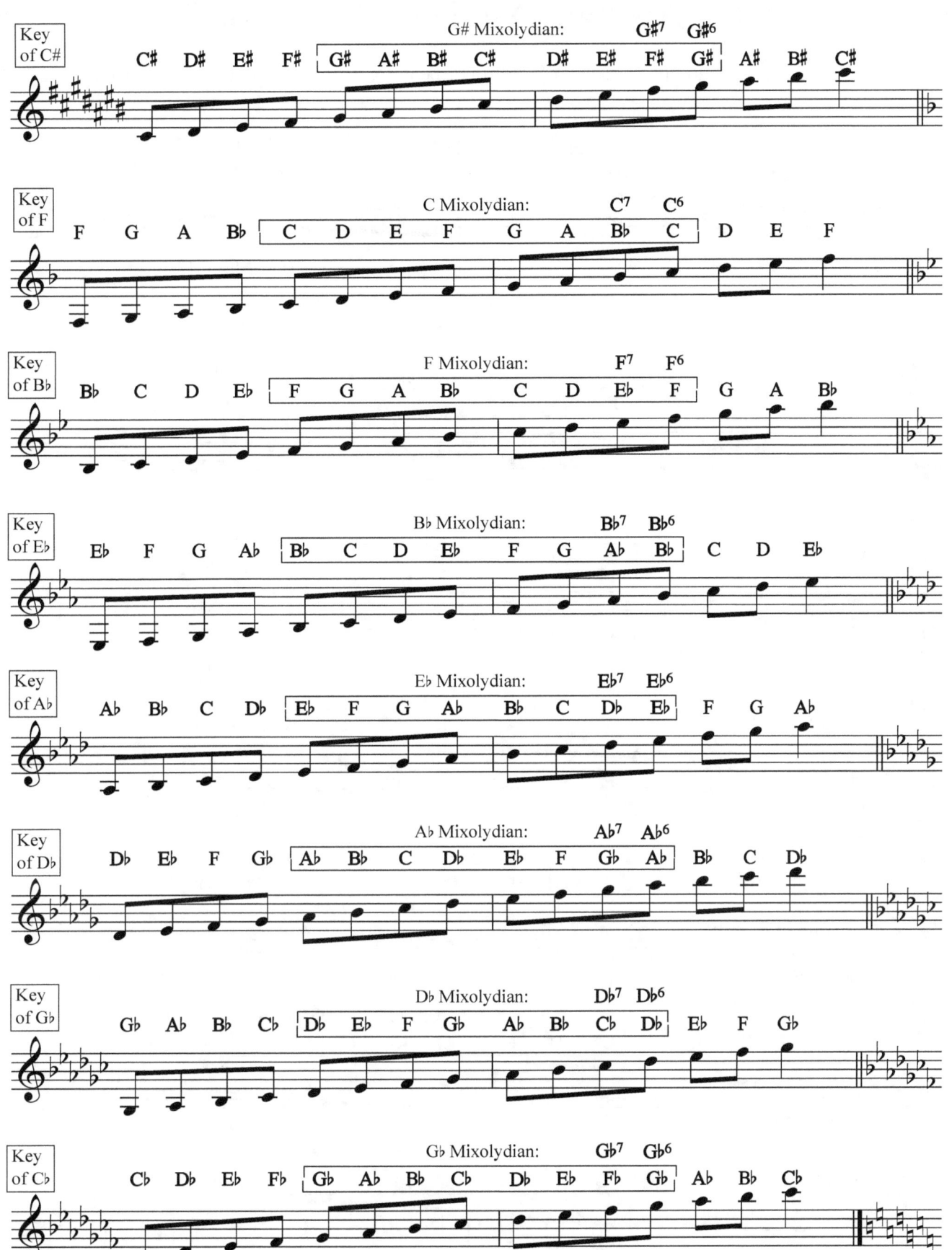

(See page 141 for fingering patterns for the mixolydian mode)

The 6th/ "Aeolian" Mode of the Major Scale

Try using the aeolian mode instead of the minor pentatonic on your next rock & roll solo...

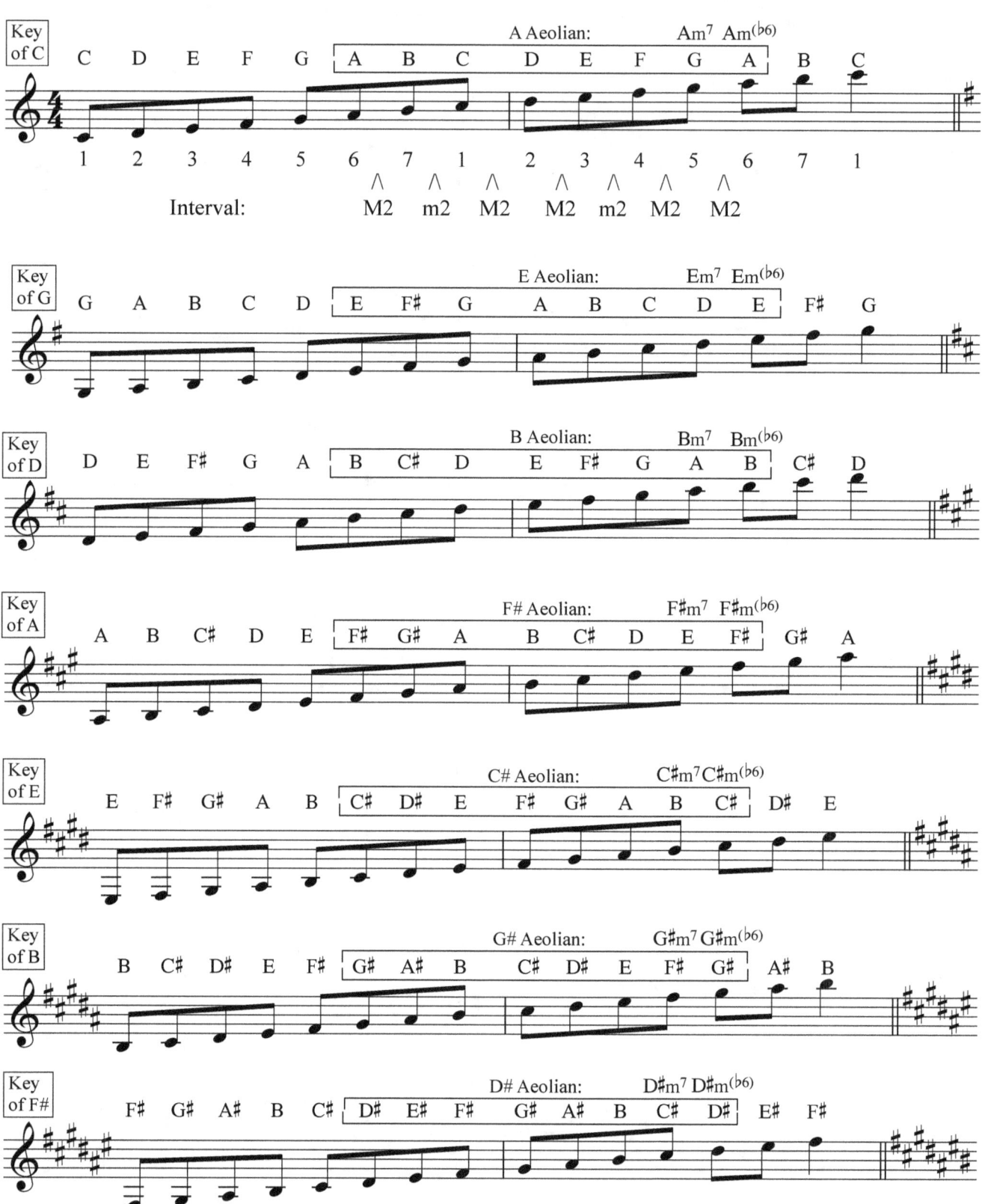

(See page 142 for fingering patterns for the aeolian mode)

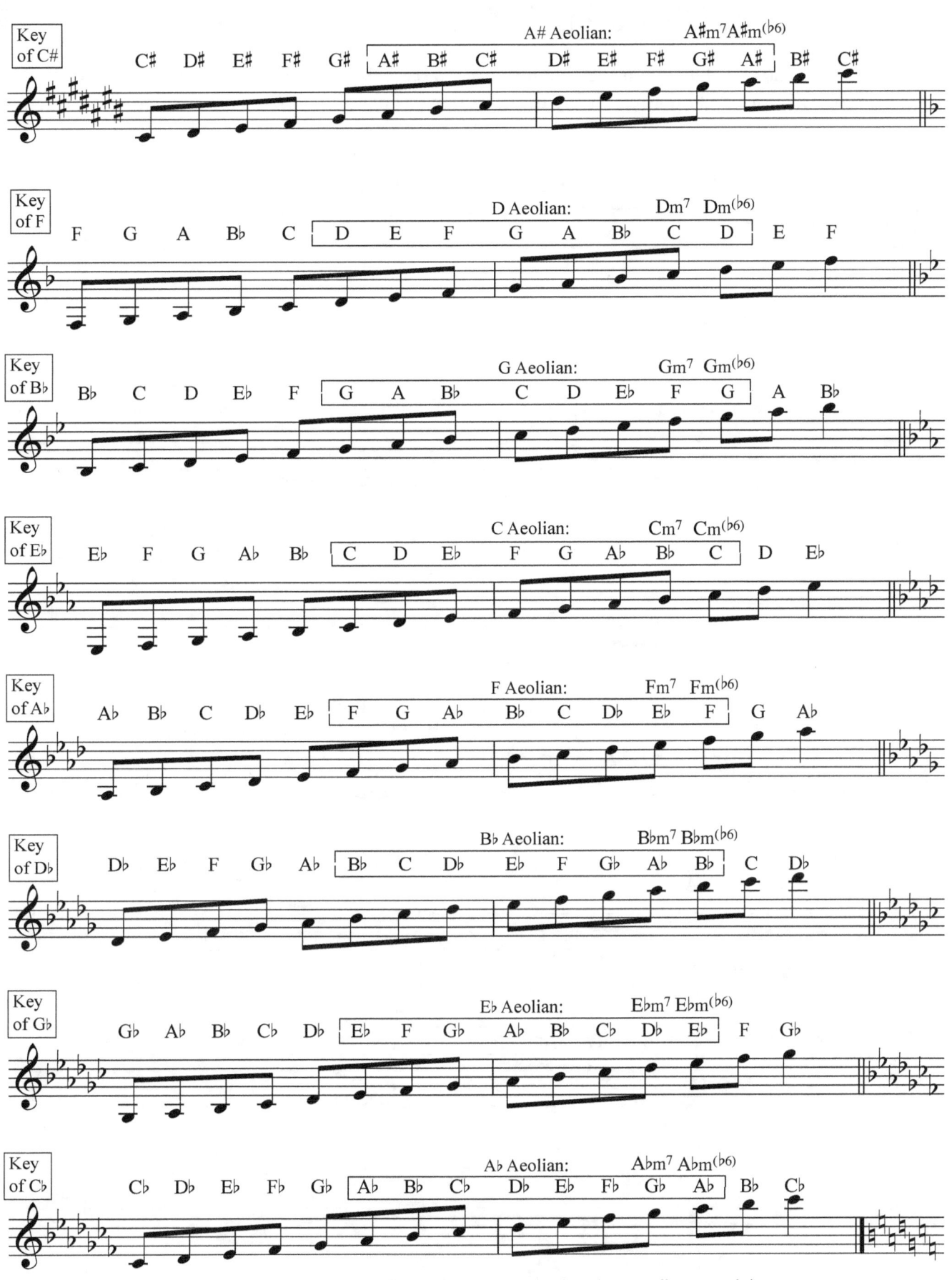

(See page 142 for fingering patterns for the aeolian mode)

The 7th/ "Locrian" Mode of the Major Scale

Min7♭9 chords? Half-diminished chords? Have a bass player lay down a groove staying on a single G note and improvise using the G locrian (A♭ major scale). It's different—but it's nice.

(See page 143 for fingering patterns for the locrian mode)

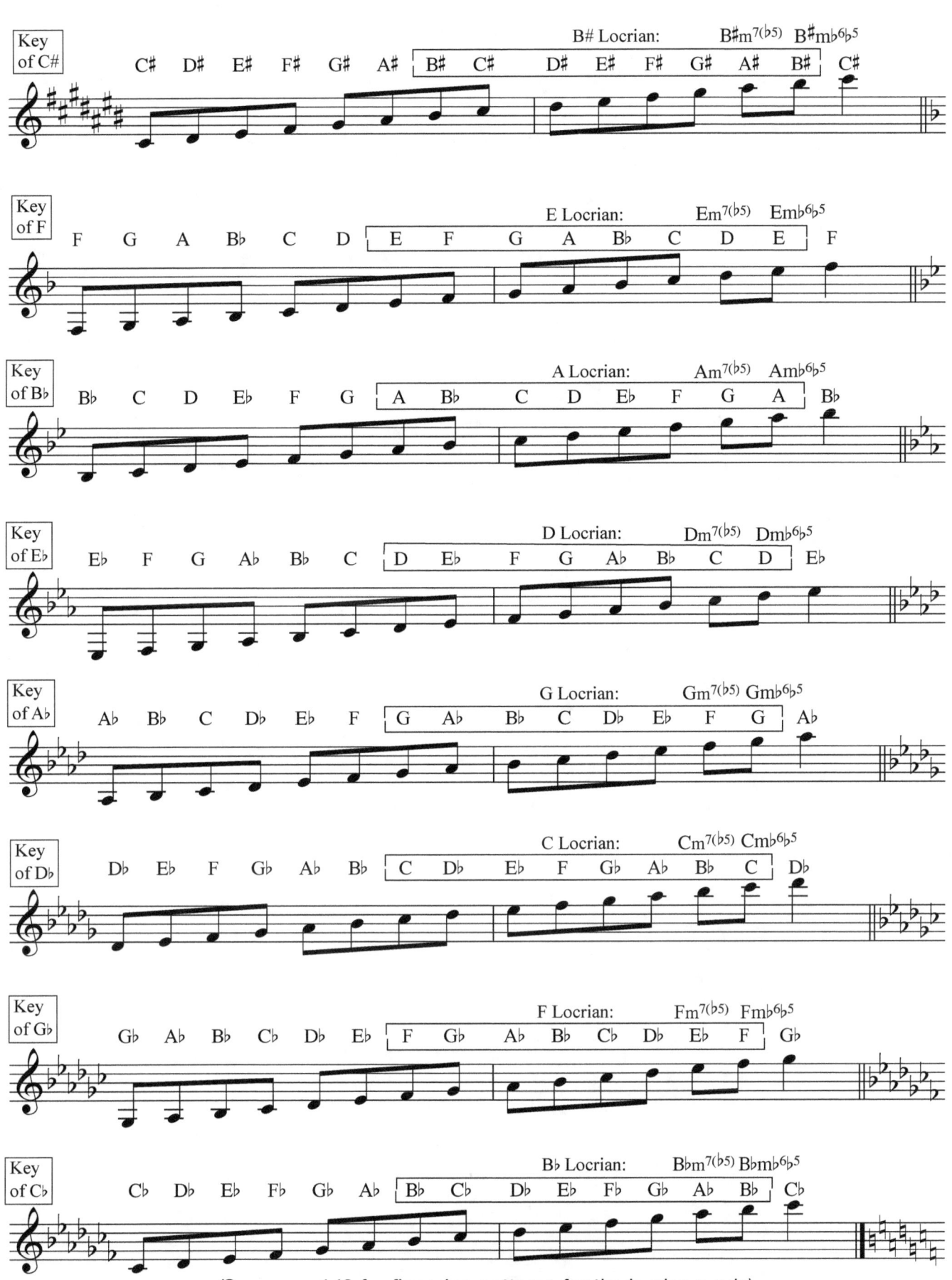

(See page 143 for fingering patterns for the locrian mode)

PART 2
The Modes of the Melodic Minor Scales

To introduce the melodic minor scales, they are spelled here, and various 2 octave fingerings (which can be used for any key) are provided in the following six pages.

2 Octave Melodic Minor Scales

A Melodic Minor

E Melodic Minor

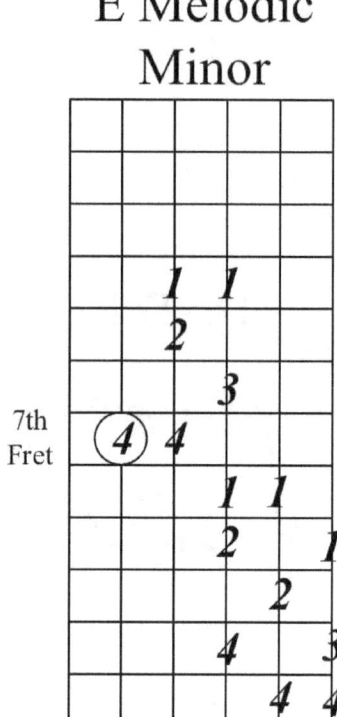

B Melodic Minor

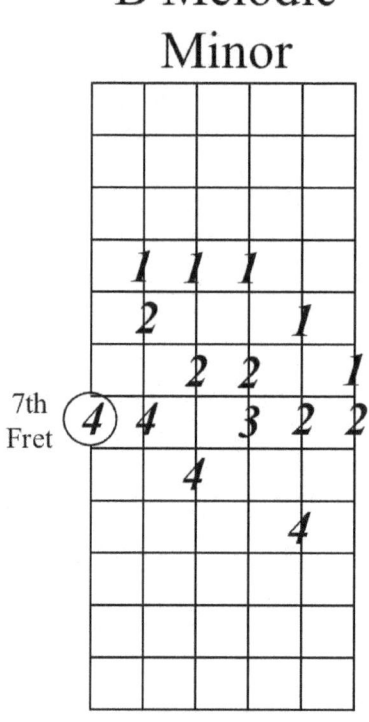

F# Melodic Minor

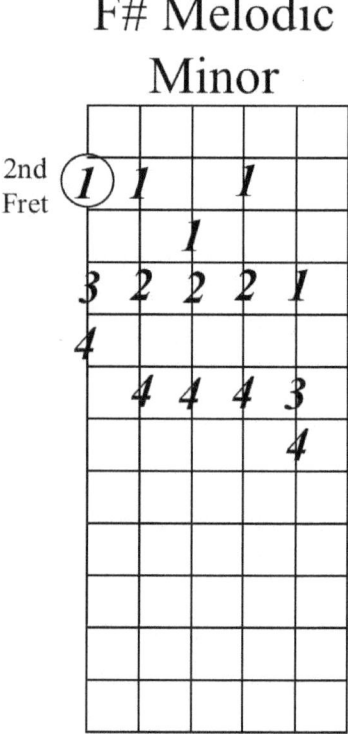

C# Melodic Minor

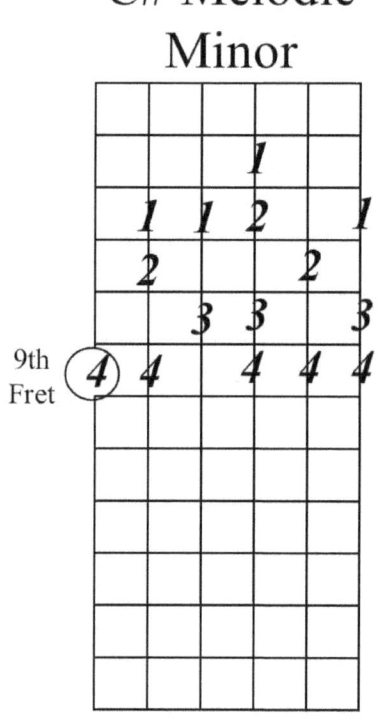

2 Octave Melodic Minor Scales

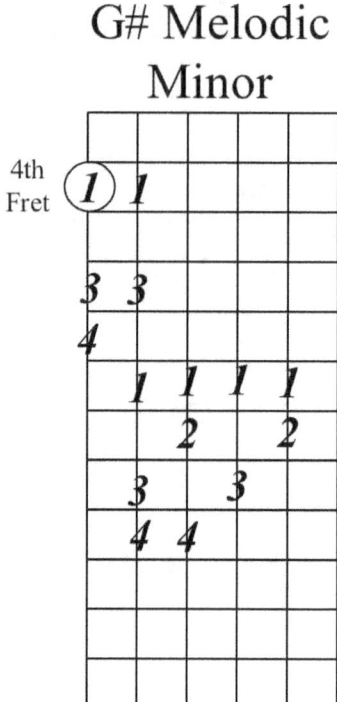
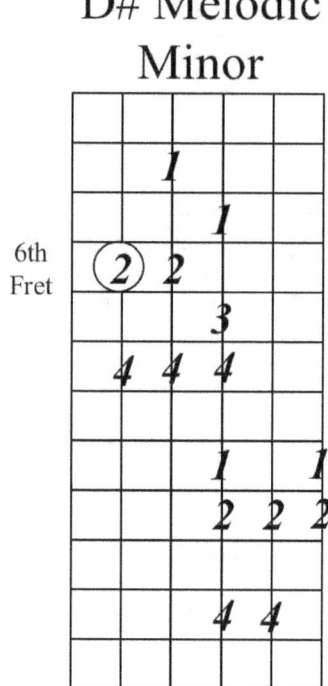
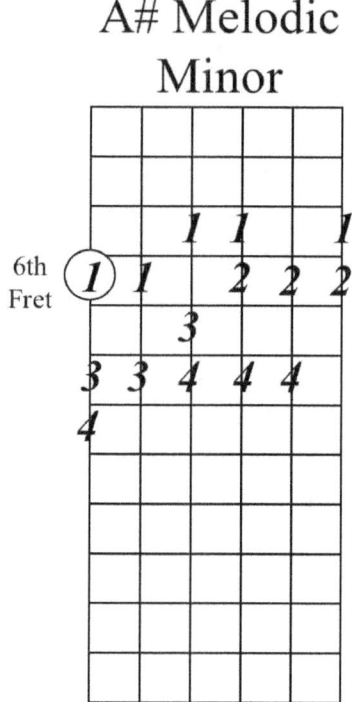
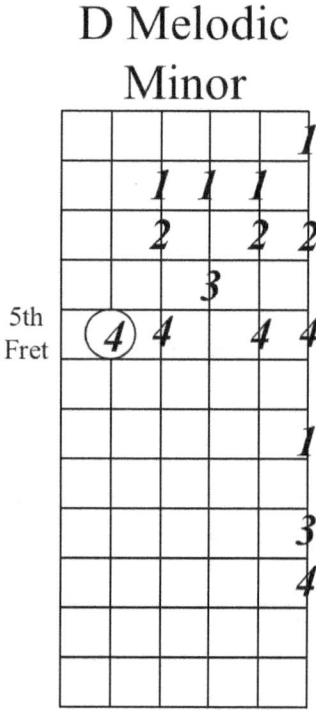
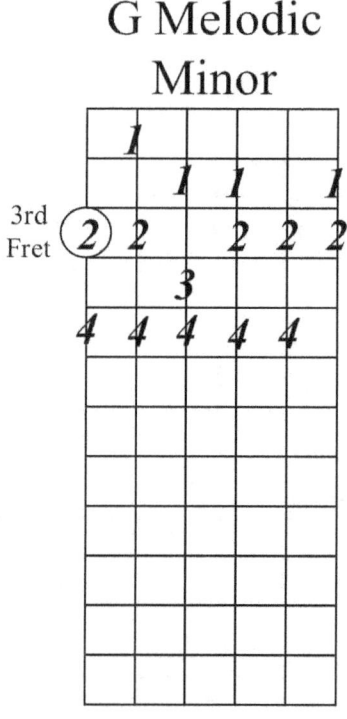

2 Octave Melodic Minor Scales

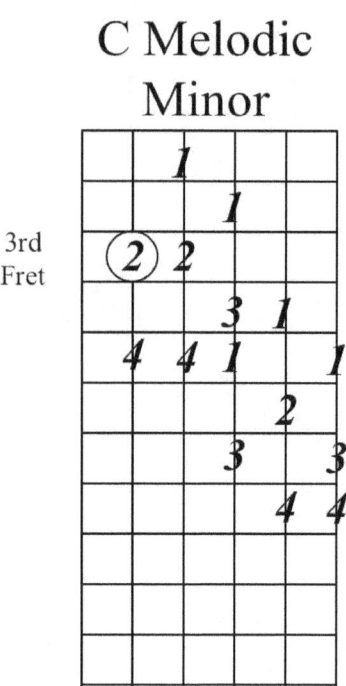
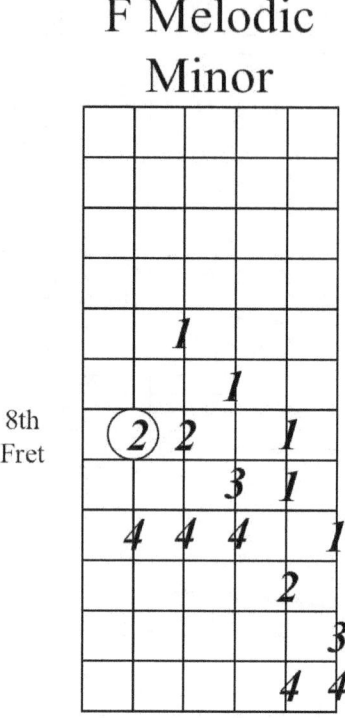
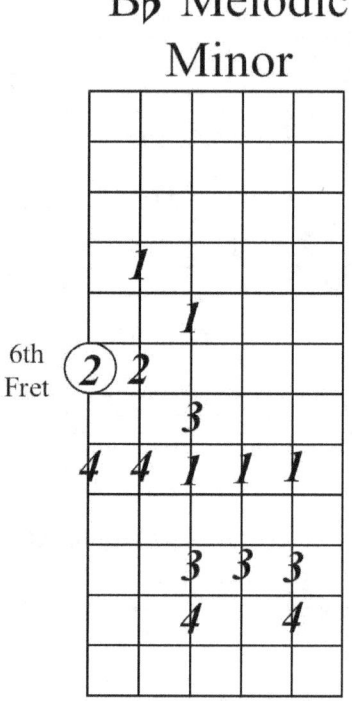
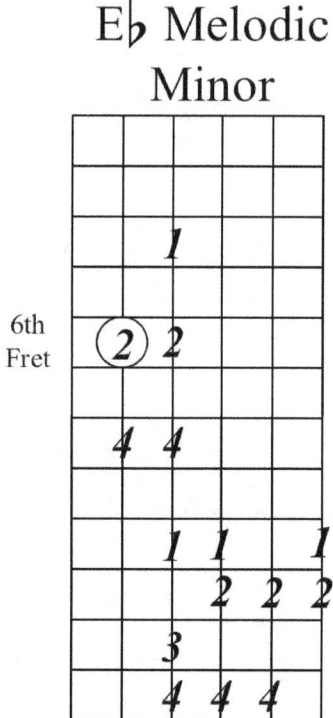
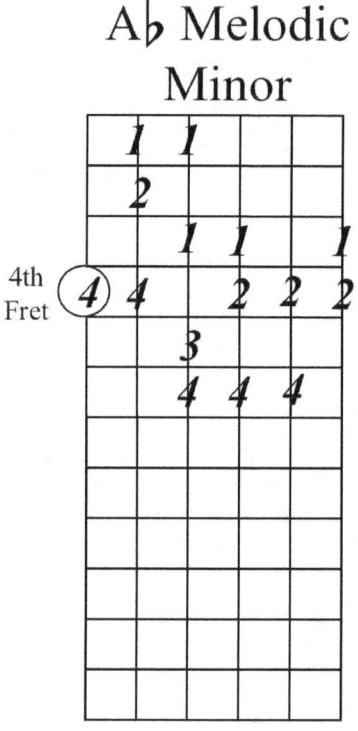

Modes of the Melodic Minor Scale

The concept of modes is not complex. Once you have memorized a major scale, identifying the modes of the major scale is simply a matter of starting the scale at each of the seven scale notes.

For example, if you take the G melodic minor scale and play it starting at the 1st scale degree (G) and go up the scale 1 octave, you have just played the 1st mode of the major scale. If you take the G major scale and play it starting at the 2nd scale degree (A) and go up the scale 1 octave, you have just played the 2nd mode of the major scale. Continuing this concept with each of the 7 scale degrees of the major scale will result in the 7 modes of the major scale.

G Melodic Minor Scale

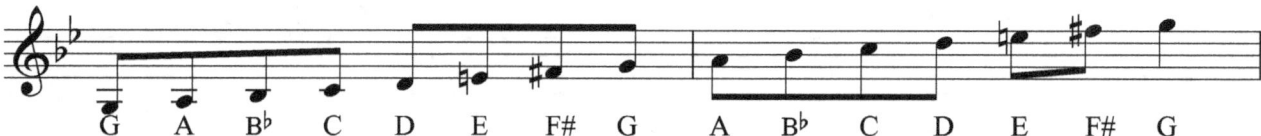

Using the G melodic minor scale as an example, the 7 modes of the melodic minor scale are presented below. Note that the 1st mode is identical to the melodic minor scale.

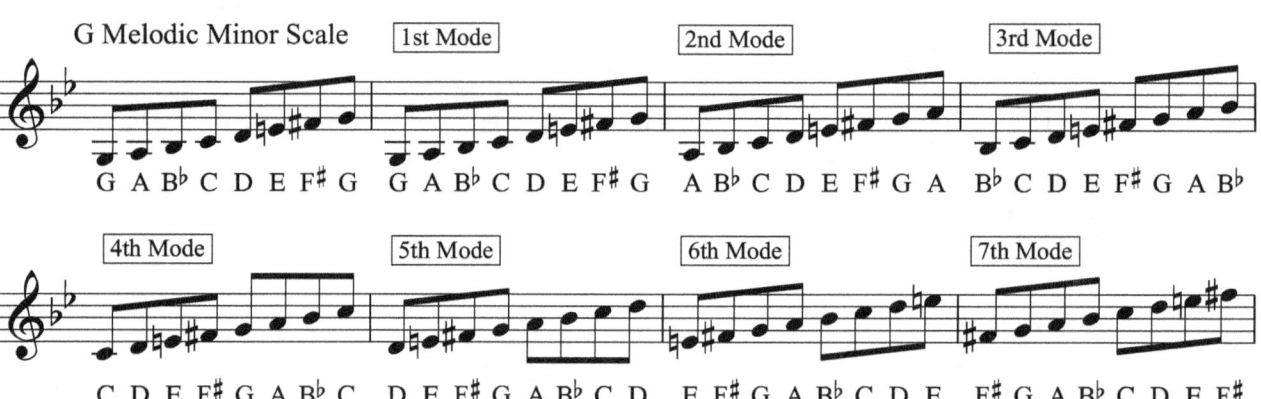

The 7 modes of the melodic minor scale correspond to the diatonic chords of the melodic minor scale. In other words, the modes can be used for improvisation over the diatonic chords. While the study of mode/chord relationships is a beneficial study, it should be viewed only as one of the many musical tools available to the improvising musician. However, building a solid knowledge base of mode/scale relationships on the guitar fretboard will reap an abundance of melodic ideas and fingering options to a guitarist who enjoys improvisation.

Melodic Minor Mode/Chord Relationships	4th mode: Dominant 7th chords
1st mode: Minor (Major7th) chords	5th mode: Dominant 7th chords
2nd mode: Minor 7 chords	6th mode: Minor 7♭5 chords
3rd mode: Major 7th (#5) chords	7th mode: Minor 7♭5 chords or Alt.7th chords

The following pages spell the melodic minor scales, and the modes nested within the melodic minor scales.

On the first row of each mode, the intervals between the notes of the mode are indicated by the following symbols found below the staff:

m2 = minor second interval

M2 = major second interval

m3 = minor third interval

M3 = major third interval

The notes making up each mode are bracketed above the staff, and suggested chords to use with each mode are shown above the brackets as seen in the example below.

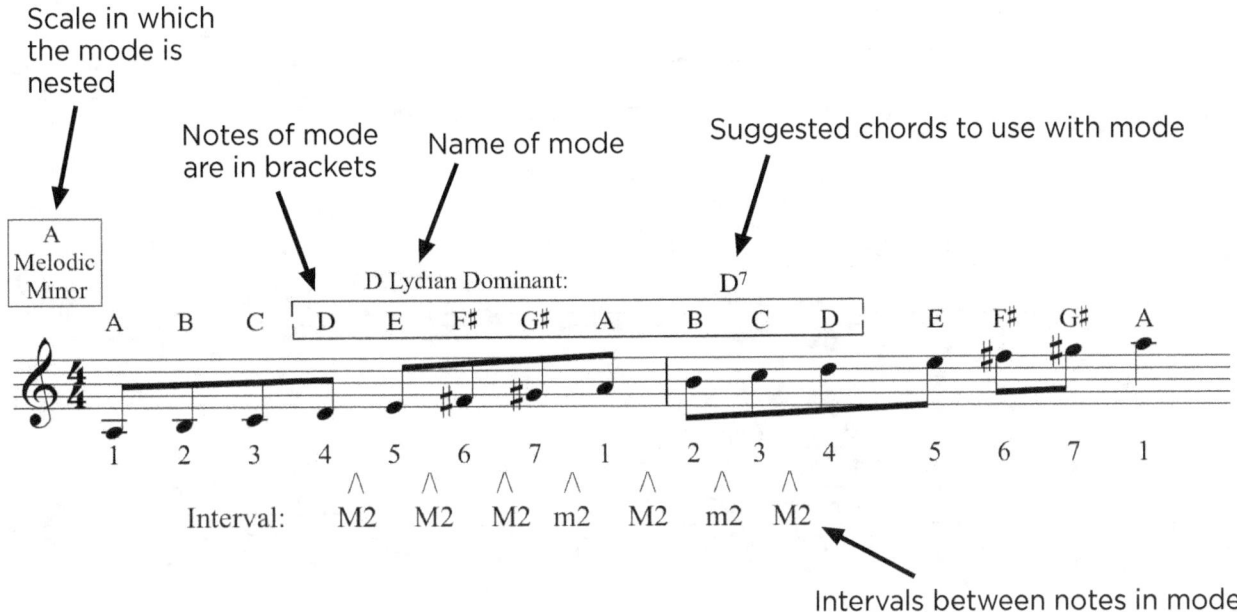

The 1st/ "Ionian ♭3" Mode of the Melodic Minor

If the melodic minor isn't clicking with you, try improvising with a strong SWING rhythm and you will find the incredible possibilites that have been hidden in this scale and its modes.

(See page 145 for fingering patterns for the ionian ♭3 mode)

(See page 145 for fingering patterns for the ionian ♭3 mode)

The 2nd/ "Dorian ♭2" Mode of the Melodic Minor Scale

The dorian ♭2 mode may not jump out at you as a great tool. However, take time to explore it.
Approach it like you are doing a movie soundtrack.
There is great stuff hidden here—but you have to find it!

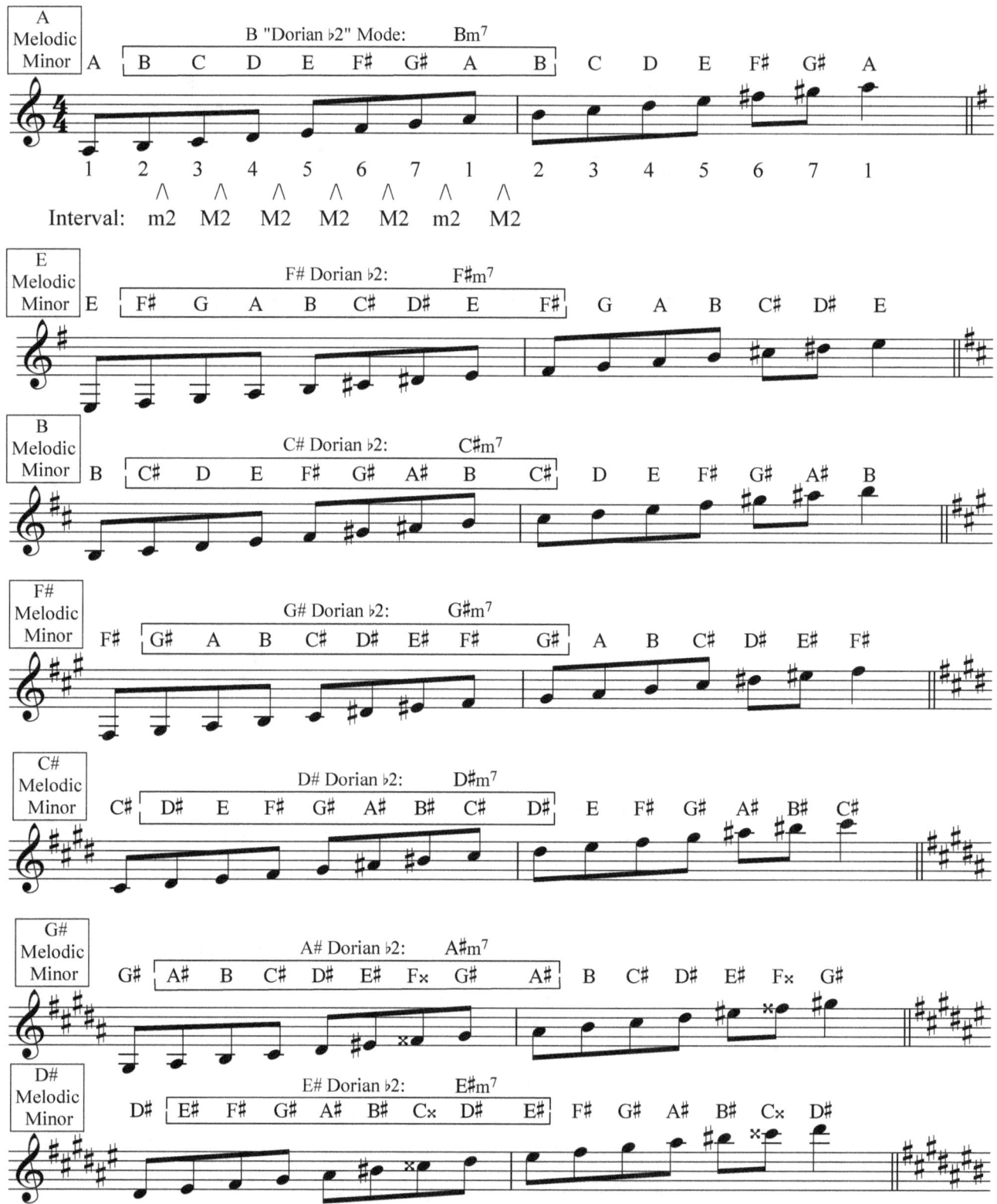

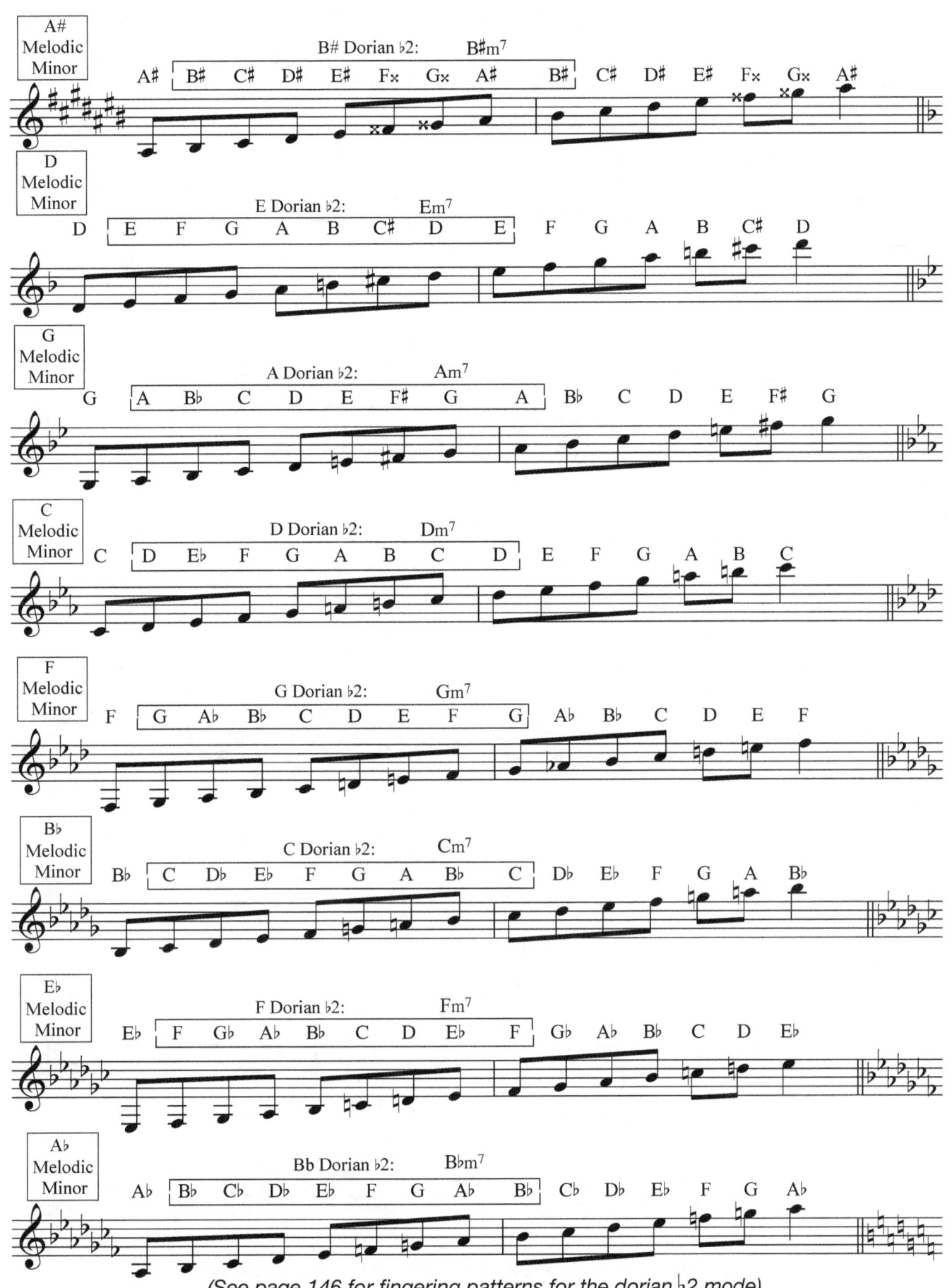

(See page 146 for fingering patterns for the dorian ♭2 mode)

The 3rd/ "Lydian Augmented" Mode of the Melodic Minor

OK, honestly, I noodled around with this mode for a couple years thinking it was one of the most awful sounding things around. BUT THEN, I found a cool melody hidden in this mode.

(See page 147 for fingering patterns for the lydian augmented mode)

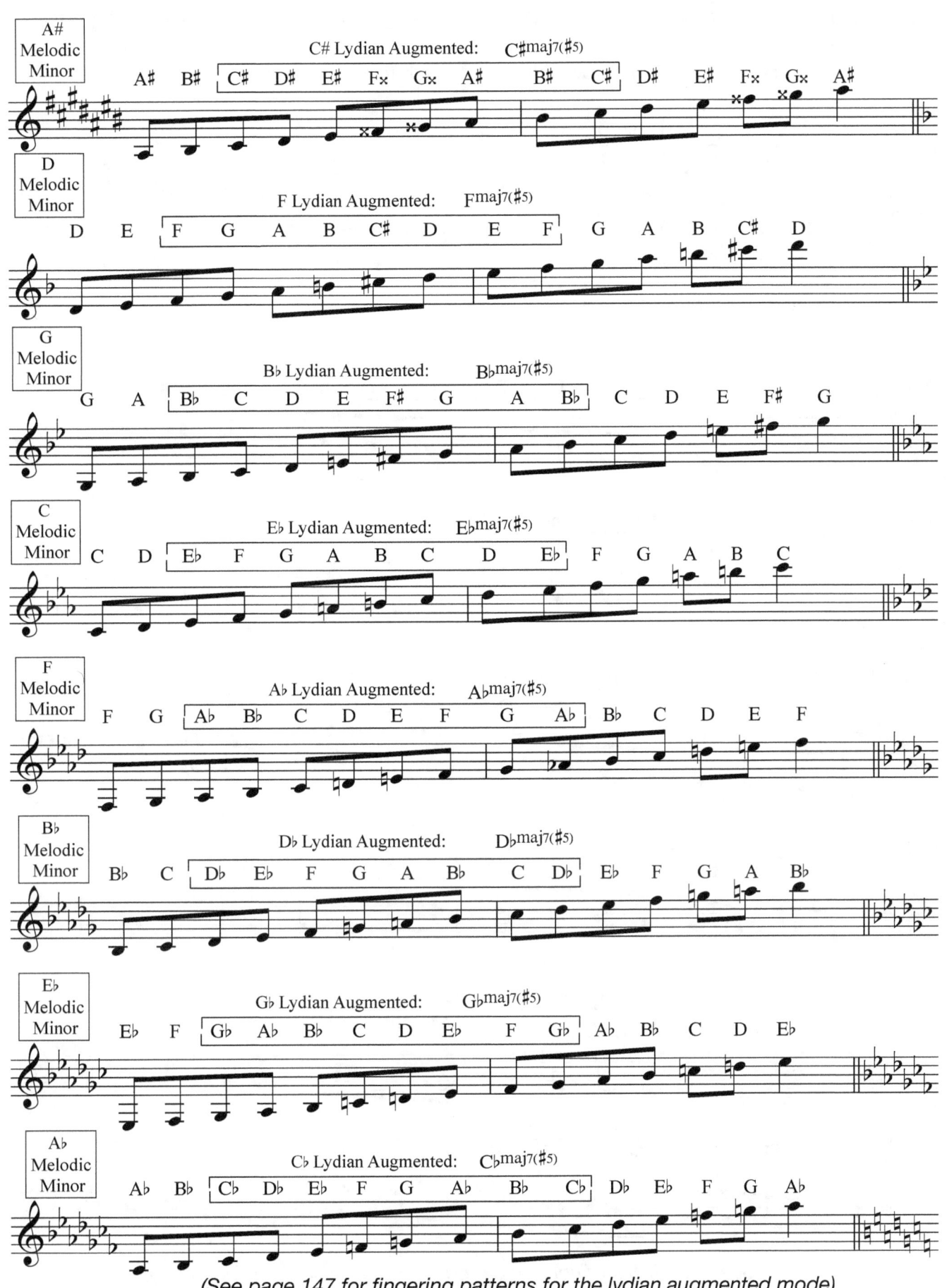

(See page 147 for fingering patterns for the lydian augmented mode)

The 4th/ "Lydian Dominant" Mode of the Melodic Minor

Try this one on a dominant 7th chord for a different flavor of funkiness.

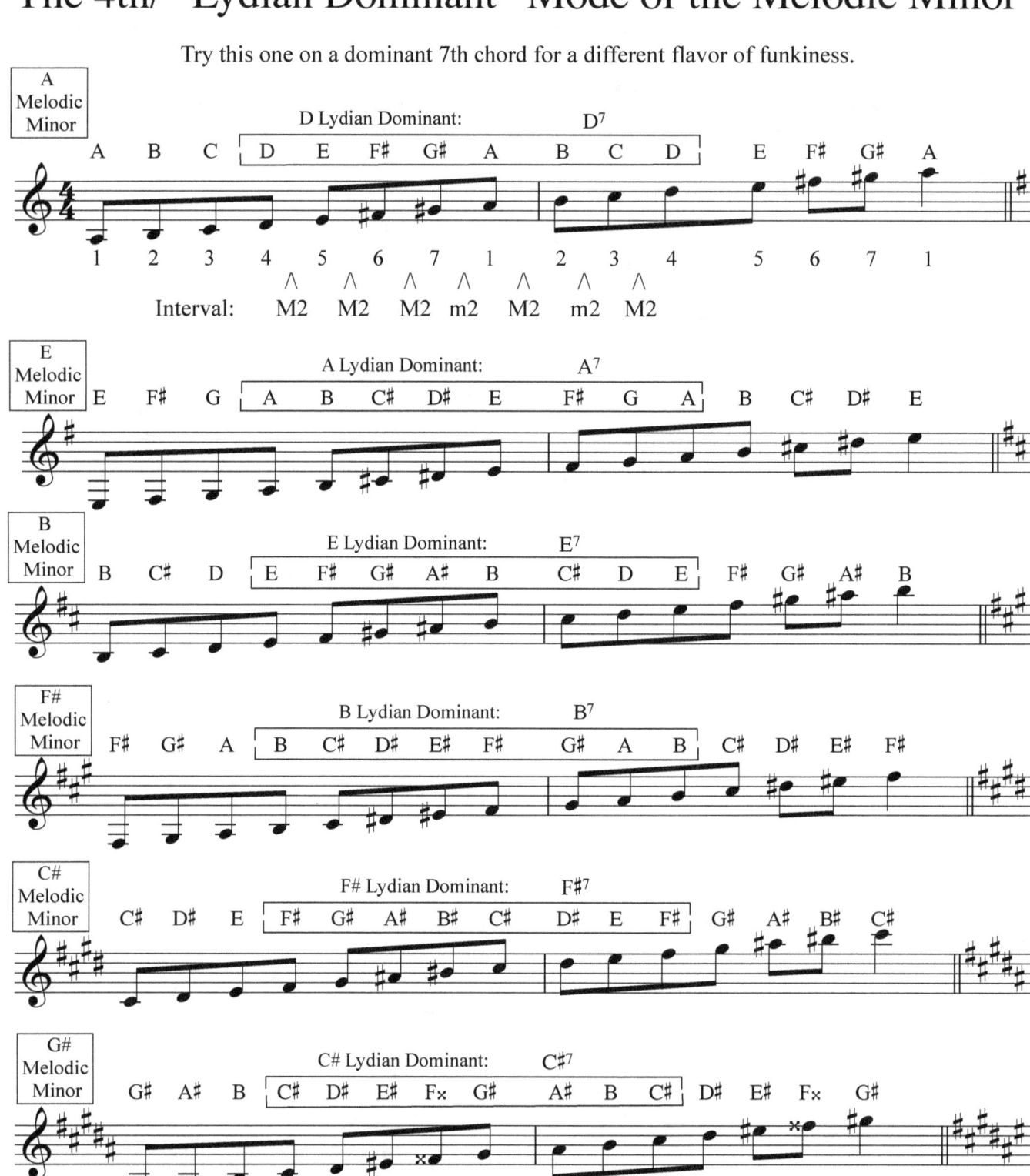

(See page 148 for fingering patterns for the lydian dominant mode)

(See page 148 for fingering patterns for the lydian dominant mode)

The 5th/ "Mixolydian ♭6" Mode of the Melodic Minor

You can get a Middle Eastern vibe here—it's a bit more subtle than the harmonic minor.

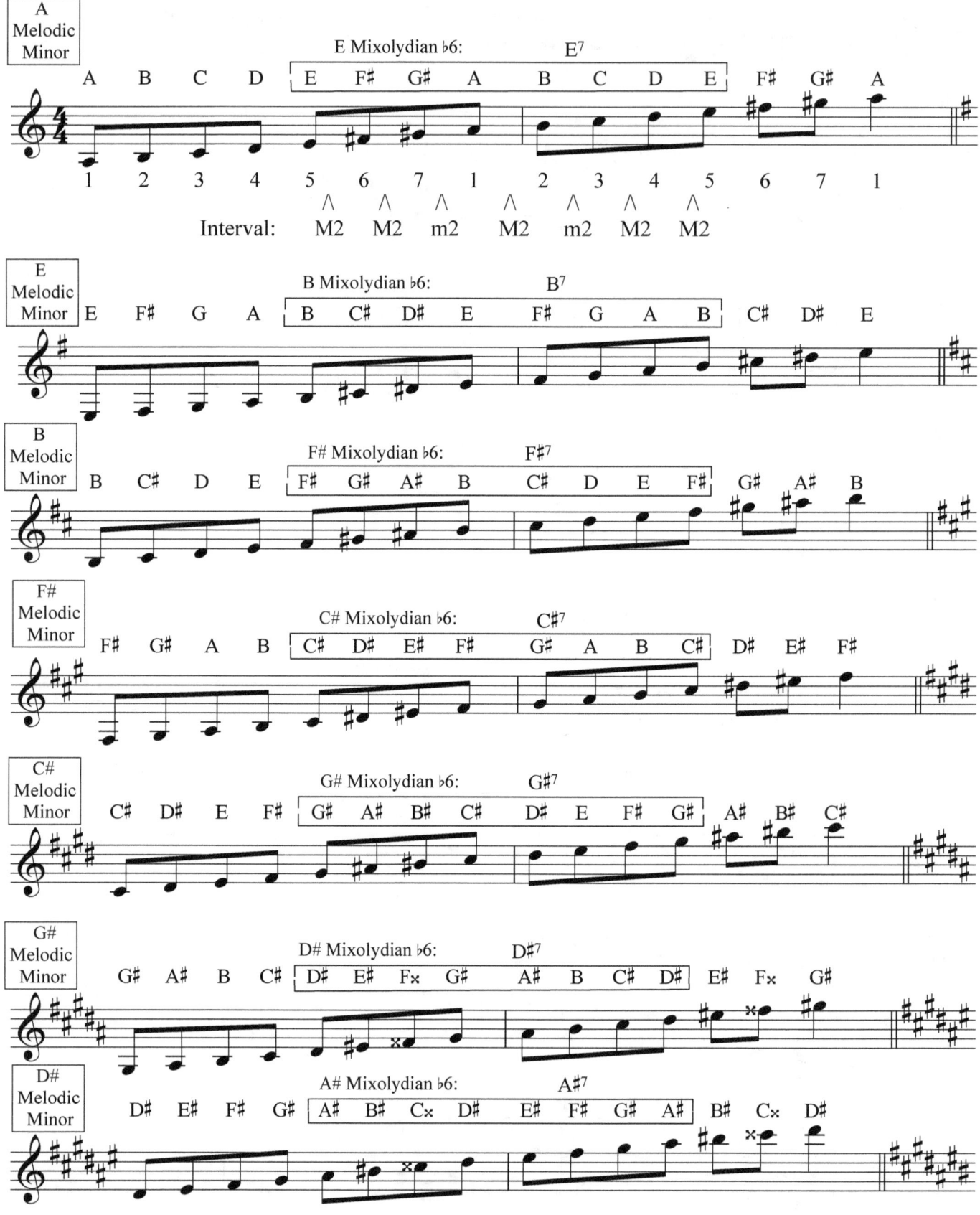

(See page 149 for fingering patterns for the mixolydian ♭6 mode)

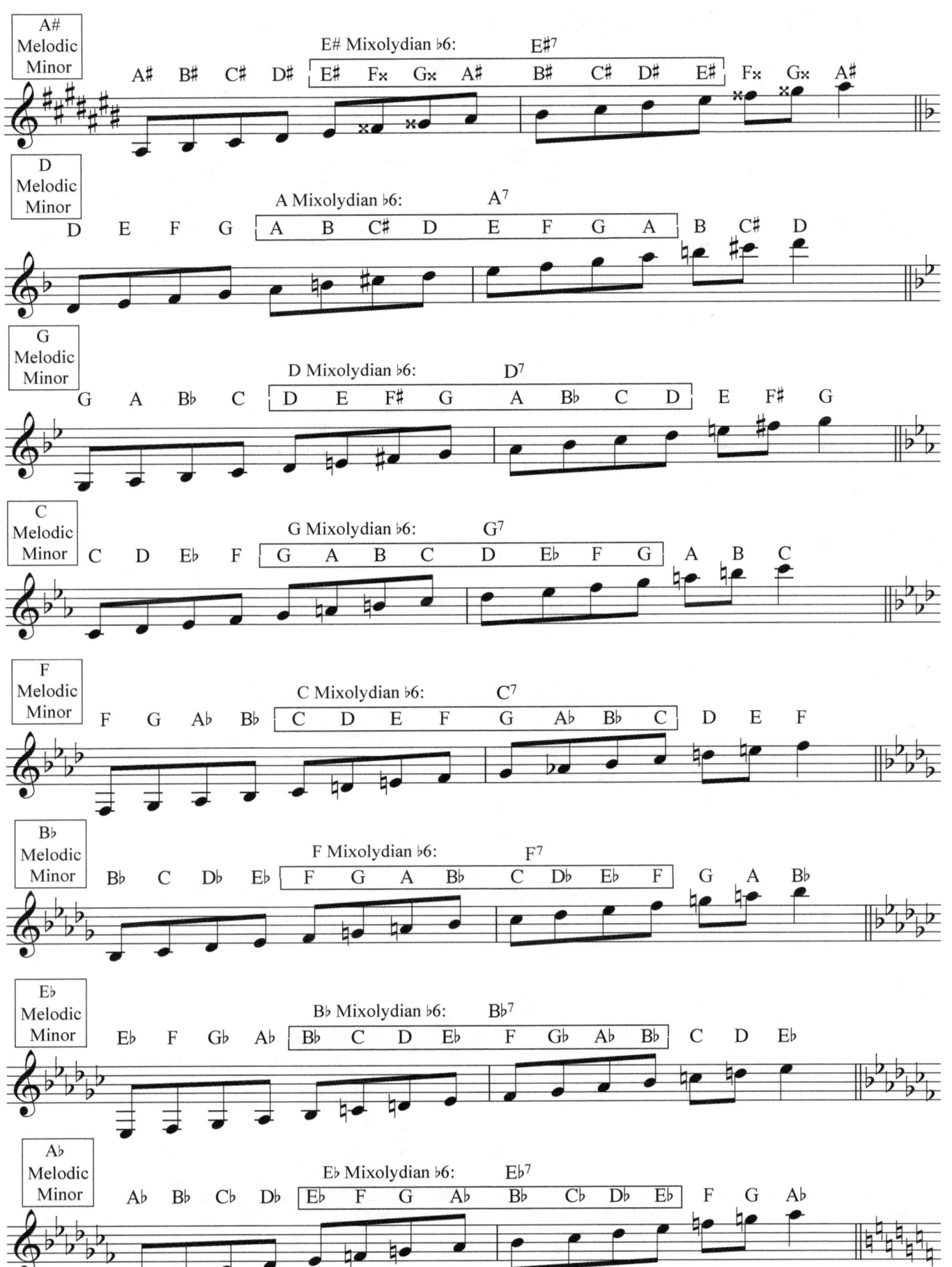

The 6th/ "Aeolian ♭5" Mode of the Melodic Minor

Try clustering ANY three or four notes from this mode and transition to another three or four note cluster. Creativity occurs! New ideas will come! Try this with any melodic minor mode.

(See page 150 for fingering patterns for the aeolian ♭5 mode)

(See page 150 for fingering patterns for the aeolian ♭5 mode)

The 7th/ "Super Locrian" Mode of the Melodic Minor

The mode is unique in that all seven notes are chord tones of the altered 7th chord (Root, 3rd, ♭5th, #5th, ♭7th, ♭9th, #9th). Anything goes with this mode over an alt. 7th chord.

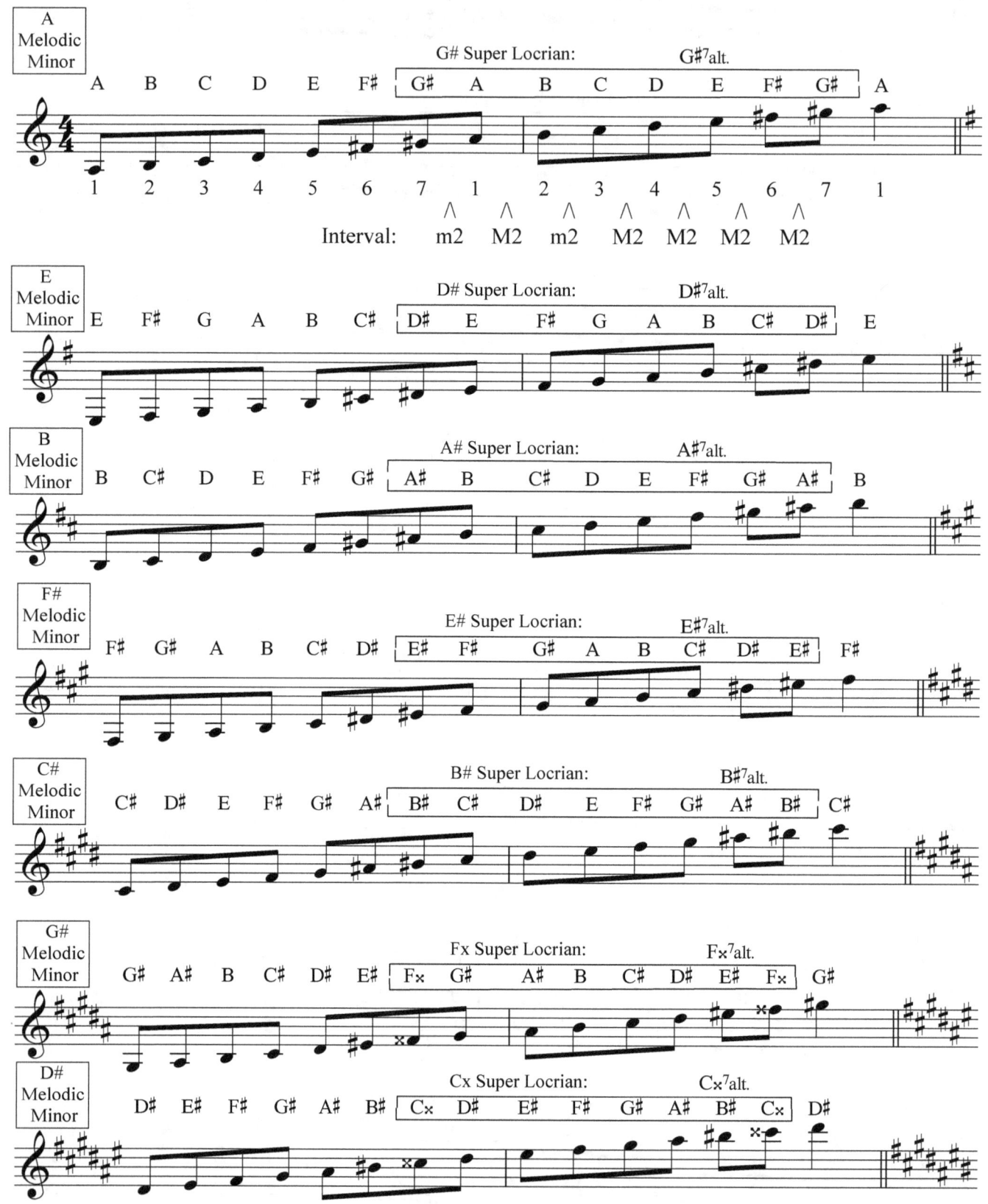

(See page 151 for fingering patterns for the super locrian mode)

(See page 151 for fingering patterns for the super locrian mode)

PART 3
The Modes of the Harmonic Minor Scales

To introduce the harmonic minor scales, they are spelled here, and various 2 octave fingerings (which can be used for any key) are provided in the following six pages.

2 Octave Harmonic Minor Scales

A Harmonic Minor

E Harmonic Minor

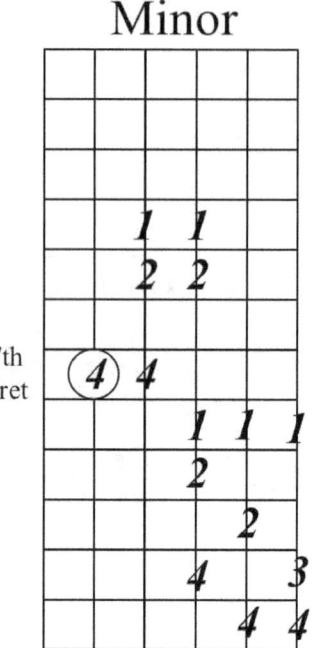

B Harmonic Minor

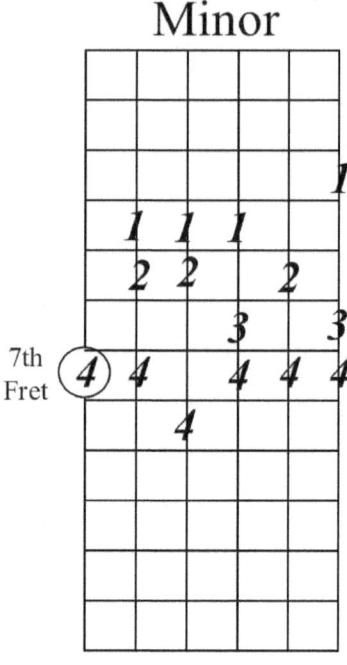

F# Harmonic Minor

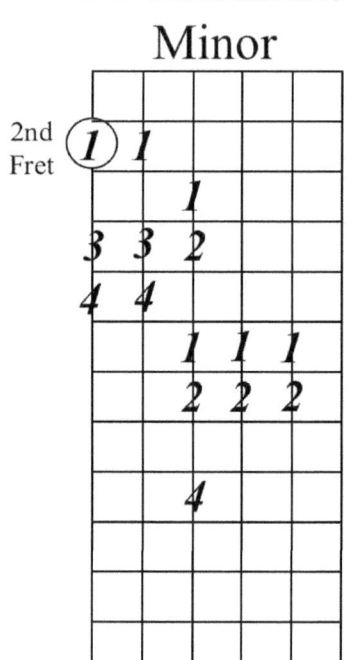

C# Harmonic Minor

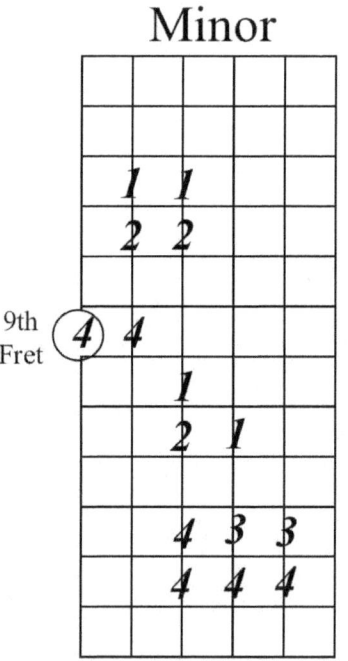

2 Octave Harmonic Minor Scales

G# Harmonic Minor

D# Harmonic Minor
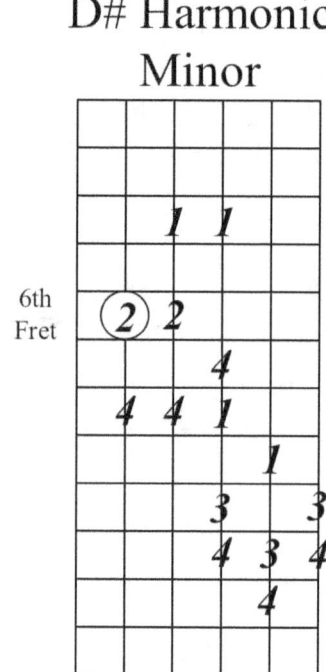

A# Harmonic Minor
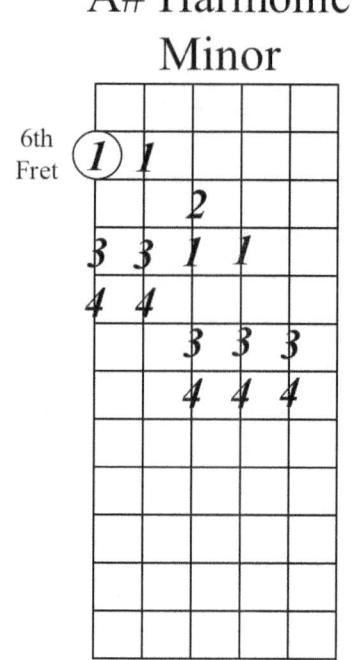

D Harmonic Minor
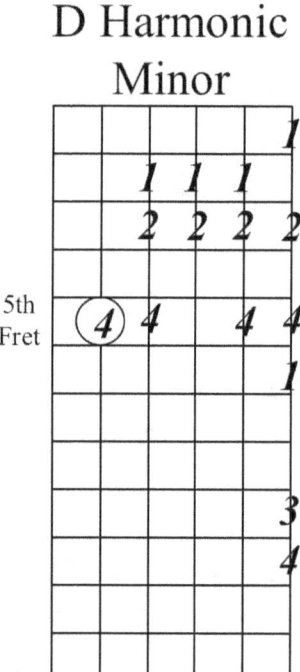

G Harmonic Minor
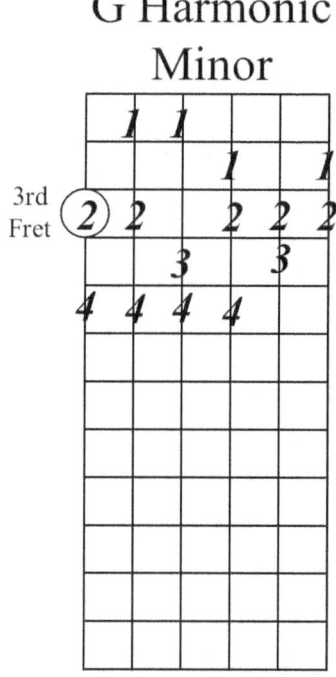

2 Octave Harmonic Minor Scales

C Harmonic Minor

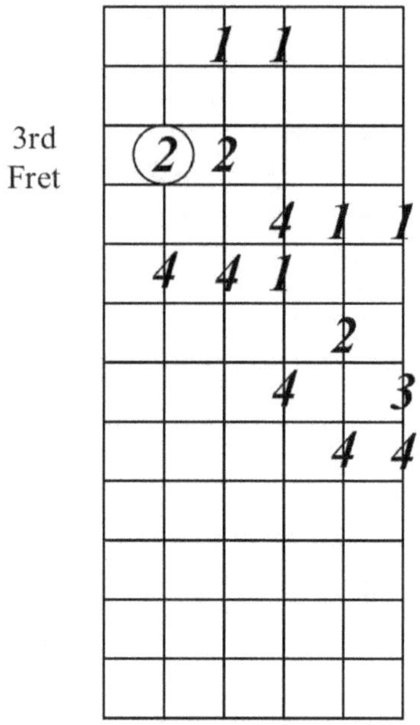

F Harmonic Minor

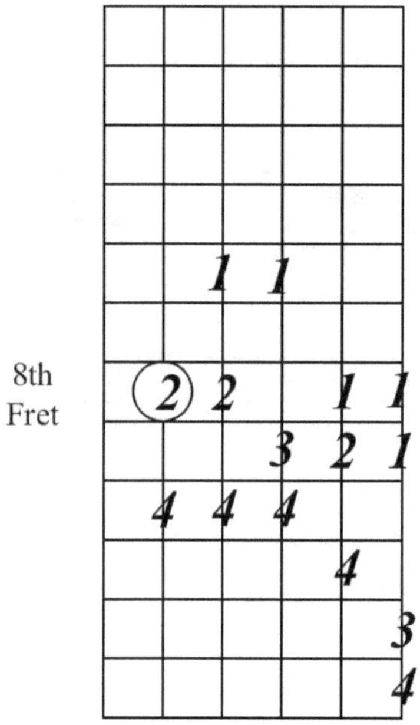

B♭ Harmonic Minor

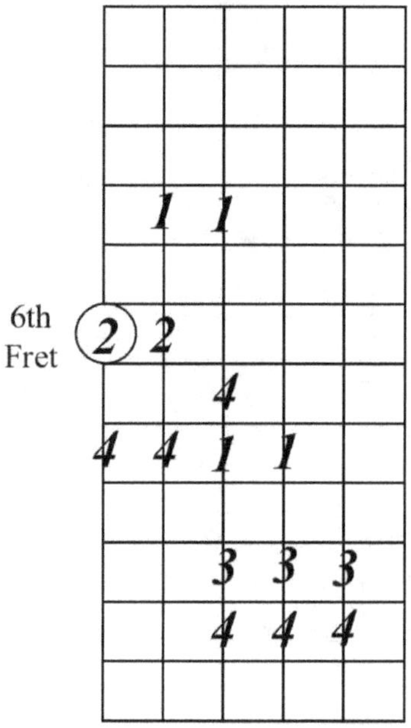

E♭ Harmonic Minor

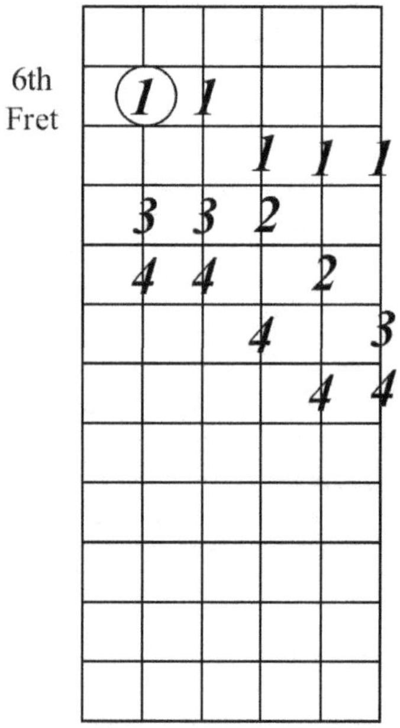

A♭ Harmonic Minor

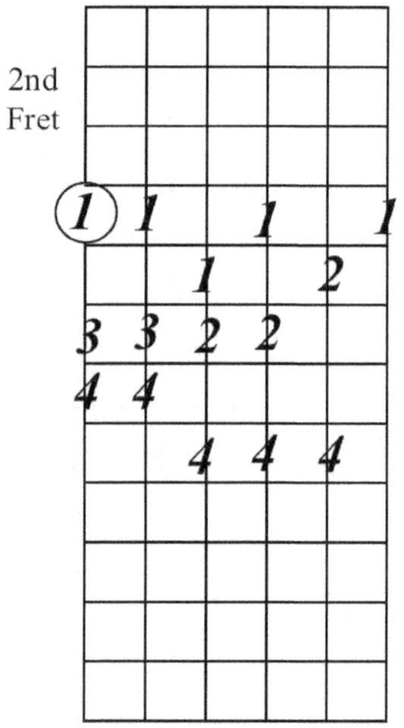

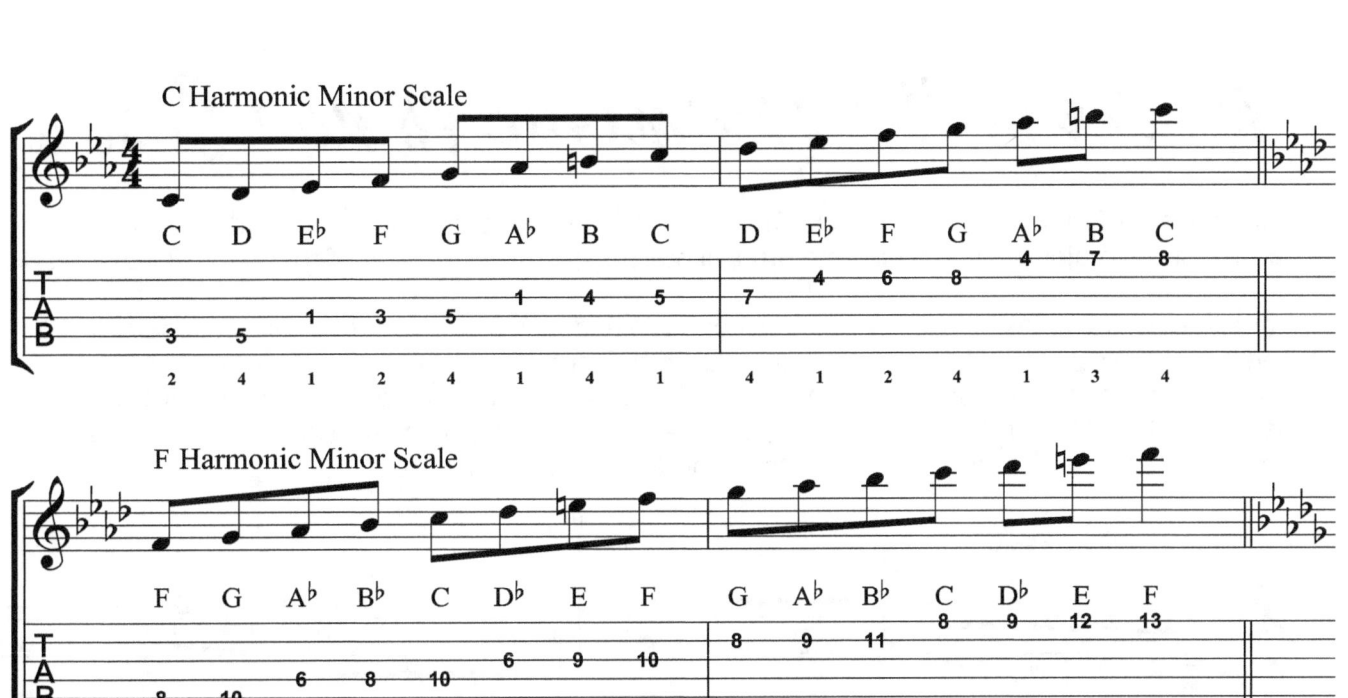

Modes of the Harmonic Minor Scale

The concept of modes is not complex. Once you have memorized a major scale, identifying the modes of the major scale is simply a matter of starting the scale at each of the seven scale notes.

For example, if you take the G harmonic minor scale and play it starting at the 1st scale degree (G) and go up the scale 1 octave, you have just played the 1st mode of the major scale. If you take the G major scale and play it starting at the 2nd scale degree (A) and go up the scale 1 octave, you have just played the 2nd mode of the major scale. Continuing this concept with each of the 7 scale degrees of the major scale will result in the 7 modes of the major scale.

G Harmonic Minor Scale

Using the G harmonic minor scale as an example, the 7 modes of the harmonic minor scale are presented below. Note that the 1st mode is identical to the harmonic minor scale.

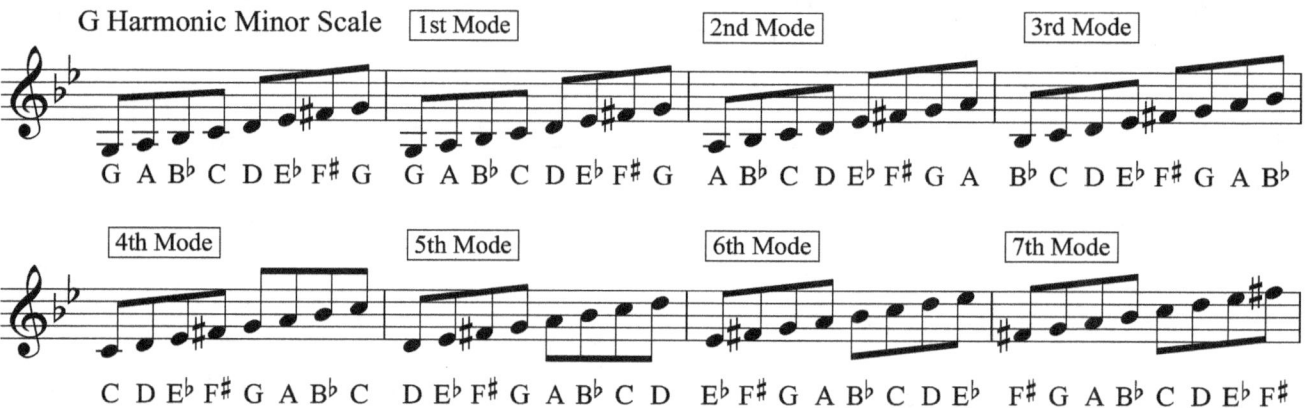

The 7 modes of the harmonic minor scale correspond to the diatonic chords of the harmonic minor scale. In other words, the modes can be used for improvisation over the diatonic chords. While the study of mode/chord relationships is a beneficial study, it should be viewed only as one of the many musical tools available to the improvising musician. However, building a solid knowledge base of mode/scale relationships on the guitar fretboard will reap an abundance of melodic ideas and fingering options to a guitarist who enjoys improvisation.

Harmonic Minor Mode/Chord Relationships	4th mode: Minor 7th chords
1st mode: Minor (Major 7th) chords	5th mode: Dominant 7th chords
2nd mode: Minor 7♭5 chords	6th mode: Major 7th chords
3rd mode: Major 7th (#5) chords	7th mode: Diminished 7th chords

The following pages spell the harmonic minor scales, and the modes nested within the harmonic minor scales.

On the first row of each mode, the intervals between the notes of the mode are indicated by the following symbols found below the staff:

m2 = minor second interval

M2 = major second interval

m3 = minor third interval

M3 = major third interval

The notes making up each mode are bracketed above the staff, and suggested chords to use with each mode are shown above the brackets as seen in the example below.

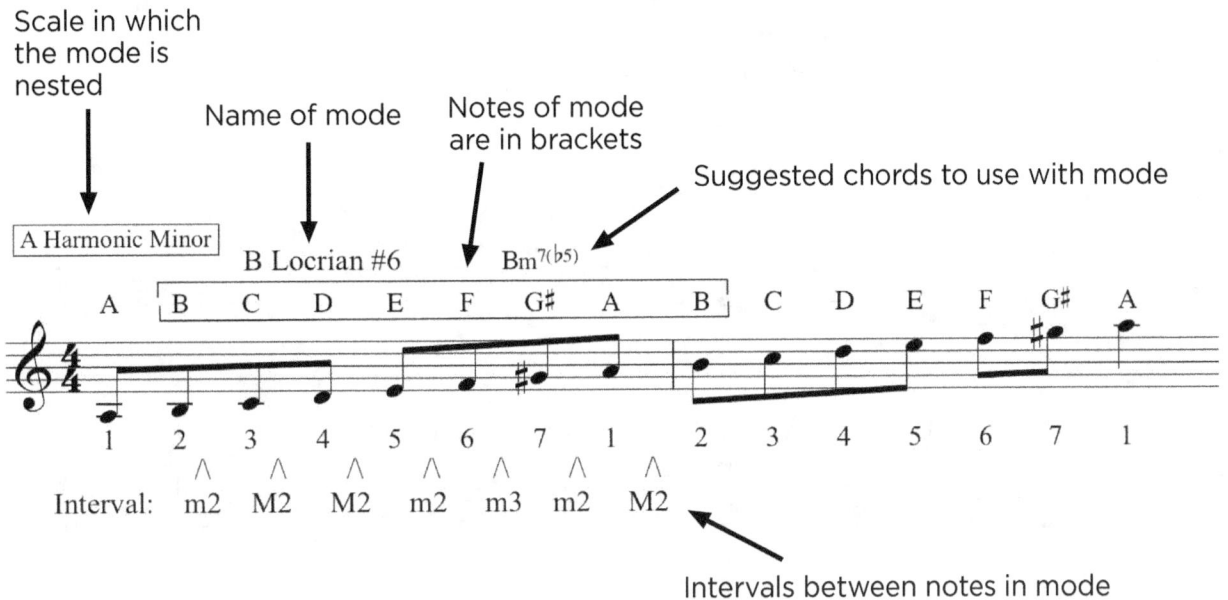

The 1st/ "Aeolian #7" Mode of the Harmonic Minor

The 1st mode is built on the 1st scale degree of the harmonic minor scale and played over minor, and minor (maj7) chords.

(See page 153 for fingering patterns for the aeolian #7 mode)

(See page 153 for fingering patterns for the aeolian #7 mode)

The 2nd/ "Locrian #6" Mode of the Harmonic Minor

The 2nd mode is played over minor 7(♭5) (a.k.a. half diminished) chords.

(See page 154 for fingering patterns for the locrian #6 mode)

(See page 154 for fingering patterns for the locrian #6 mode)

The 3rd/ "Ionian #5" Mode of the Harmonic Minor

The 3rd mode can be played over maj7(#5) chords. Yep, the maj7(#5) is weird sounding at first. But trust me, there is good music hidden here—but you will need to seek it to find it.

(See page 155 for fingering patterns for the ionian #5 mode)

The 4th/ "Dorian #4" Mode of the Harmonic Minor

The 4th mode plays over minor 7th chords very nicely.

(See page 156 for fingering patterns for the dorian #4 mode)

(See page 156 for fingering patterns for the dorian #4 mode)

The 5th/ "Phrygian Dominant" Mode of the Harmonic Minor

(See page 157 for fingering patterns for the phrygian dominant mode)

(See page 157 for fingering patterns for the phrygian dominant mode)

The 6th/ "Lydian #2" Mode of the Harmonic Minor

Try playing this mode over major 7th chords to get a different spin on these chords.
I love playing things that surprise the listener—but that work.

(See page 158 for fingering patterns for the lydian #2 mode)

(See page 158 for fingering patterns for the lydian #2 mode)

The 7th/ "Super Locrian ♭♭7" Mode of the Harmonic Minor

Looking for something to play over diminished 7th chords? Here ya go!

(See page 159 for fingering patterns for the super locrian ♭♭7 mode)

(See page 159 for fingering patterns for the super locrian ♭♭7 mode)

Just learn one small piece at a time.

PART 4
The Symmetric and the Pentatonic Scales

The Half Step/Whole Step Diminished Scale

The half step/whole step scale is a symmetrical scale containing eight notes.
There are only 3 half step/whole step scales, each of which can have four different notes as the root.

(See page 161 for fingering patterns for the half step/whole step scale)

(See page 161 for fingering patterns for the half step/whole step scale)

The Whole Step/Half Step Diminished Scale

The whole step/half step scale is a symmetrical scale containing eight notes.
There are only three whole step half/step scales, each of which can have four different notes as the root.
Use this scale over diminished and dominant ♭9 chords.

(See page 162 for fingering patterns for the whole step/half step scale)

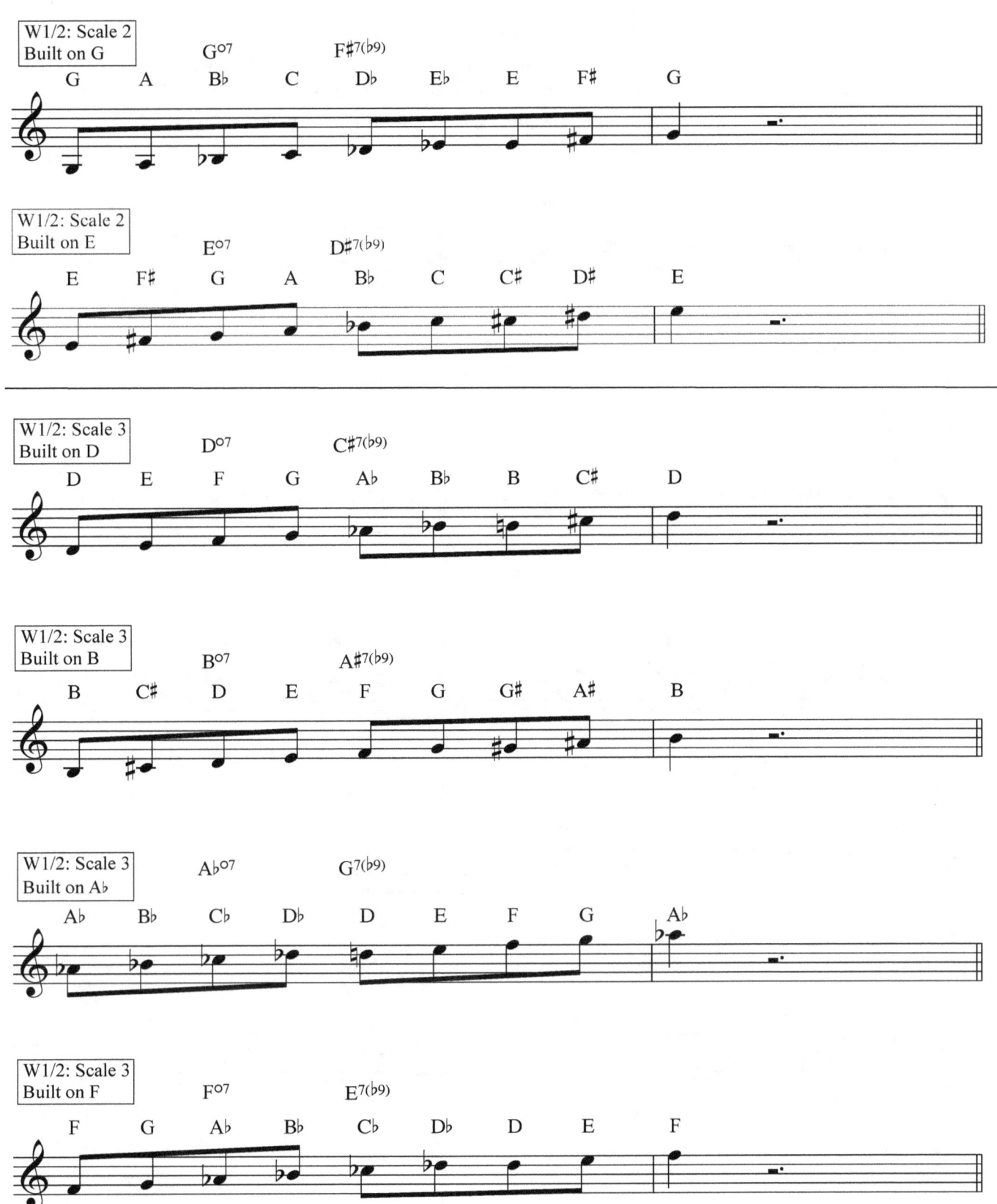

(See page 162 for fingering patterns for the whole step/half step scale)

The Whole Tone Scale

The Whole Tone Scale is made up of six notes as shown below.
There are really only two different whole tone scales. One starts on C and the other on C#.
The whole tone scale is typically played over a dominant #5 chord (e.g. C7#5).

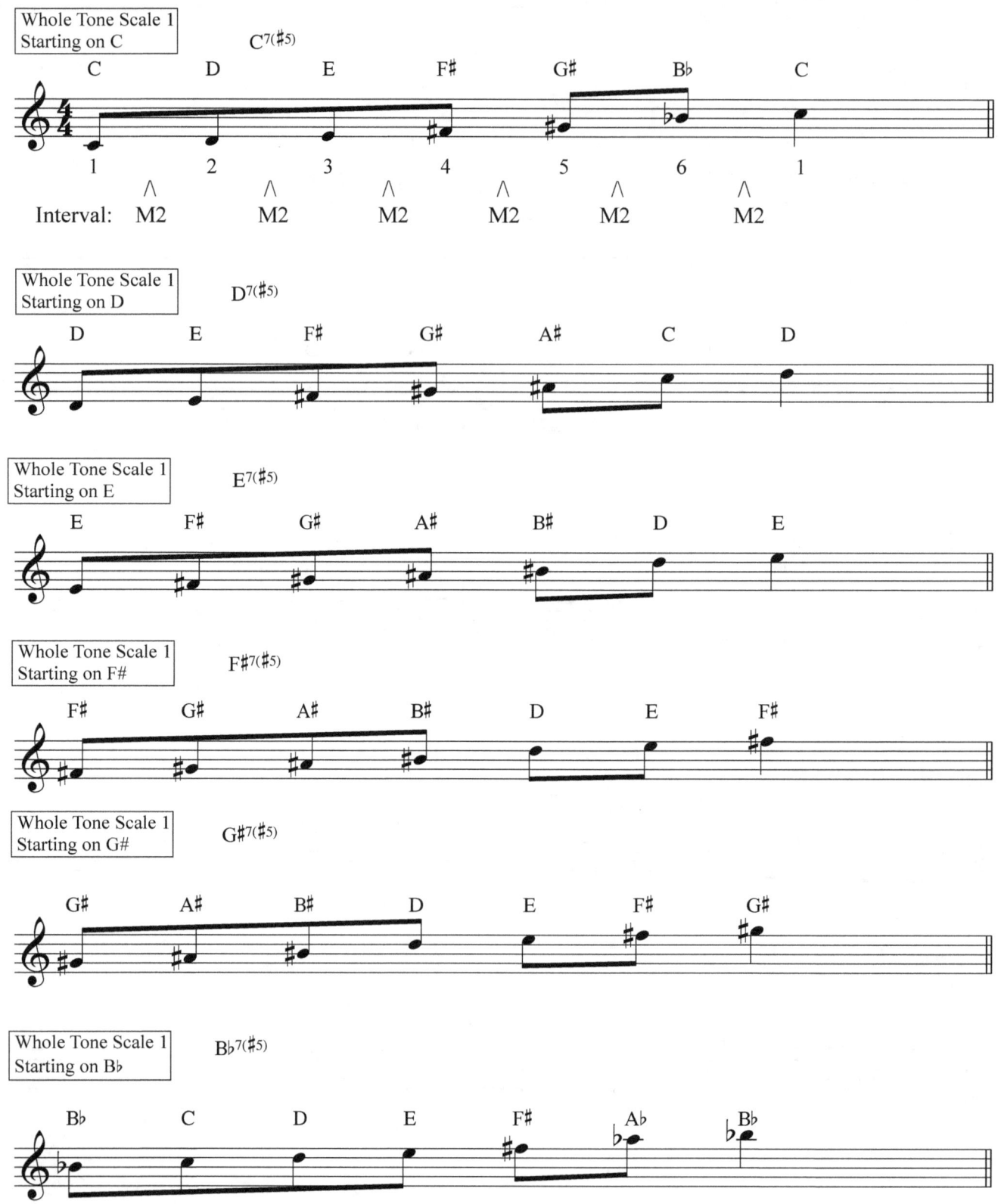

(See page 163 for fingering patterns for the whole tone scale)

(See page 163 for fingering patterns for the whole tone scale)

The Major Pentatonic Scale

To play "outside," play a lick in C major pentatonic over a progression in C, then take that same lick up a half step to C# and repeat, then bring it back down to C and repeat. Once you get the hang of it, you are hooked.

(See page 164 for fingering patterns for the major pentatonic scale)

(See page 164 for fingering patterns for the major pentatonic scale)

The Minor Pentatonic Scale

With only five notes, the minor pentatonic is almost a hybrid of scale and arpeggio. The wider spacing from the minor third intervals results in a natural melodic outcome when using this scale.

(See page 165 for fingering patterns for the minor pentatonic scale)

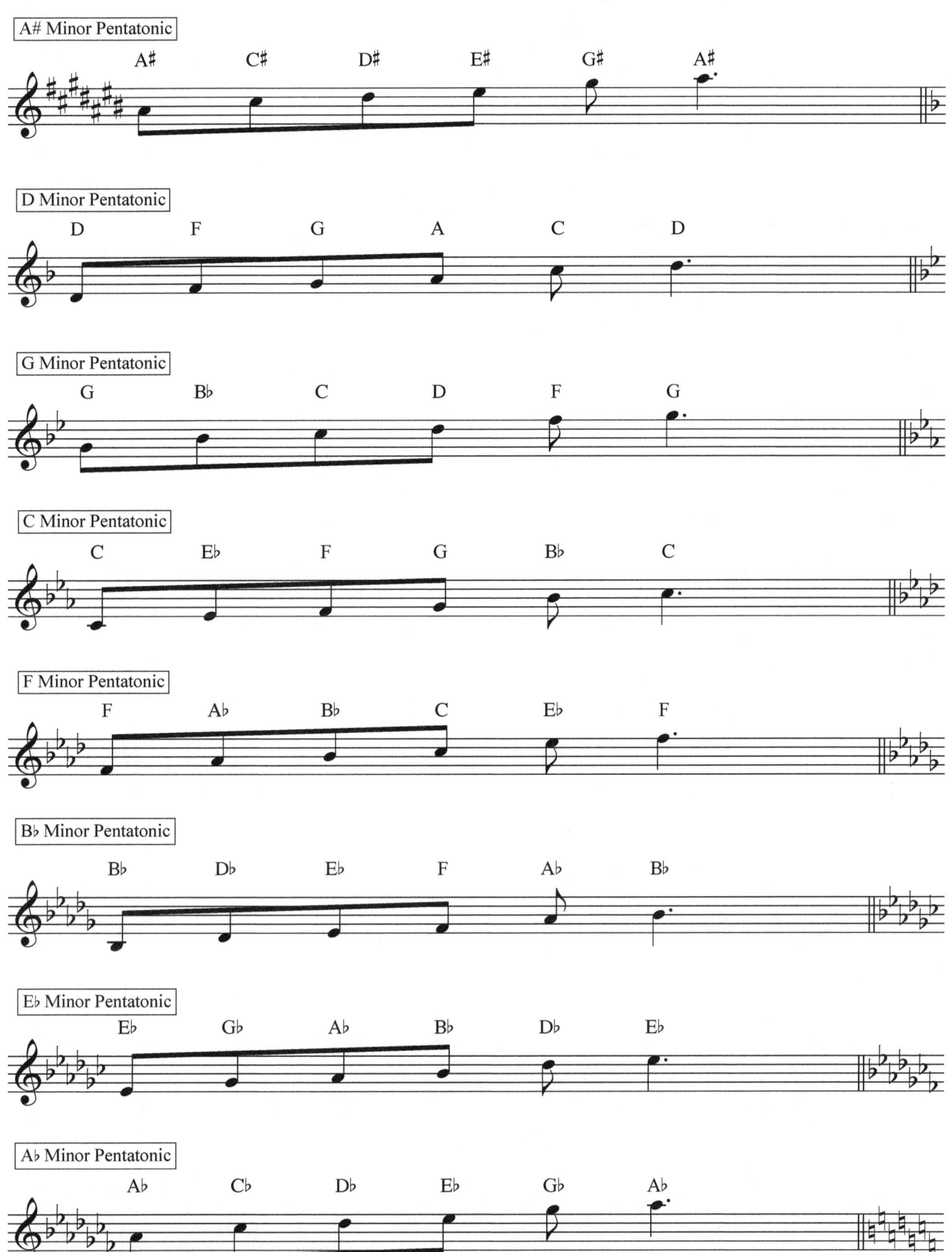

(See page 165 for fingering patterns for the minor pentatonic scale)

PART 5
The Arpeggios

Diatonic 7th Chords of the Major Scales

The concept of diatonic chords is very simple. Diatonic chords are made up exclusively of notes in a scale. For example, consider the G major scale:

By starting with the first note (G) and building a chord using every other note in the scale (G, B, D, F#) a GM7 chord is constructed. Moving to the second note in the scale (A) and again building a chord using every other note (A, C, E, G) produces an Am7 chord. Using this principle to build a chord upon every note in the scale yields the following results:

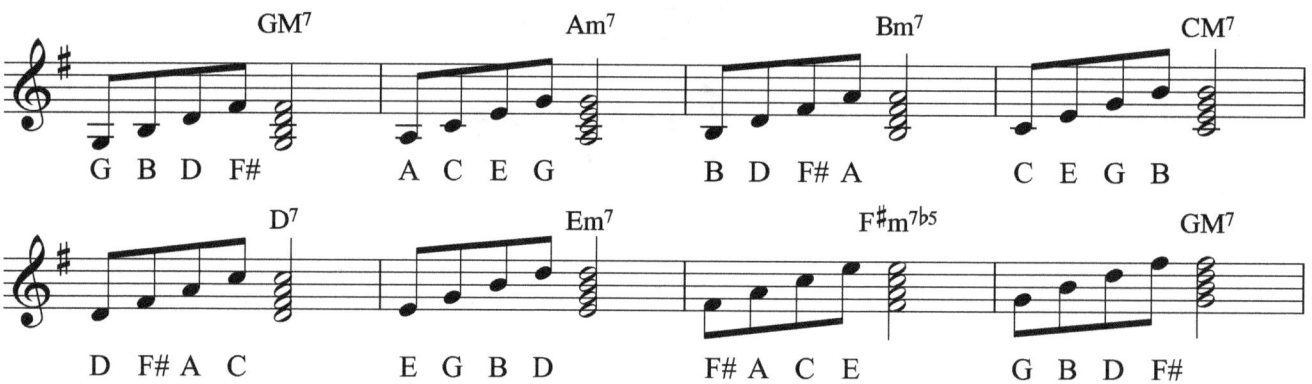

When building diatonic chords using major scales, the chords built on the first and fourth notes of the scale will always be major 7th chords, those built on the second, third, and sixth notes in the scale will always be minor 7th chords, those built on the fifth note in the scale will always be dominant 7th chords, and those built on the seventh note in the scale will always be minor 7th flat 5 (half-diminished) chords.

Diatonic chord built on 1st note in major scale:	Major 7th
Diatonic chord built on 2nd note in major scale:	Minor 7th
Diatonic chord built on 3rd note in major scale:	Minor 7th
Diatonic chord built on 4th note in major scale:	Major 7th
Diatonic chord built on 5th note in major scale:	Dominant 7th
Diatonic chord built on 6th note in major scale:	Minor 7th
Diatonic chord built on 7th note in major scale:	Minor 7th flat 5

By memorizing the table above, you will be able to quickly identify and construct diatonic chords from any major scale.

Diatonic 6th Chords of the Major Scales

The concept of diatonic 6th chords is again very simple. Diatonic 6th chords are made up exclusively of notes in a scale. For example, consider the G major scale:

Start with the first note (G) and build a chord using every other note in the scale (G, B, D) to build a triad, then add the next note in the scale (E) to form a G6 chord (G,B,D,E).
Using this same principle with the second note in the scale (A) produces an Am6 chord (A,C,E,F#).
Using this approach to build a sixth chord upon every note in the scale yields the following results:

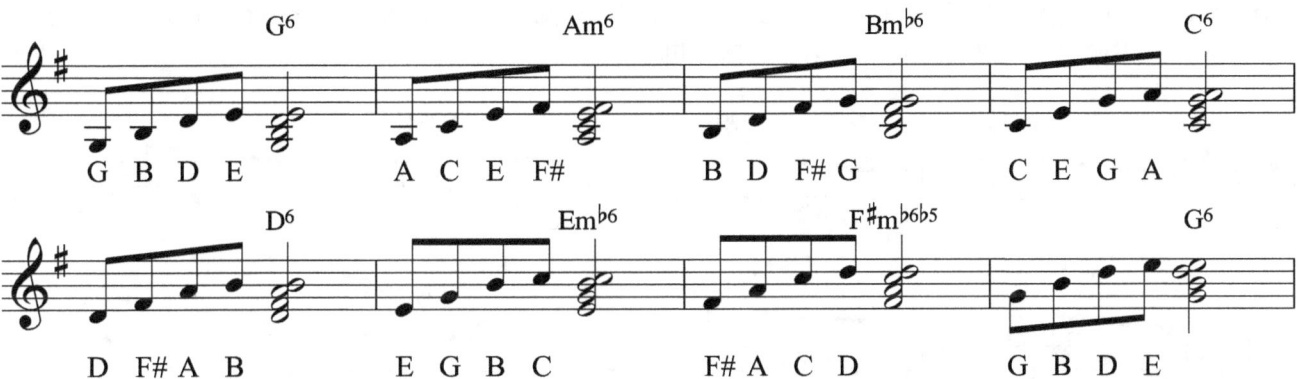

When building diatonic chords using major scales, the chords built on the first, fourth, and fifth notes of the scale will always be major 6th chords, those built on the second note in the scale will always be minor 6th chords, those built on the third and sixth notes in the scale will always be minor flat 6 chords, and those built on the seventh note in the scale will always be minor flat 6 flat 5 chords.

Diatonic chord built on 1st note in major scale:	Major 6th
Diatonic chord built on 2nd note in major scale:	Minor 6th
Diatonic chord built on 3rd note in major scale:	Minor flat 6th
Diatonic chord built on 4th note in major scale:	Major 6th
Diatonic chord built on 5th note in major scale:	Major 6th
Diatonic chord built on 6th note in major scale:	Minor flat 6th
Diatonic chord built on 7th note in major scale:	Minor flat 6th flat 5

By memorizing the table above, you will be able to quickly identify and construct diatonic chords from any major scale.

Diatonic 7th Chords of the Melodic Minor

The concept of diatonic 7th chords in the melodic minor scales is identical to that of the major and harmonic minor scales. Diatonic 7th chords are made up exclusively of notes in a scale. For example, consider the G melodic minor scale:

By starting with the first note (G) and building a chord using every other note in the scale (G, B♭, D, F#) a Gm(M7) chord is constructed. Moving to the second note in the scale (A) and again building a chord using every other note (A, C, E, G) produces an Am7 chord. Using this principle to build a chord upon every note in the scale yields the following results:

When building diatonic chords using melodic minor scales, the chords built on the first note of the scale will always be minor major 7th chords; those built on the second note in the scale will always be minor 7th chords; those built on the third note in the scale will always be major 7th sharp 5 chords; those built on the fourth and fifth notes of the scale will always be dominant 7th chords; and those built on the sixth and seventh notes of the scale will always be minor 7th flat 5 chords.

Diatonic chord built on 1st note in melodic minor:	Minor major 7th
Diatonic chord built on 2nd note in melodic minor:	Minor 7th
Diatonic chord built on 3rd note in melodic minor:	Major 7th sharp 5
Diatonic chord built on 4th note in melodic minor:	Dominant 7th
Diatonic chord built on 5th note in melodic minor:	Dominant 7th
Diatonic chord built on 6th note in melodic minor:	Minor 7th flat 5
Diatonic chord built on 7th note in melodic minor:	Minor 7th flat 5

By memorizing the table above, you will be able to quickly identify and construct diatonic chords from any melodic minor scale.

Diatonic 7th Chords of the Harmonic Minor

The concept of diatonic 7th chords in the harmonic minor scales is identical to that of the major scales. Diatonic 7th chords are made up exclusively of notes in a scale. For example, consider the G harmonic minor scale:

By starting with the first note (G) and building a chord using every other note in the scale (G, B♭, D, F#) a Gm(M7) chord is constructed. Moving to the second note in the scale (A) and again building a chord using every other note (A, C, E♭, G) produces an Am7♭5 chord. Using this principle to build a chord upon every note in the scale yields the following results:

When building diatonic chords using harmonic minor scales, the chords built on the first note of the scale will always be minor major 7th chords; those built on the second note in the scale will always be minor 7th flat 5 chords; those built on the third note in the scale will always be major 7th sharp 5 chords; those built on the fourth note of the scale will always be minor 7th chords; those built on the fifth note of the scale will always be dominant 7th chords; those built on the sixth note of the scale will always be major 7th chords; and those built on the seventh note in the scale will always be diminished 7th chords.

Diatonic chord built on 1st note in harmonic minor:	Minor major 7th
Diatonic chord built on 2nd note in harmonic minor:	Minor 7th flat 5
Diatonic chord built on 3rd note in harmonic minor:	Major 7th sharp 5
Diatonic chord built on 4th note in harmonic minor:	Minor 7th
Diatonic chord built on 5th note in harmonic minor:	Dominant 7th
Diatonic chord built on 6th note in harmonic minor:	Major 7th
Diatonic chord built on 7th note in harmonic minor:	Diminished 7th

By memorizing the table above, you will be able to quickly identify and construct diatonic chords from any harmonic minor scale.

The Major 7th Arpeggio

The major 7th arpeggio is found nested within the 1st and 4th modes of the major scale and the 6th mode of the harmonic minor scale.

(See page 167 for fingering patterns for the major 7th arpeggio)

(See page 167 for fingering patterns for the major 7th arpeggio)

The Major 6th Arpeggio

The major 6th arpeggio is found nested within the 1st and 4th modes of the major scale.

(See page 168 for fingering patterns for the major 6th arpeggio)

(See page 168 for fingering patterns for the major 6th arpeggio)

The Dominant 7th Arpeggio

The dominant 7th arpeggio is found nested within the 5th mode of the major scale, the 5th mode of the harmonic minor scale, and the 4th and 5th modes of the melodic minor scale.

(See page 169 for fingering patterns for the dominant 7th arpeggio)

(See page 169 for fingering patterns for the dominant 7th arpeggio)

The Dominant 7th(♭5) Arpeggio

The dominant 7th(♭5) arpeggio is simply a dominant 7th arpeggio with the 5th of the chord flatted a half step. Notice this arpeggio is nested inside the whole tone scale.

(See page 170 for fingering patterns for the dominant 7th flat 5 arpeggio)

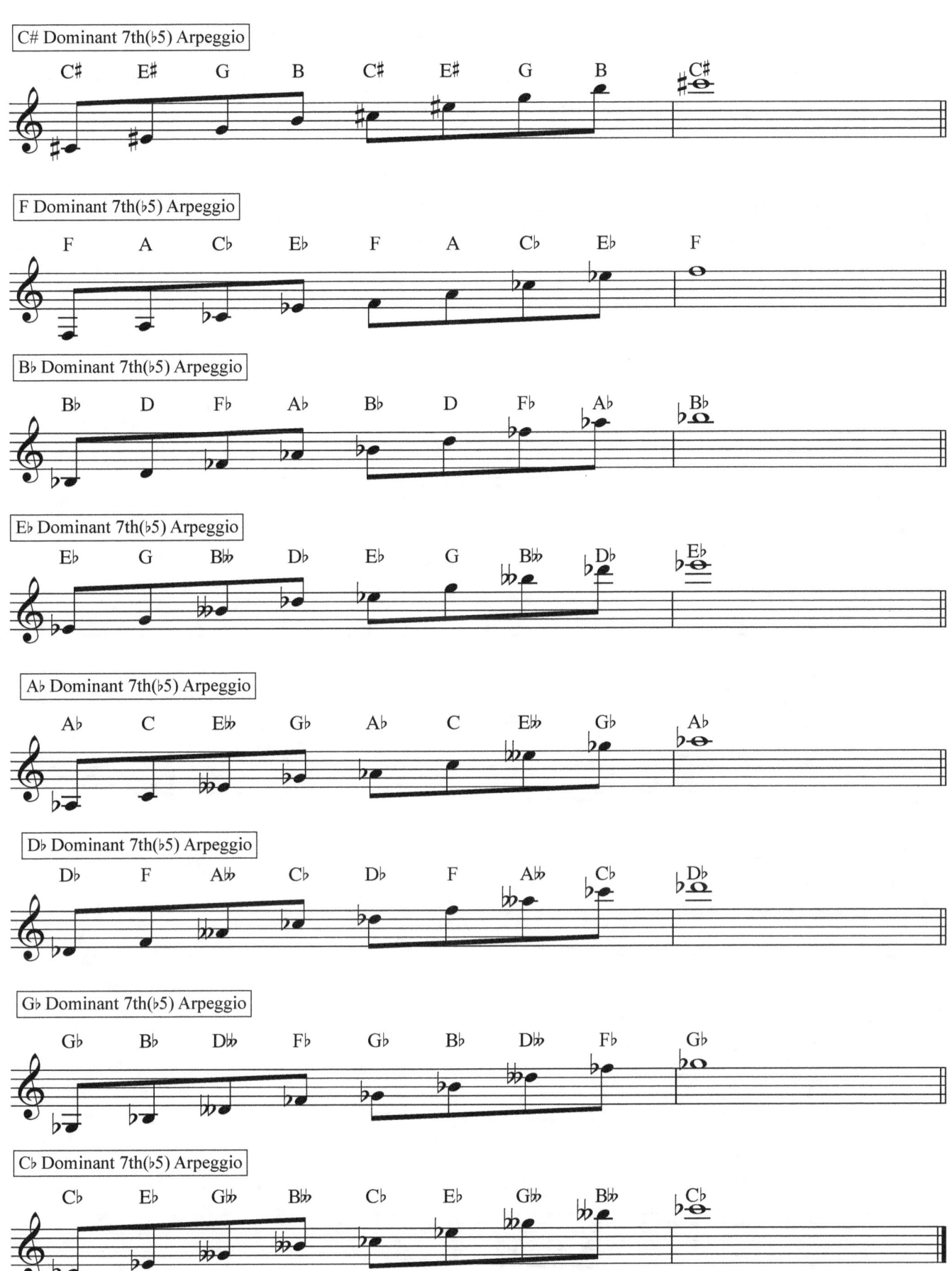

(See page 170 for fingering patterns for the dominant 7th flat 5 arpeggio)

The Dominant 7th(#5) Arpeggio

The dominant 7th(#5) arpeggio's simply a dominant 7th arpeggio with the 5th of the chord sharped a half step. This arpeggio is nested within the whole tone scale.

(See page 171 for fingering patterns for the dominant 7th sharp 5 arpeggio)

(See page 171 for fingering patterns for the dominant 7th sharp 5 arpeggio)

The Minor 7th Arpeggio

The minor 7th arpeggio is found nested within the 2nd, 3rd, and 4th modes of the major scale, the 4th mode of the harmonic minor scale, and the 2nd mode of the melodic minor scale.

(See page 172 for fingering patterns for the minor 7th arpeggio)

(See page 172 for fingering patterns for the minor 7th arpeggio)

The Minor 7th (♭5) Arpeggio

The minor 7th (♭5) arpeggio (also called the "half diminished" arpeggio) is found nested within the 7th mode of the major scale, the 2nd mode of the harmonic minor scale, and the 6th and 7th modes of the melodic minor scale.

(See page 173 for fingering patterns for the minor 7th flat 5 arpeggio)

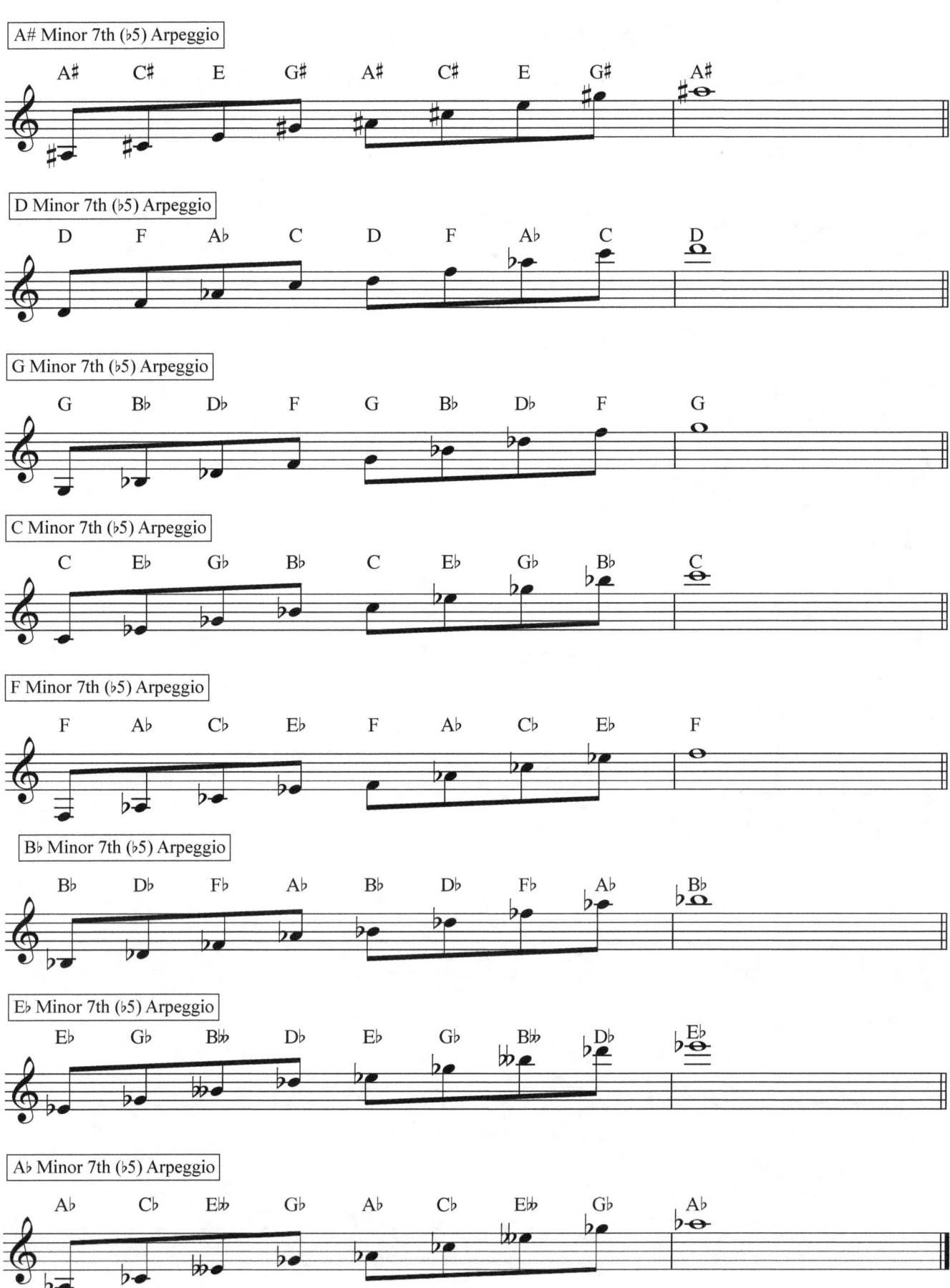

(See page 173 for fingering patterns for the minor 7th flat 5 arpeggio)

The Minor 6th Arpeggio

The minor 6th arpeggio is found nested within the 2nd mode of the major scale.

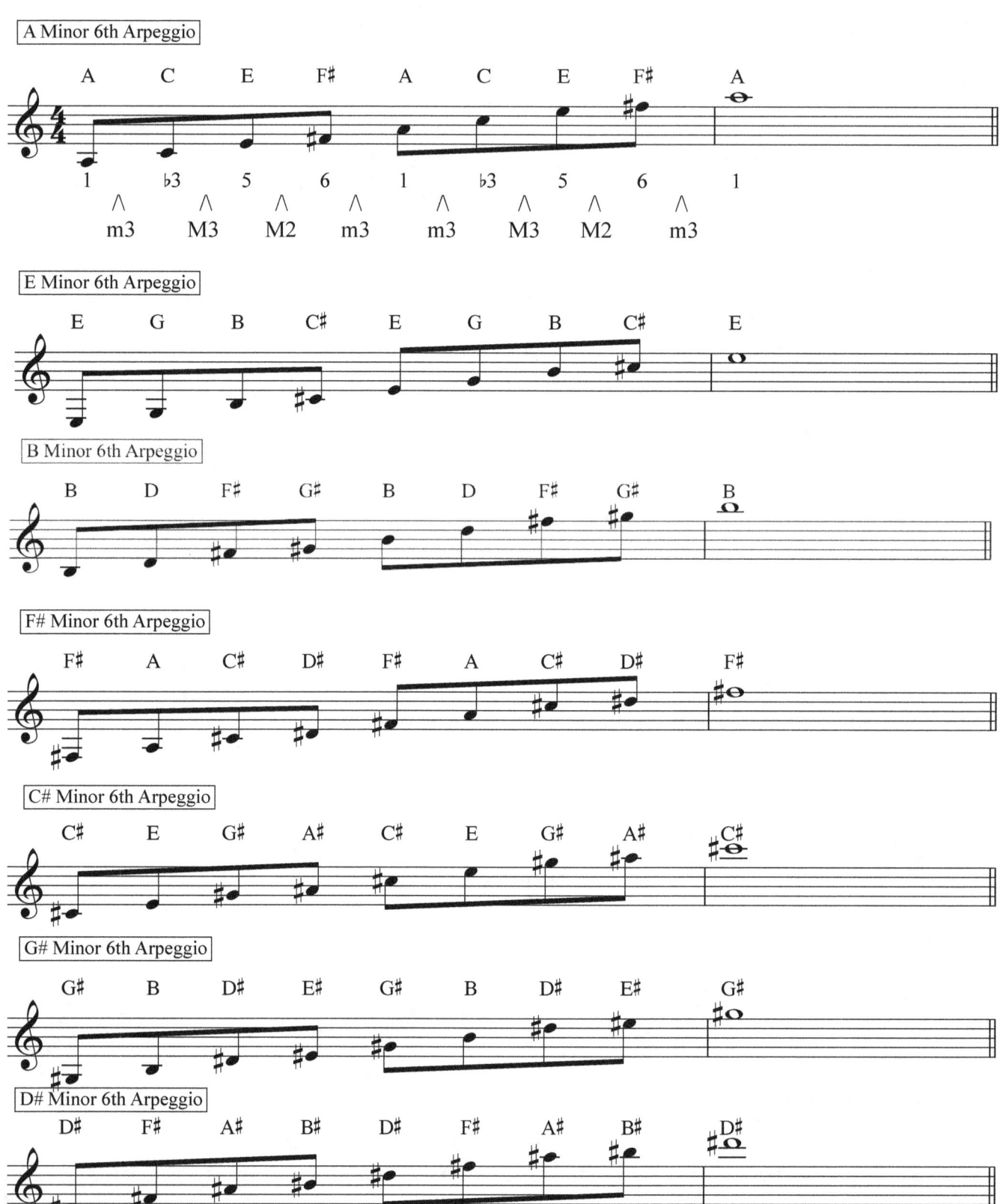

(See page 174 for fingering patterns for the minor 6th arpeggio)

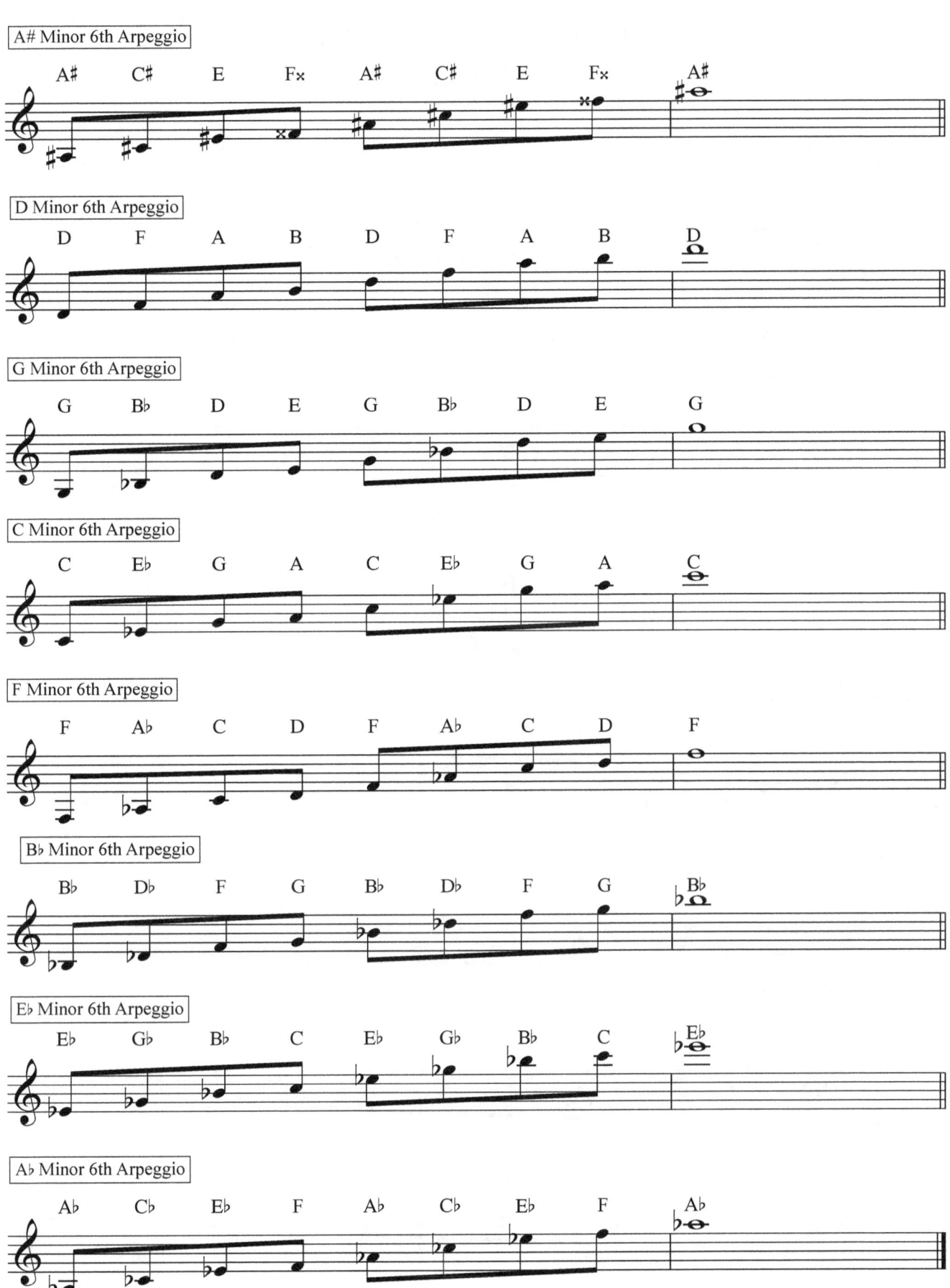

(See page 174 for fingering patterns for the minor 6th arpeggio)

The Minor ♭6th Arpeggio

Noodle around in the the minor ♭6th arpeggio, then the minor 6th arpeggio to notice the different flavors these two arpeggios possess.

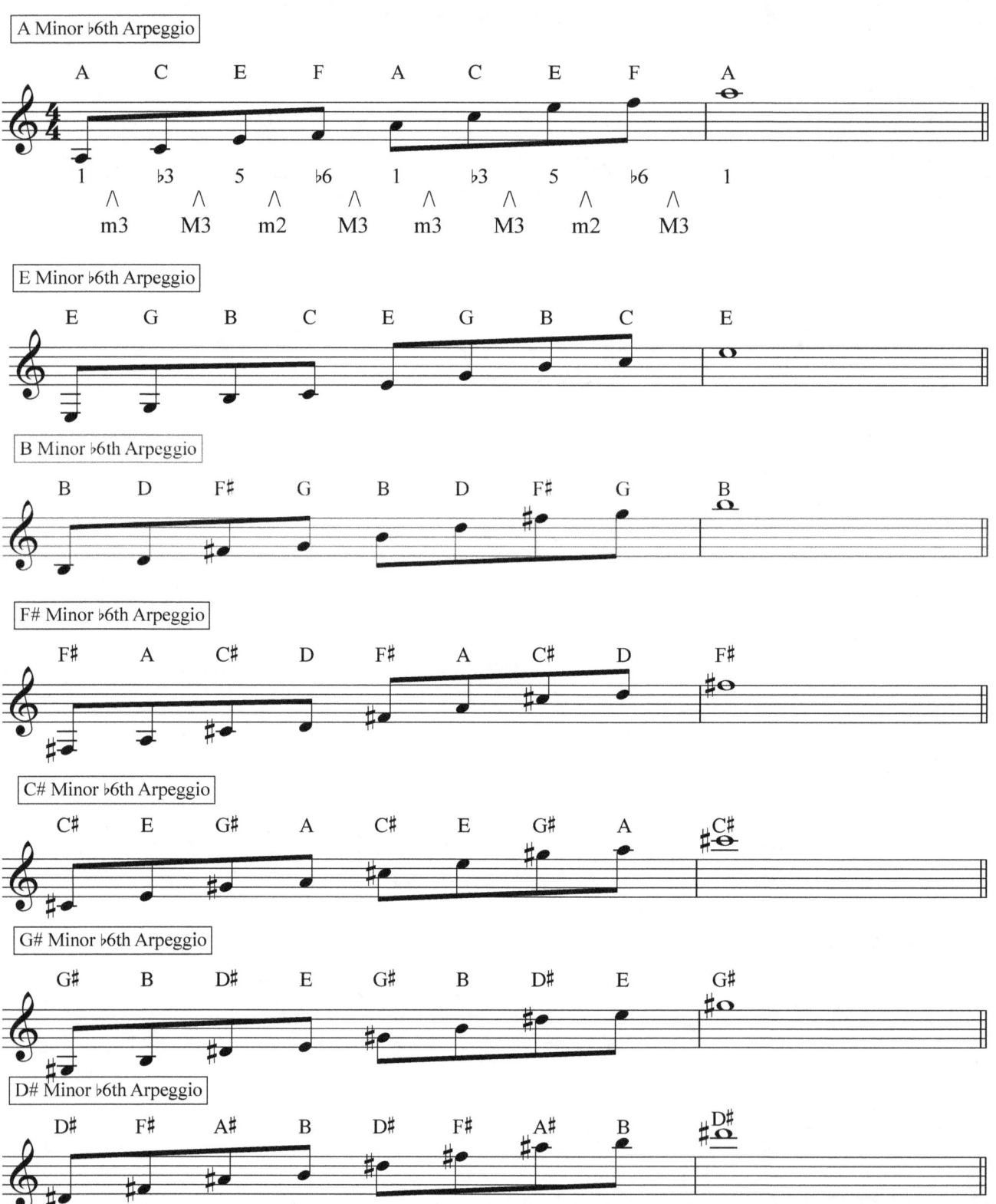

(See page 175 for fingering patterns for the minor flat 6th arpeggio)

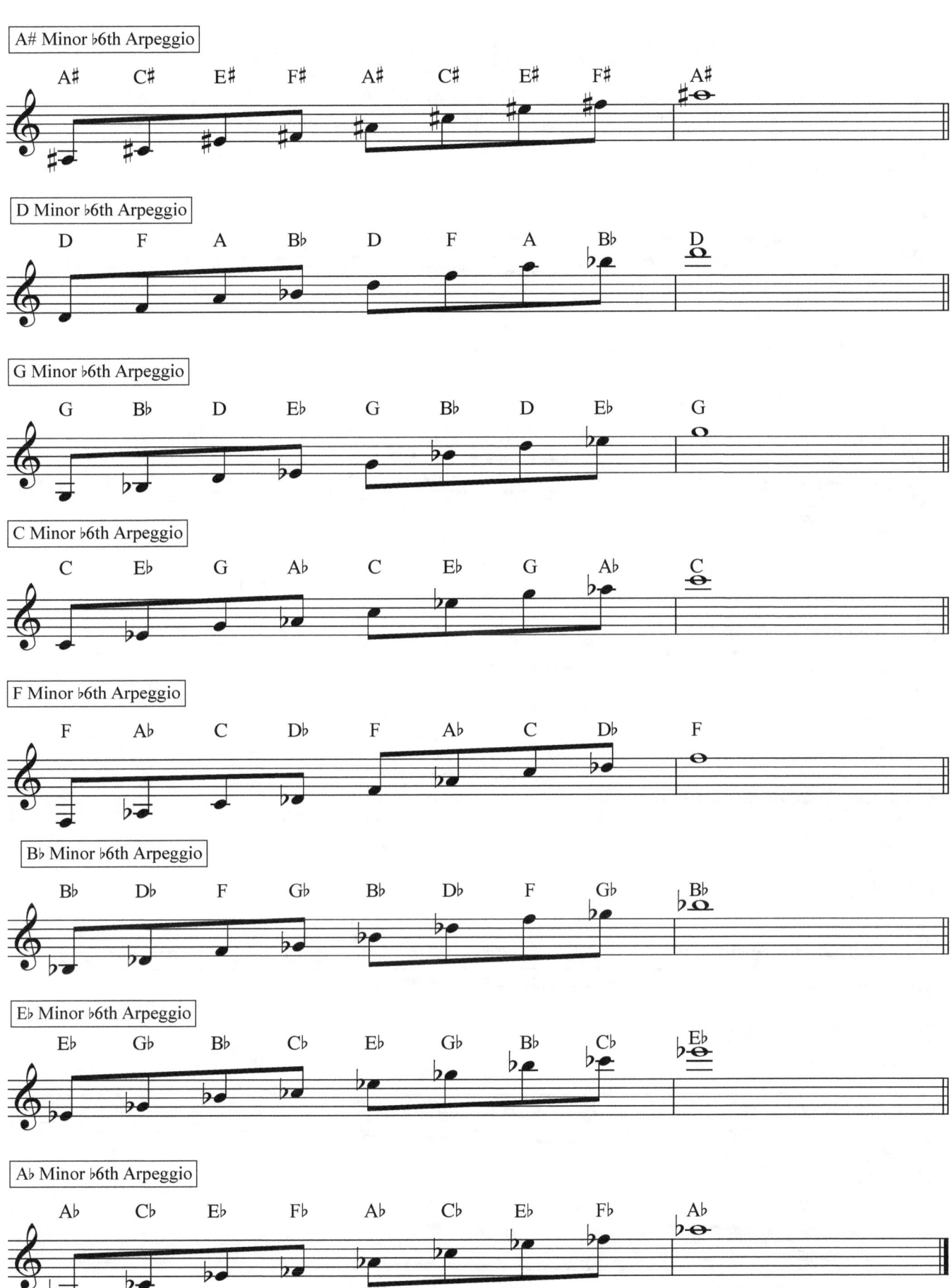

(See page 175 for fingering patterns for the minor flat 6th arpeggio)

The Minor ♭6th (♭5) Arpeggio

The minor ♭6th(♭5) arpeggio is found nested within the 7th mode of the major scale.
Notice that an Am♭6(♭5) has the same notes (A, C, E♭, F) as an F7 chord (F, A, C, E♭)

(See page 176 for fingering patterns for the minor flat 6th flat 5 arpeggio)

(See page 176 for fingering patterns for the minor flat 6th flat 5 arpeggio)

The Minor (Maj7th) Arpeggio

This one works good in jazz against a minor chord—play it with a swing feel.
Good training for the fingers.

(See page 177 for fingering patterns for the minor major 7th arpeggio)

(See page 177 for fingering patterns for the minor major 7th arpeggio)

The Major 7th(#5) Arpeggio

The major 7th(#5) arpeggio is found nested within the 3rd modes of the harmonic minor and melodic minor scales. If you experiment long enough, you will find some cool melodies here.

(See page 178 for fingering patterns for the major 7th sharp 5 arpeggio)

The Diminished 7th Arpeggio

The diminished 7th arpeggio is found nested within the 7th mode of the harmonic minor scale.

(See page 179 for fingering patterns for the diminished 7th arpeggio)

(See page 179 for fingering patterns for the diminished 7th arpeggio)

Review of the Arpeggios

The various arpeggios covered in this book are presented here—all built on C—so that you can see how the chord tones are altered to create their various sounds.

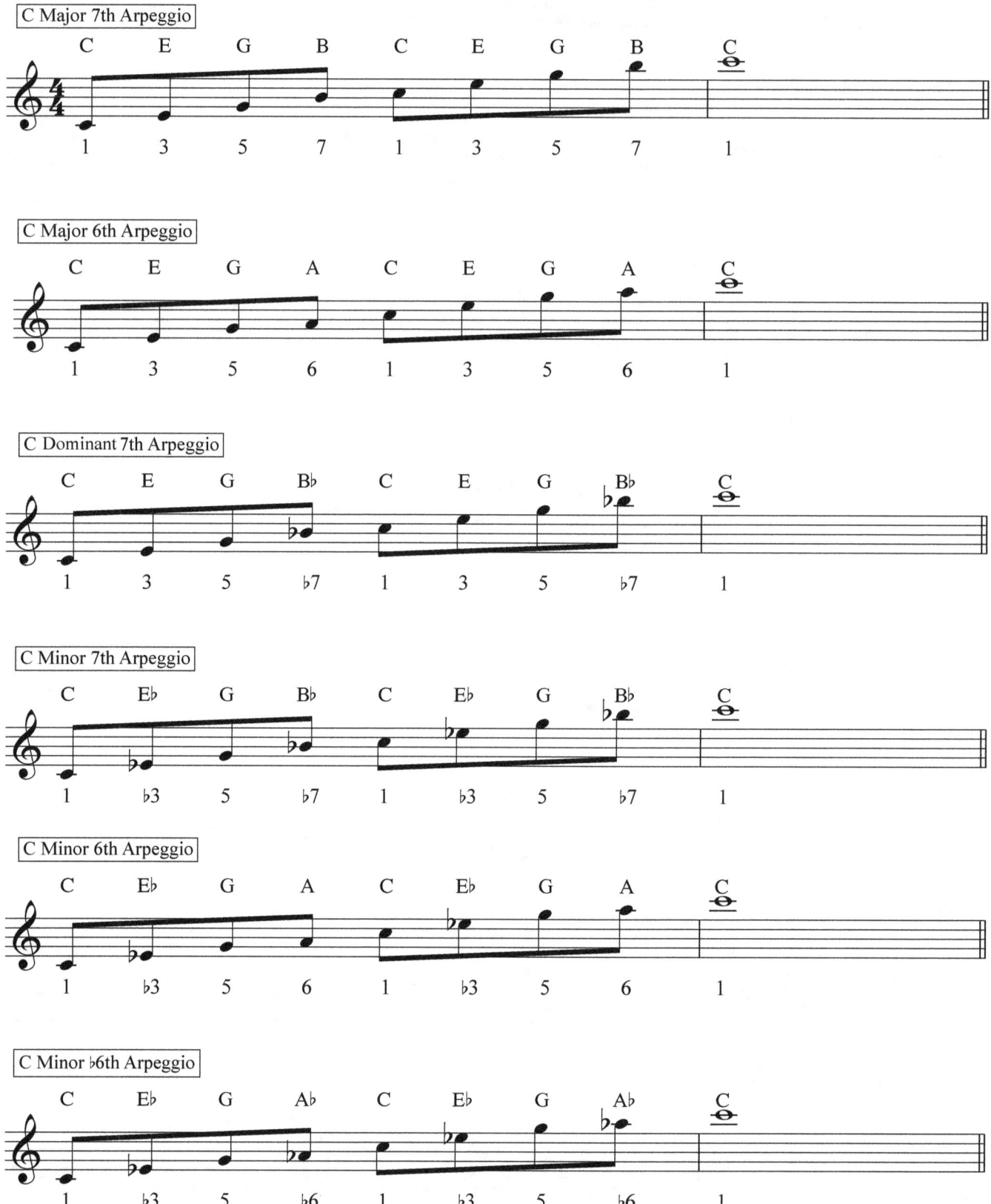

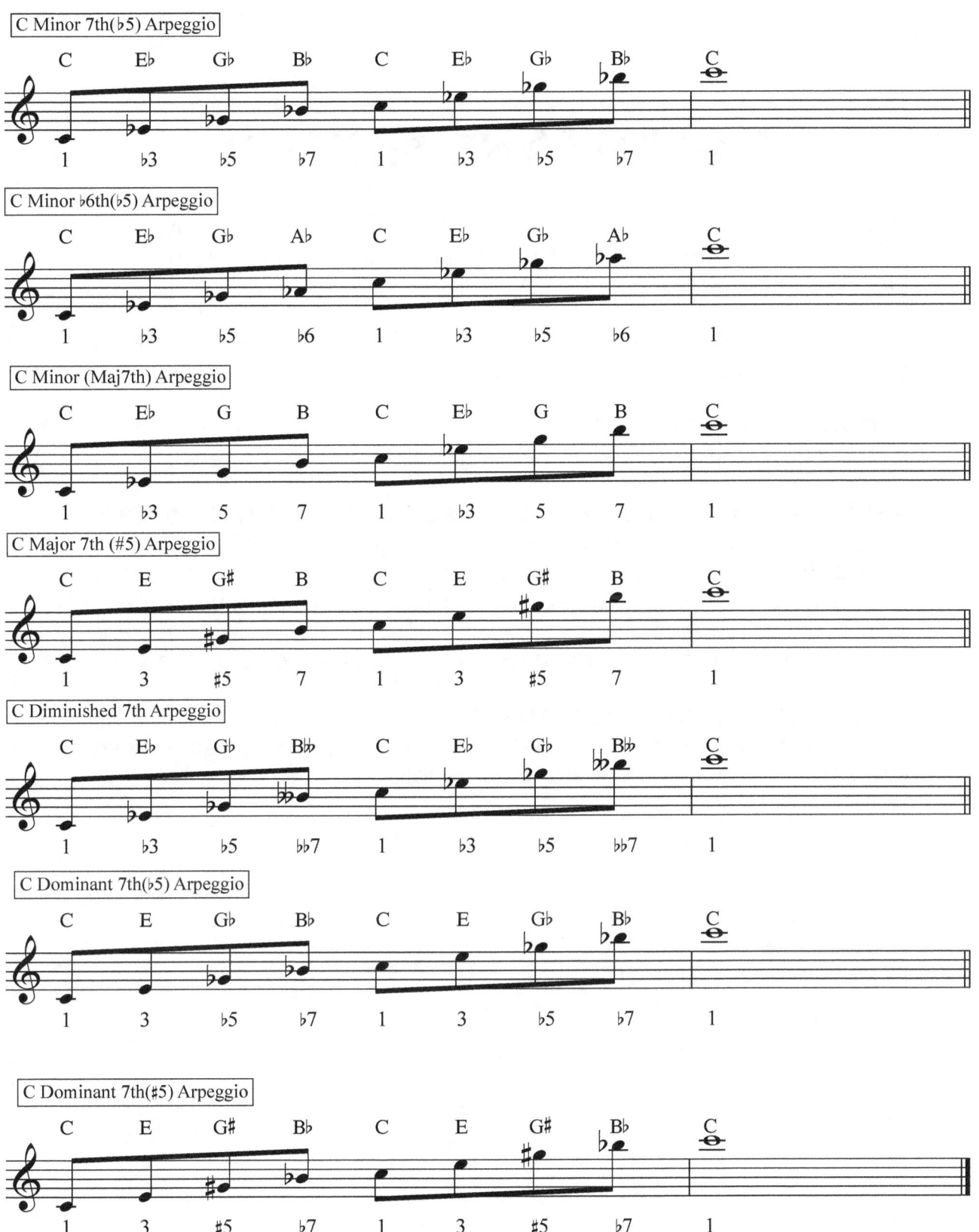

IMPORTANT NOTE!!!

In the next section of the book some of the finger patterns may be challenging at first—especially those which require extending the fourth finger two frets from the third finger.

While training your hands and muscle memory to play these patterns do the following...

KEEP YOUR HANDS RELAXED
Do NOT allow tension to exist in your hands, wrists, or fingers.

USE THE LIGHTEST POSSIBLE TOUCH FOR FRETTING THE NOTES
Do NOT press down more than you have to when fretting the notes, as this fights against speed and wears out your hands/joints. Practice the patterns which are difficult slowly and with minimal fretting pressure—in fact you can practice them by just laying your fingers on the strings and not pressing down at all (as if you were playing a harmonic on the string).

DO NOT OVEREXTEND YOUR FINGERS
If at first a stretch seems beyond the range of your fingers, slightly shift the position of your entire hand to accomplish fretting the note.

SECTION 2

Learning the Fingerings

This section of the book contains the fingering patterns used to logically play the scales, modes, and arpeggios which were spelled out in Section 1 of this book.

It may seem a vast number of fingering patterns to learn, however, following the approach below will make memorization of these patterns MUCH easier.

      1 - Memorize the 12 fingerings for the 1st Mode of the major scale
      2 - Then memorize the fingering for the other modes of the major scale

Then use the same approach for the melodic minor and harmonic minor. You will find this approach makes learning these fingerings much more efficient.

Once the fingerings have been memorized, don't just play them from the lowest note to the highest and back down. Noodle around and see what licks come easy to each pattern.

Example of How to Play the Fingering patterns Shown in the Block Diagrams

After you have memorized the patterns, try noodling around in them rather than merely playing them straight up and straight down. Find what licks are EASY to play in each pattern. These fingering patterns follow the 6 Fret Chromatic Concept explained on page 8. Any exceptions to that concept are noted with an asterisk (*).

The example below shows the D dorian mode, the Dm7 and Dm6 arpeggios starting on the fourth finger of the fifth string.

Begin on the circled note,
Play up to the highest possible note,
Play down to the lowest possible note,
Play back up to the circled note.

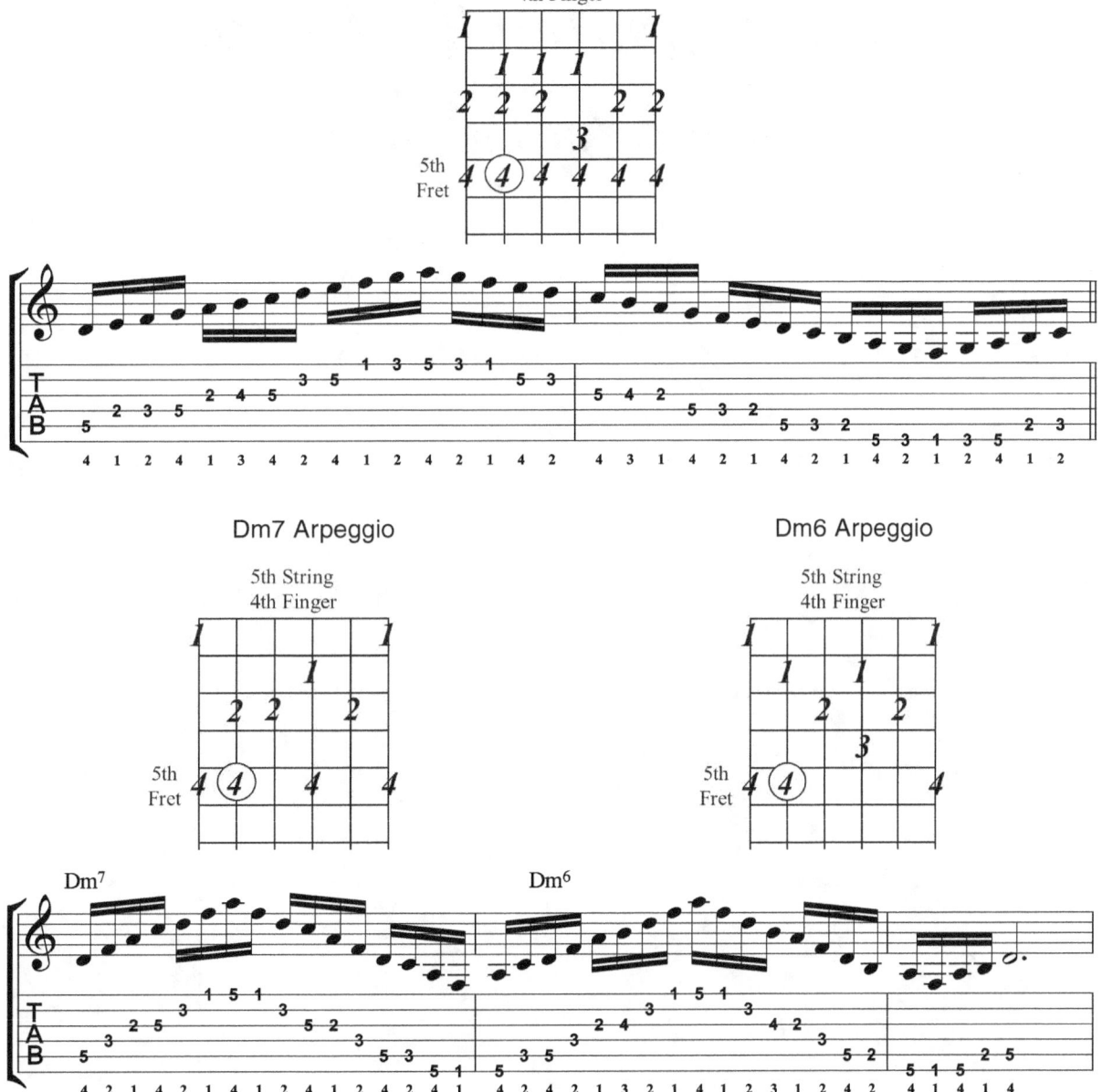

PART 6
Fingerings for the Modes of the Major Scale

Tip: Memorizing the 12 patterns for the 1st mode will greatly enhance the speed at which you will be able to memorize the fingerings for the other 6 modes.

The 1st/ "Ionian" Mode of the Major Scale

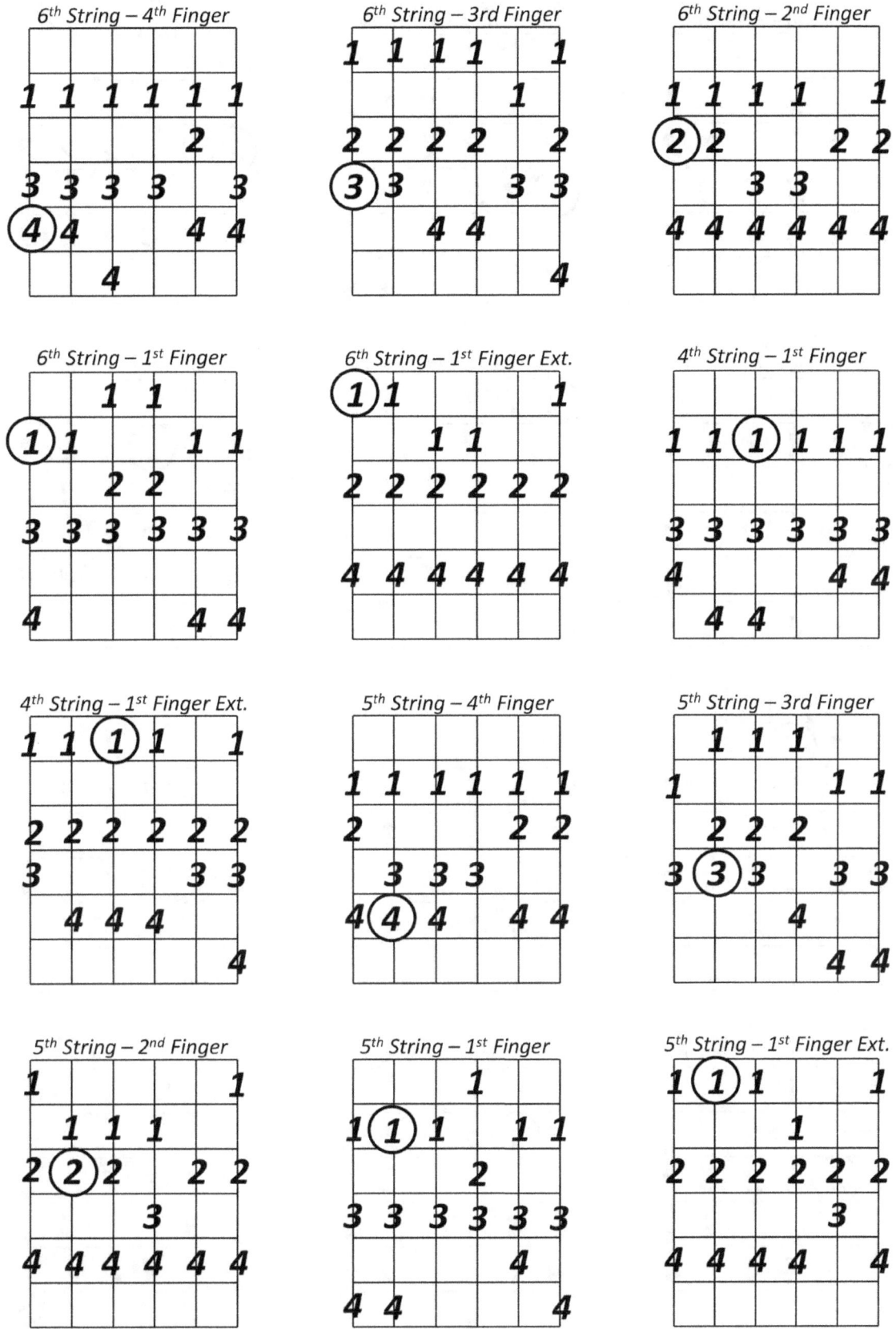

(See pages 24–25 to view the spelling of the ionian modes)

The 2nd/"Dorian" Mode of the Major Scale

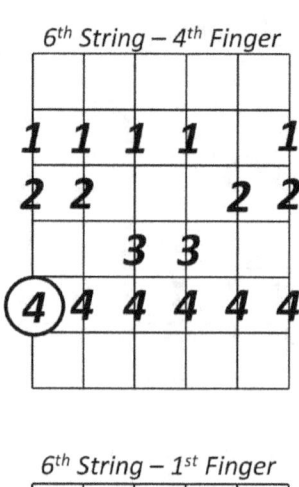
6th String – 4th Finger

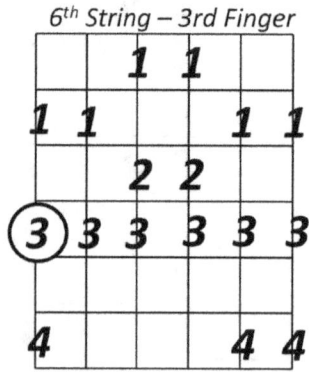
6th String – 3rd Finger

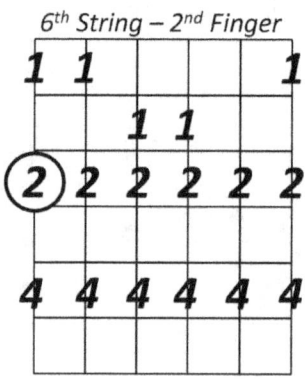
6th String – 2nd Finger

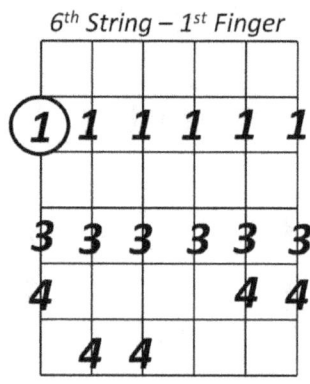
6th String – 1st Finger

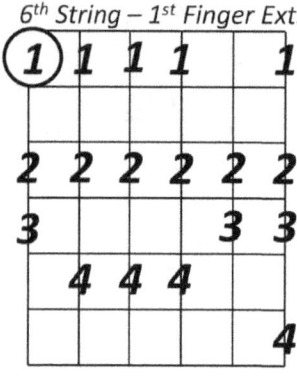
6th String – 1st Finger Ext.

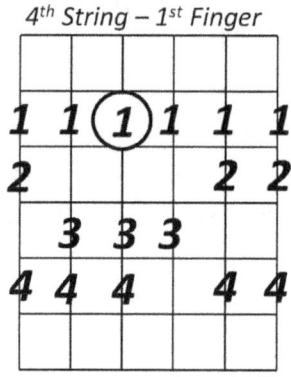
4th String – 1st Finger

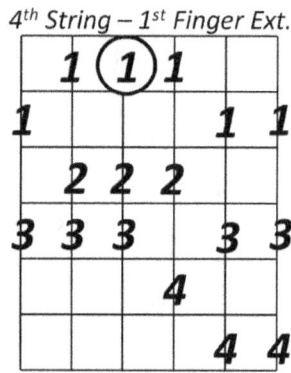
4th String – 1st Finger Ext.

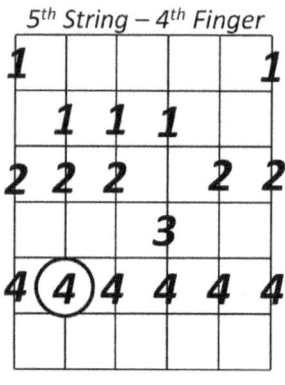
5th String – 4th Finger

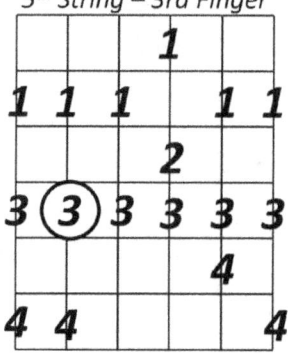
5th String – 3rd Finger

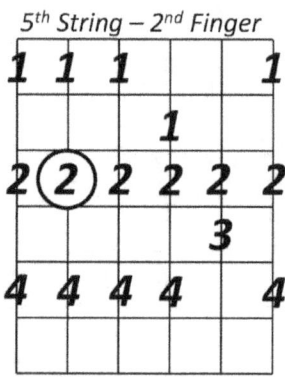
5th String – 2nd Finger

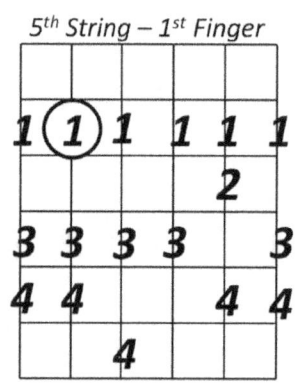
5th String – 1st Finger

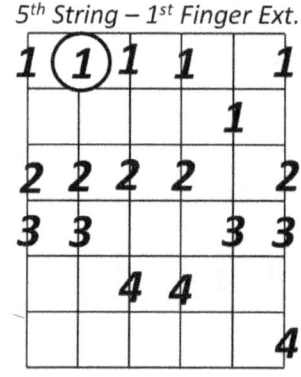
5th String – 1st Finger Ext.

(See pages 26–27 to view the spelling of the dorian modes)

The 3rd/"Phrygian" Mode of the Major Scale

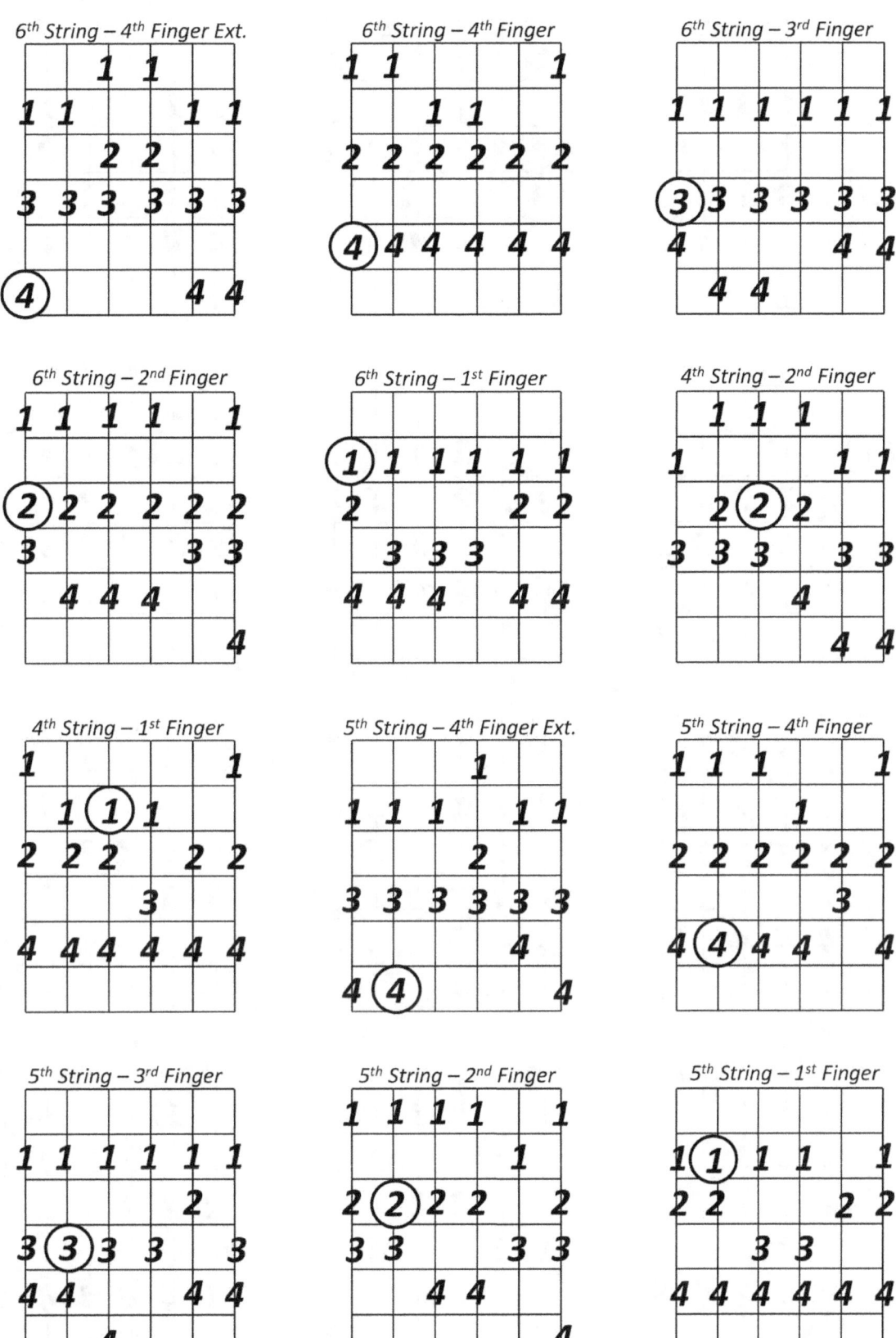

(See pages 28–29 to view the spelling of the phrygian modes)

The 4th/"Lydian" Mode of the Major Scale

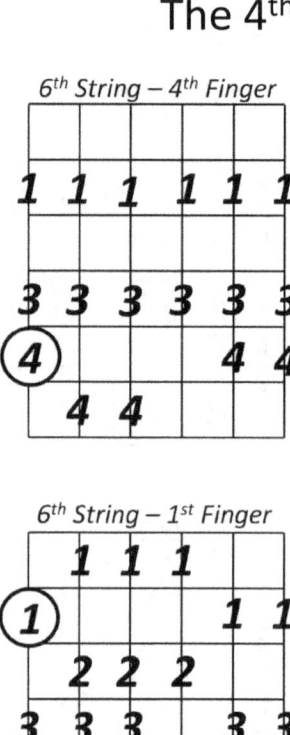
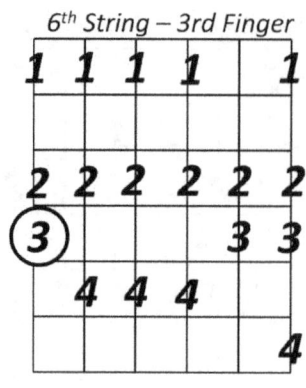
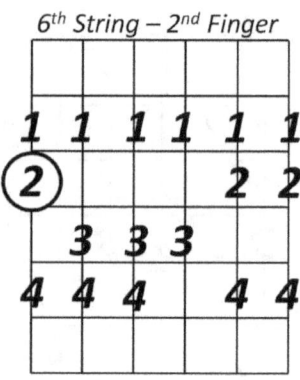
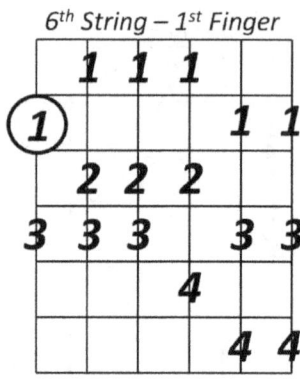
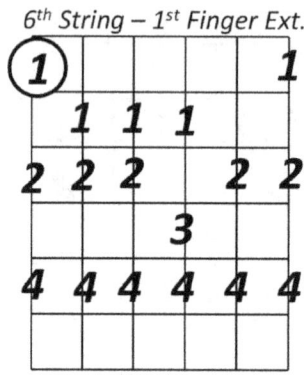
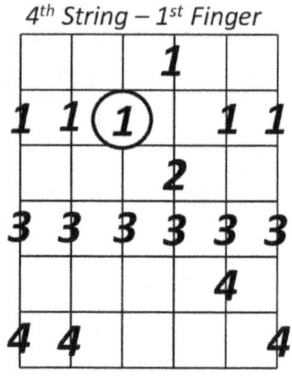
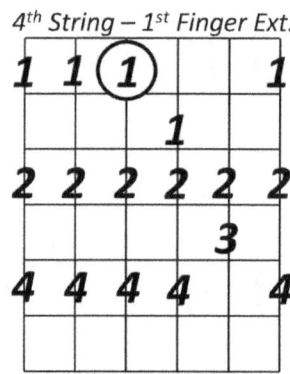
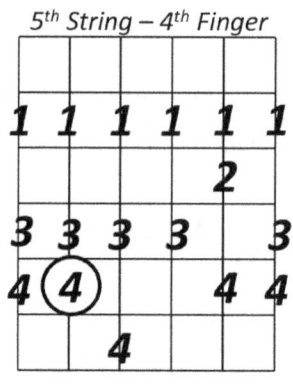
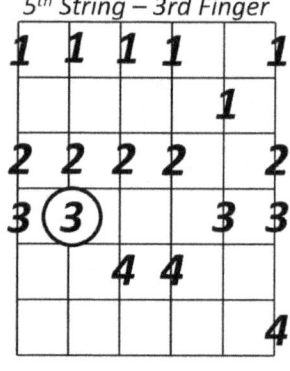
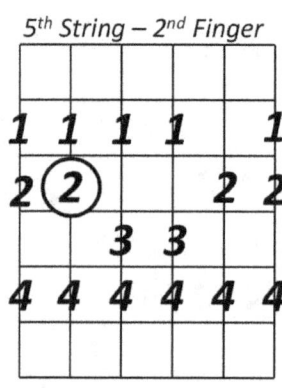
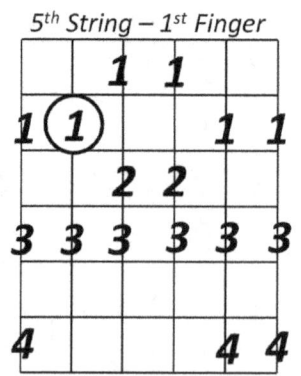
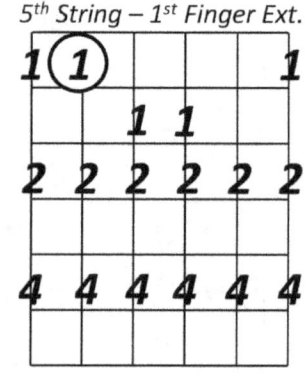

(See pages 30–31 to view the spelling of the lydian modes)

The 5th/"Mixolydian" Mode of the Major Scale

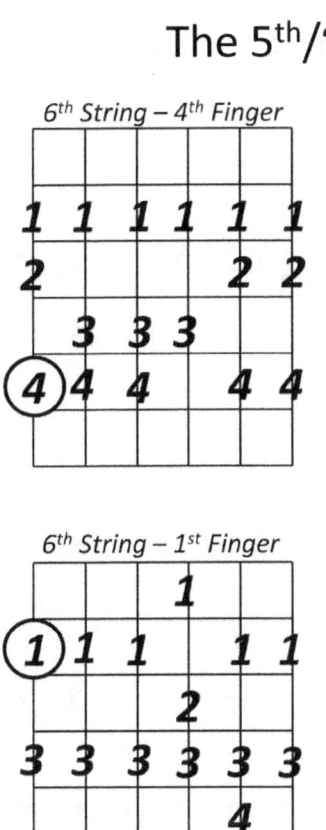
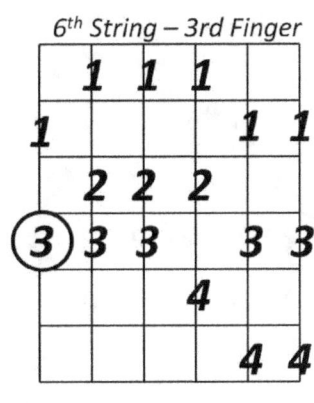
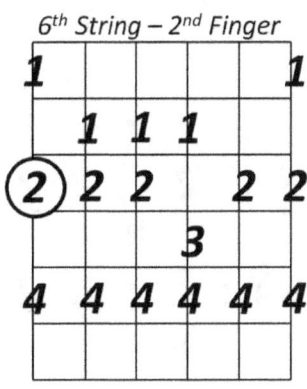
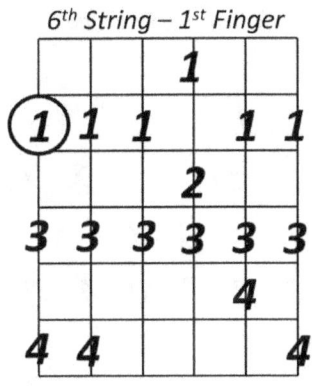
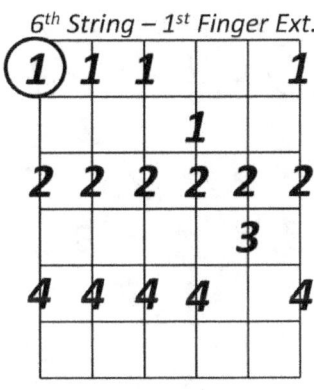
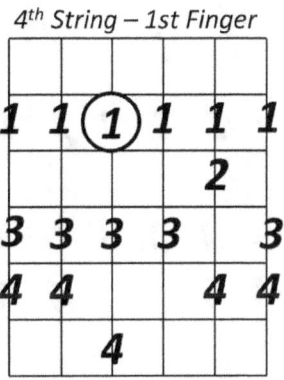
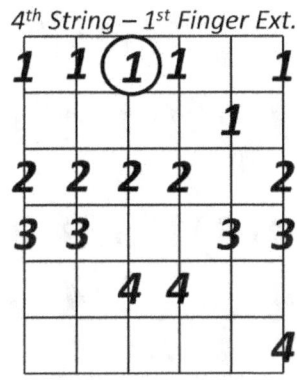
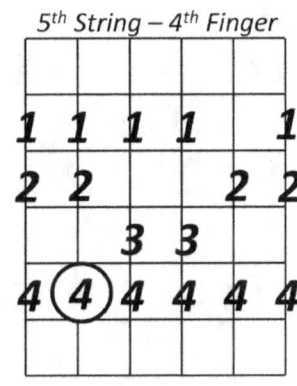
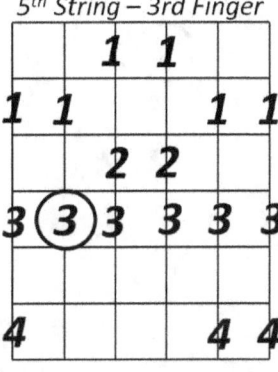
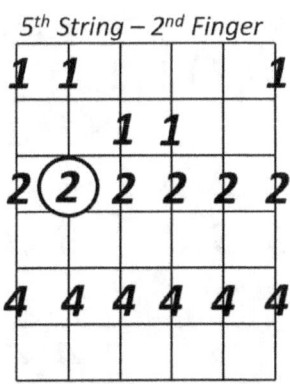
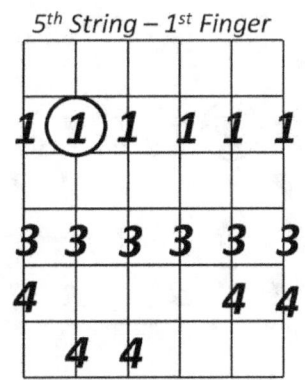
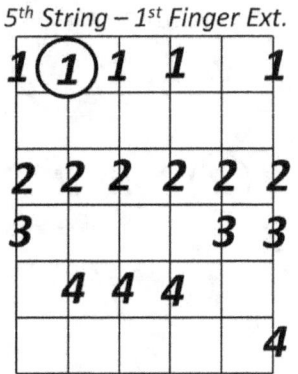

(See pages 32–33 to view the spelling of the mixolydian modes)

The 6th/"Aeolian" Mode of the Major Scale

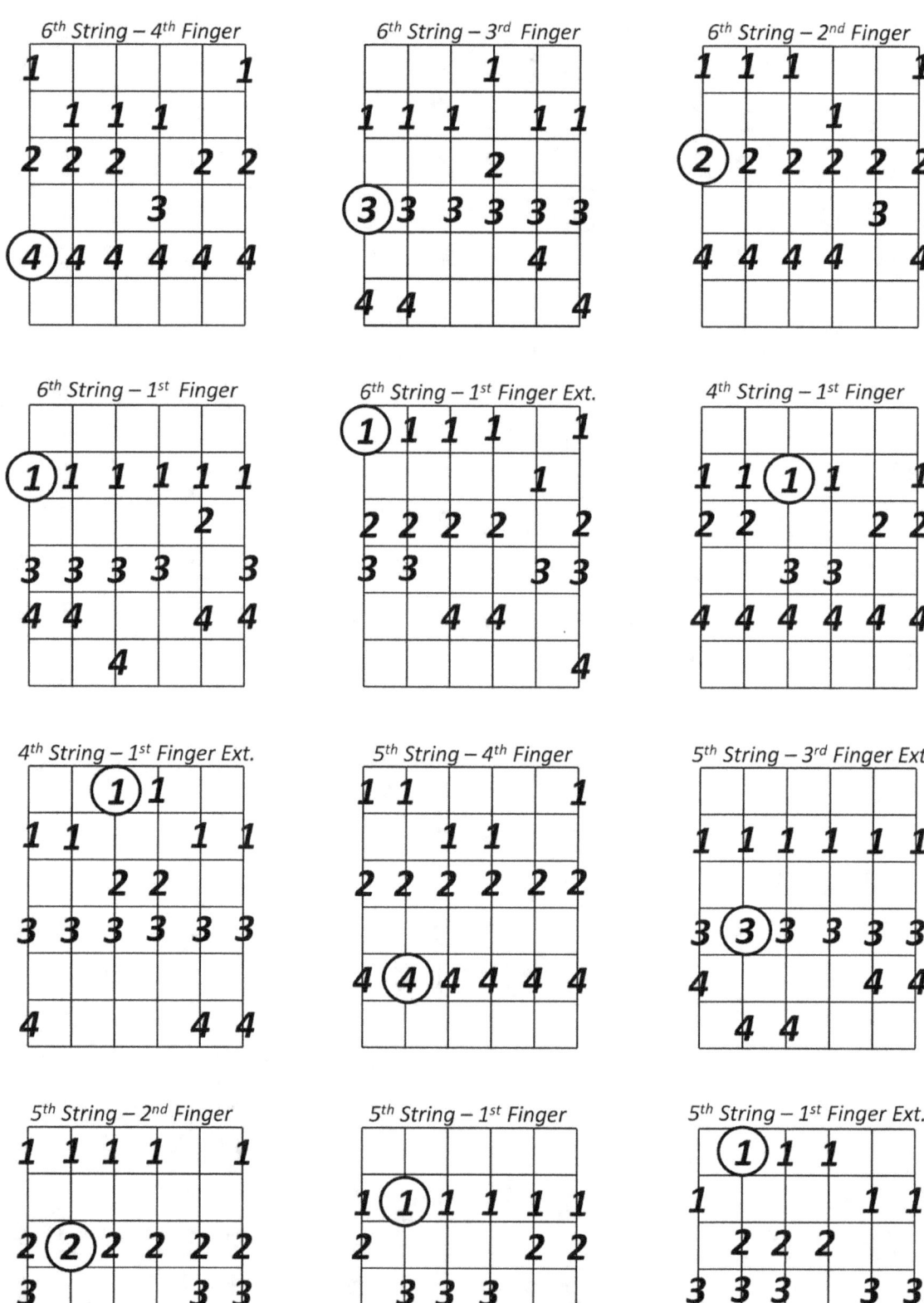

(See pages 34–35 to view the spelling of the aeolian modes)

The 7th/"Locrian" Mode of the Major Scale

6th String – 4th Finger Ext.
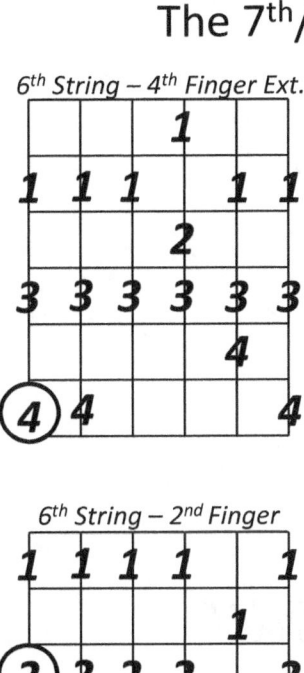

6th String – 4th Finger
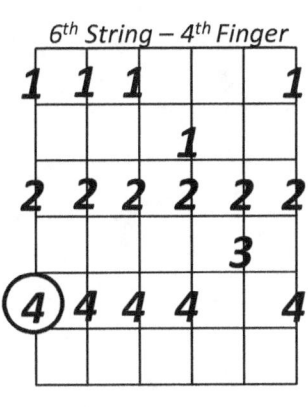

6th String – 3rd Finger
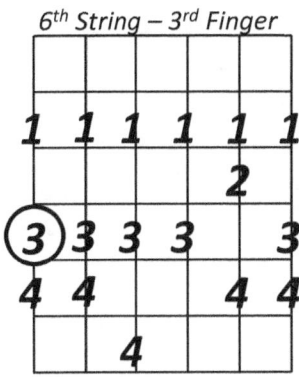

6th String – 2nd Finger
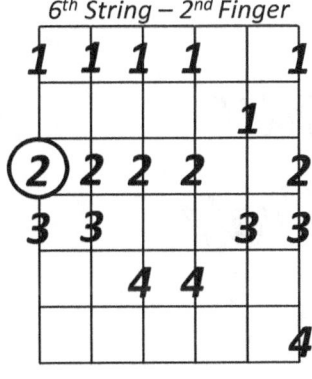

6th String – 1st Finger
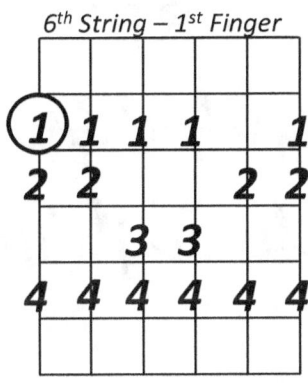

4th String – 2nd Finger
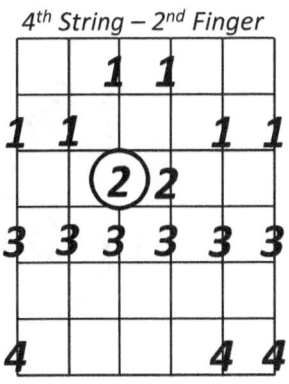

4th String – 1st Finger
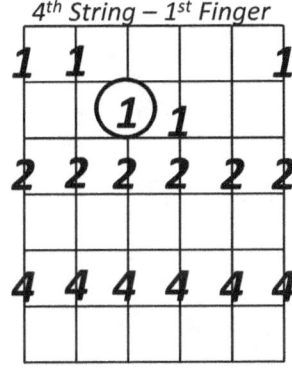

5th String – 4th Finger Ext.
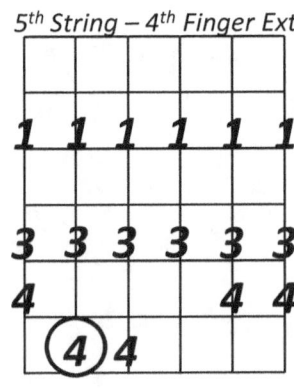

5th String – 4th Finger
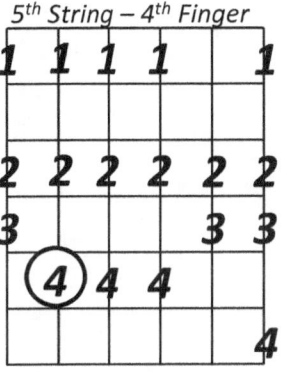

5th String – 3rd Finger
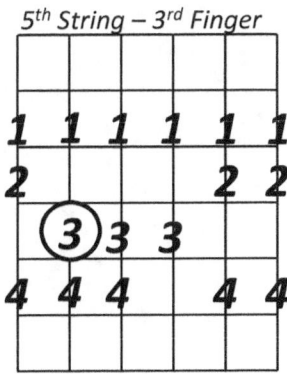

5th String – 2nd Finger
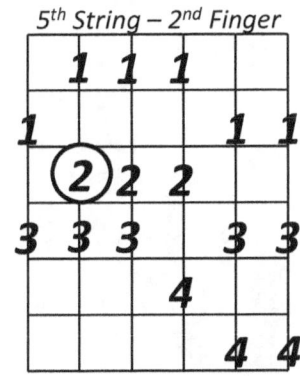

5th String – 1st Finger
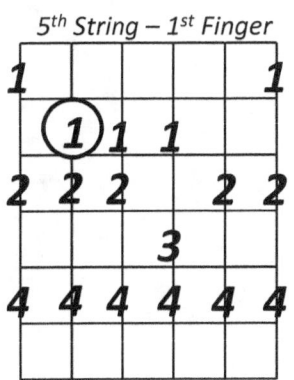

(See pages 36–37 to view the spelling of the locrian modes)

PART 7
Fingerings for the Modes of the Melodic Minor Scale

The 1st/"Ionian ♭3" Mode of the Melodic Minor Scale

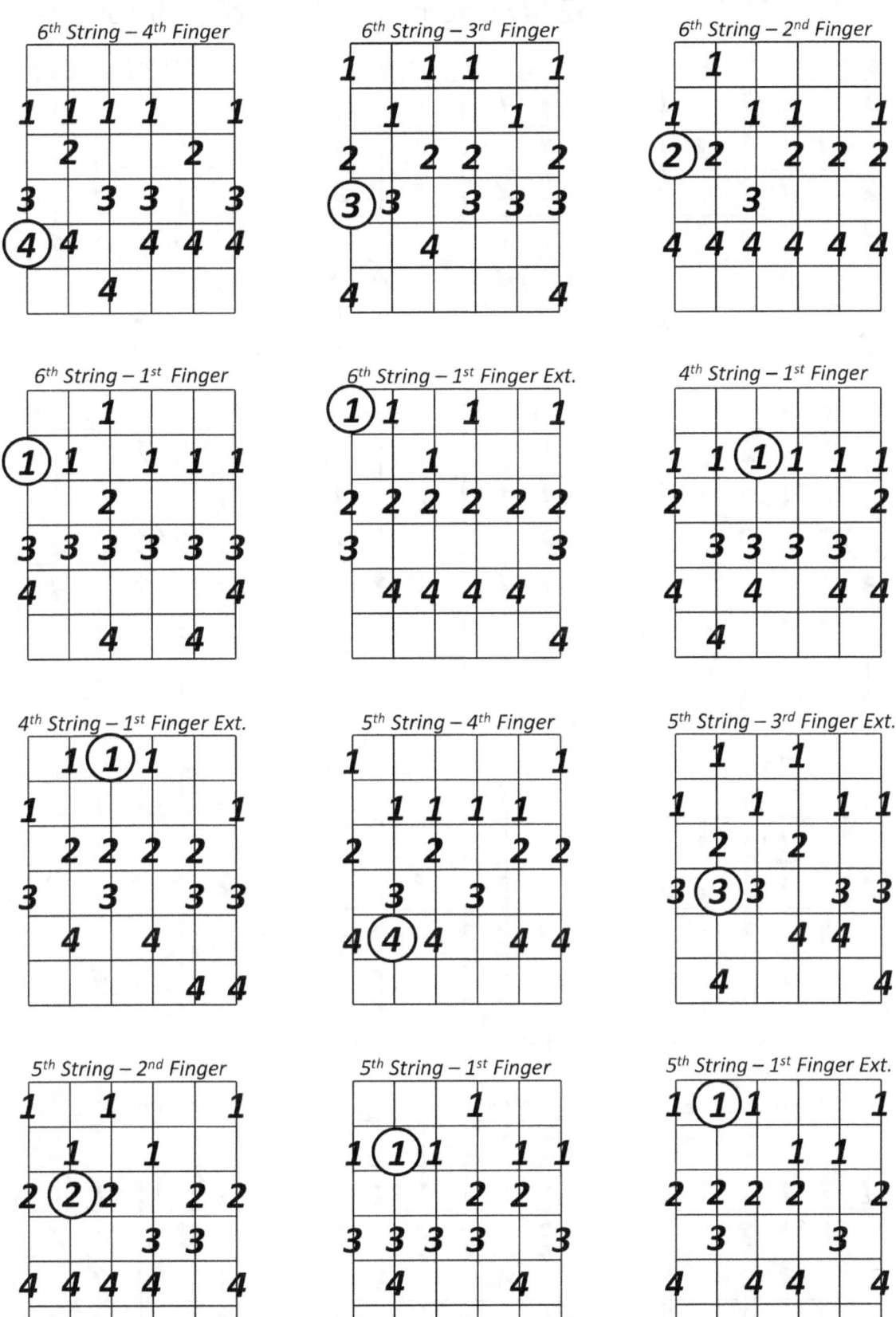

(See pages 48–49 to view the spelling of the ionian ♭3 modes)

The 2nd/"Dorian ♭2" Mode of the Melodic Minor Scale

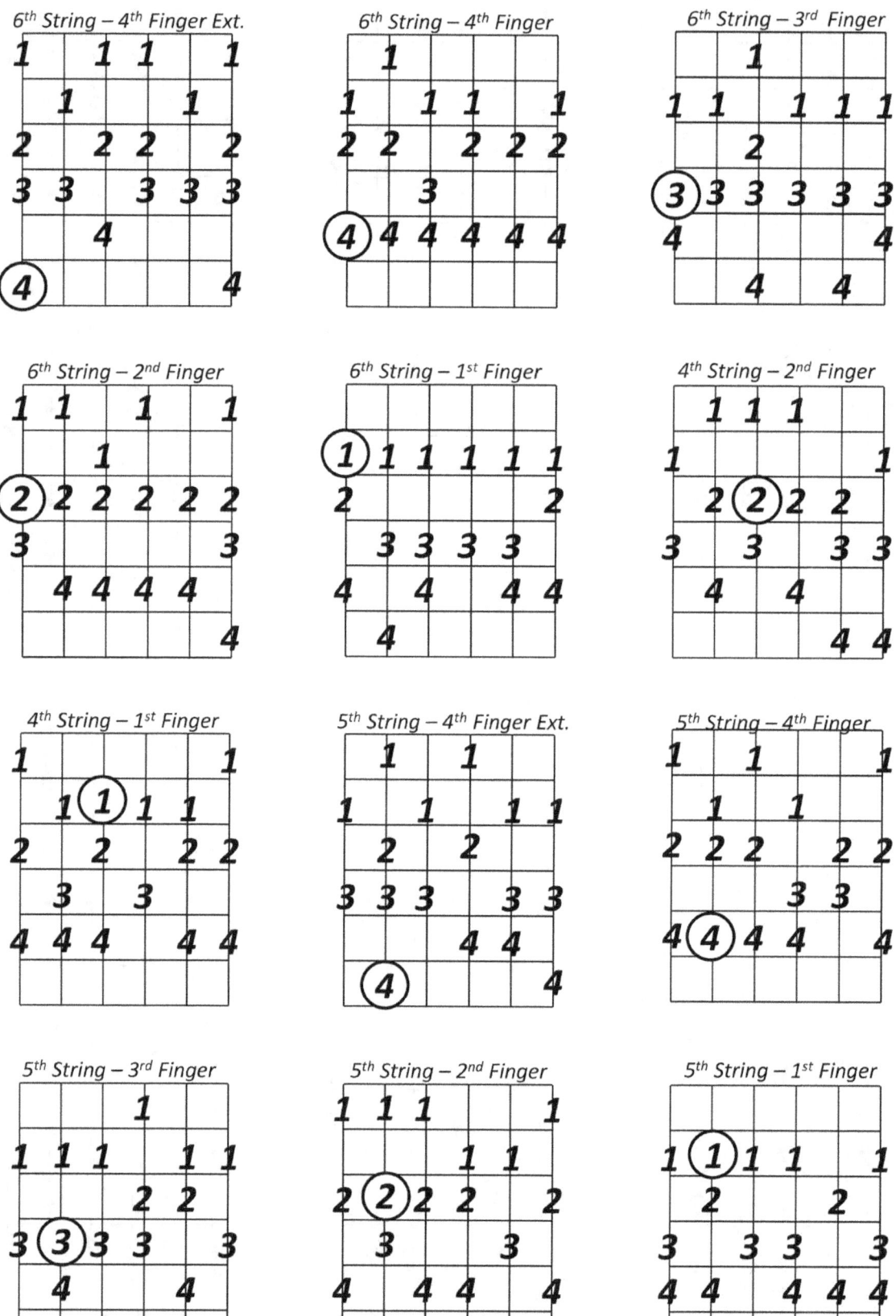

(See pages 50–51 to view the spelling of the dorian ♭2 modes)

The 3rd/"Lydian Augmented" Mode of the Melodic Minor Scale

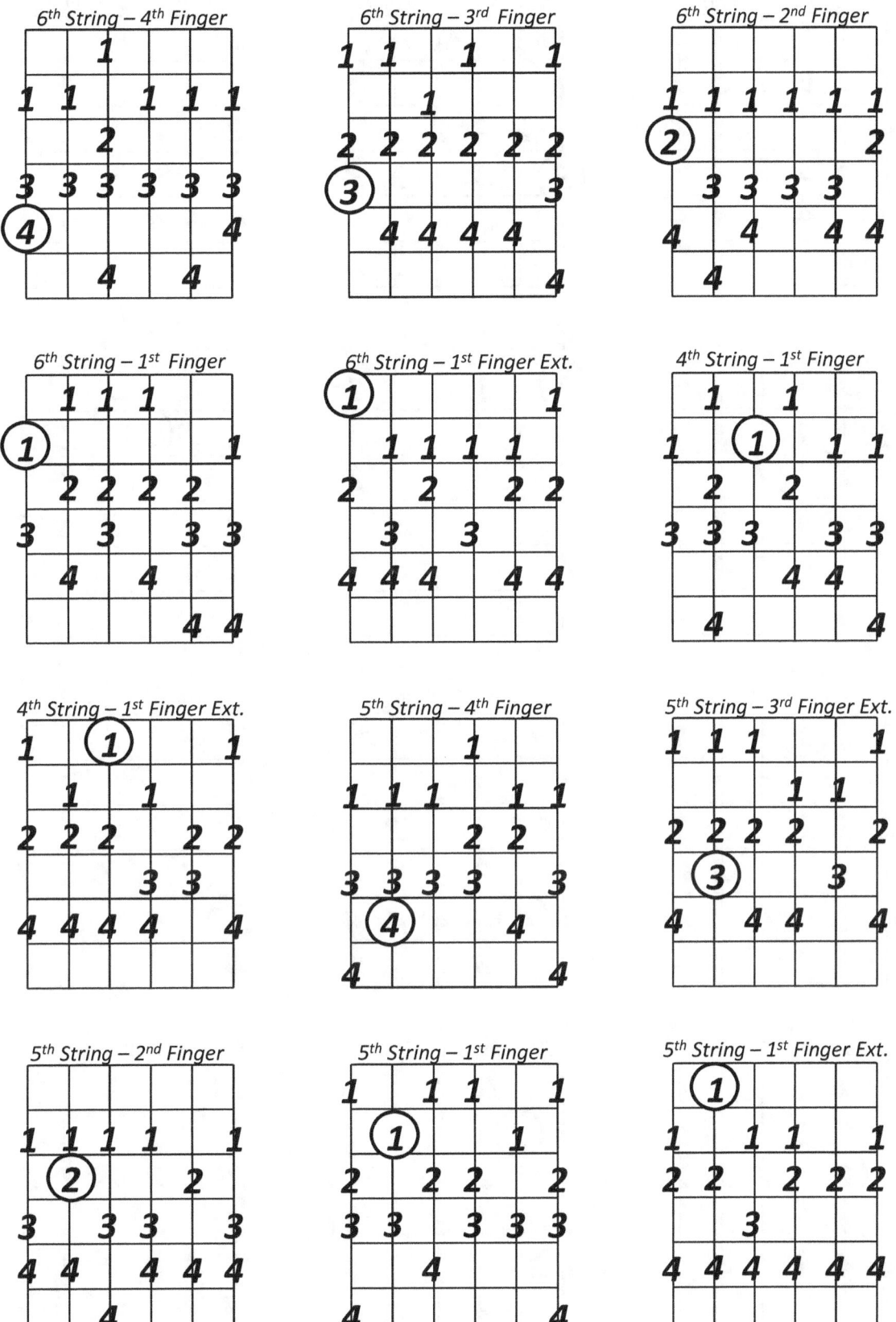

(See pages 52–53 to view the spelling of the lydian augmented modes)

The 4th/"Lydian Dominant" Mode of the Melodic Minor Scale

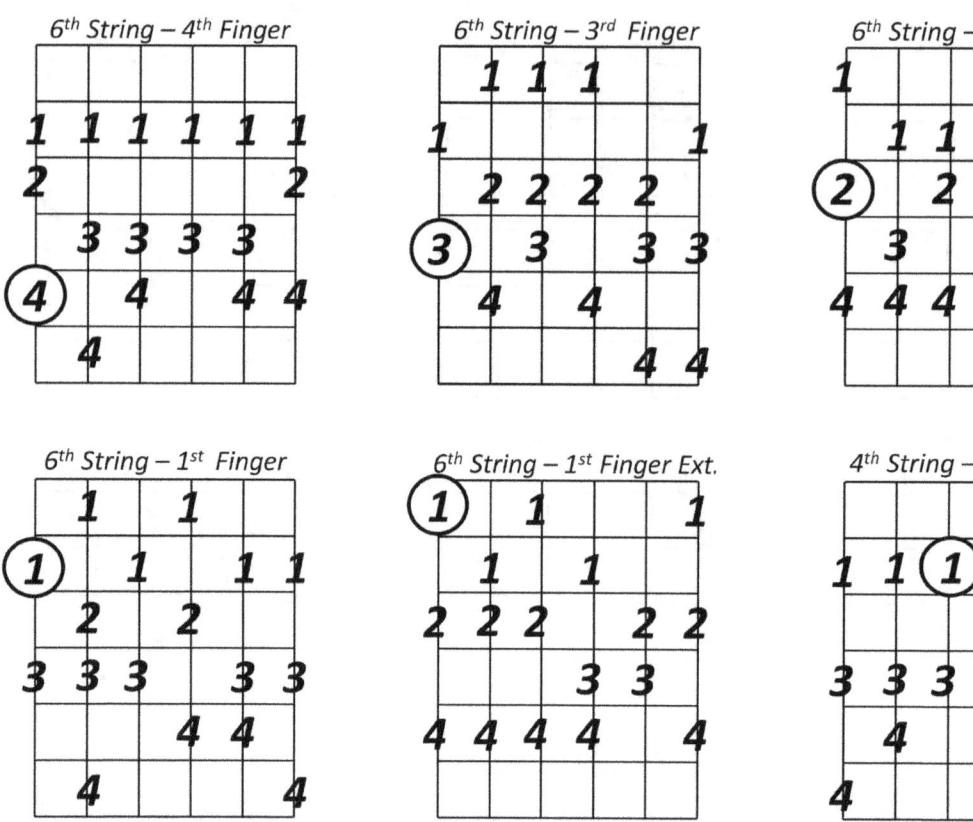
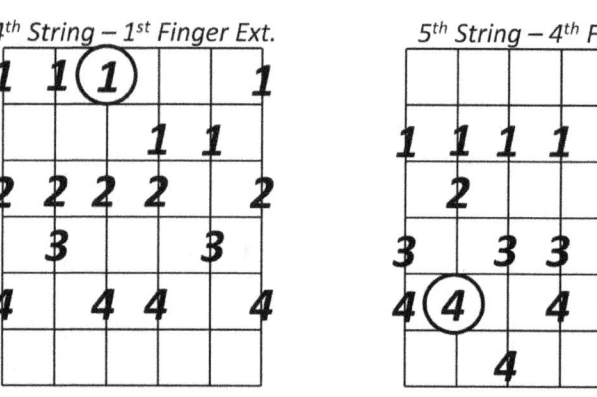
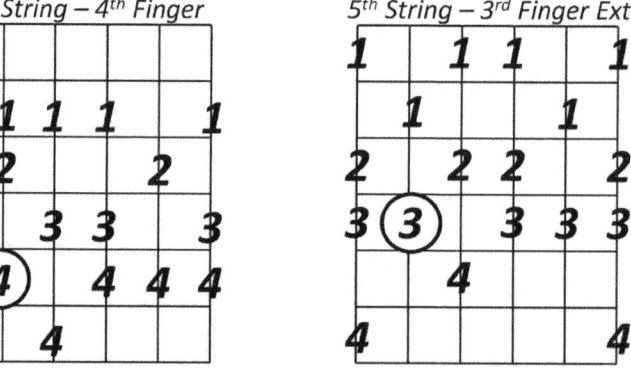
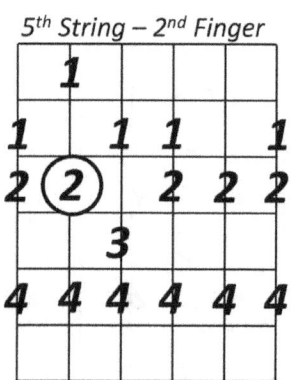
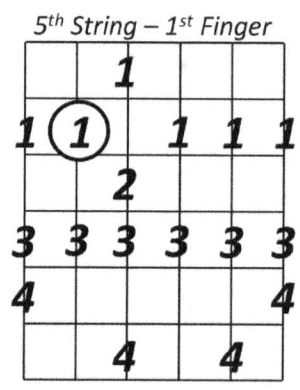
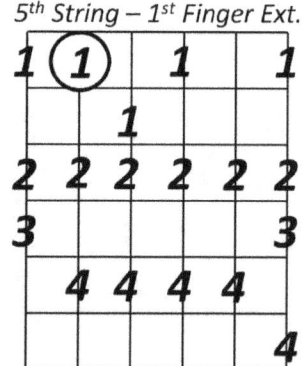

(See pages 54–55 to view the spelling of the lydian dominant modes)

The 5th/"Mixolydian ♭6" Mode of the Melodic Minor Scale

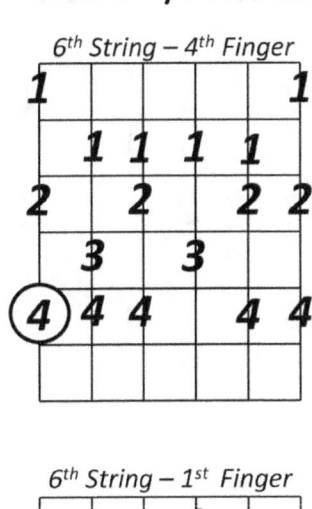
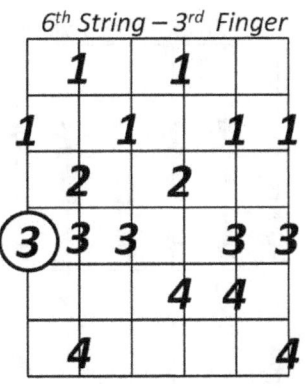
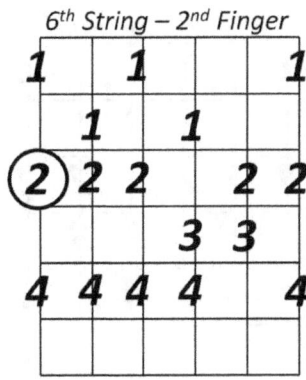
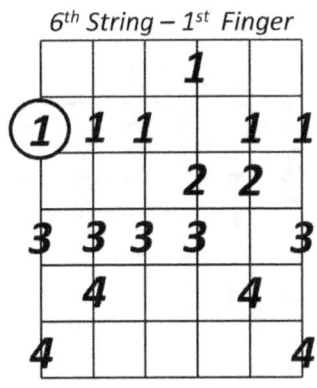
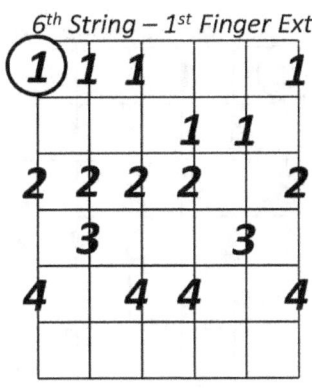
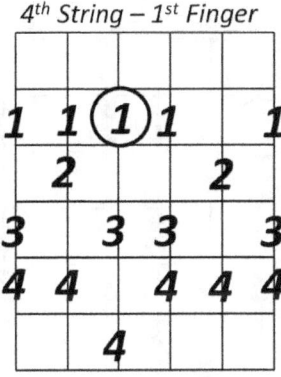
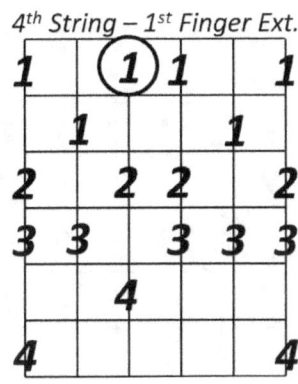
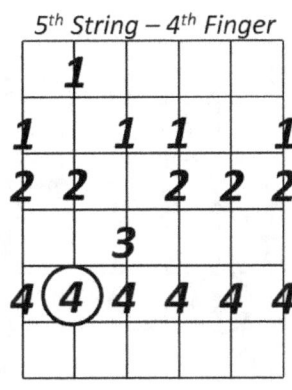
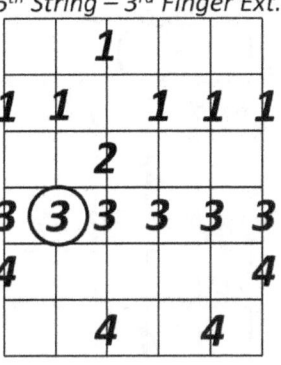
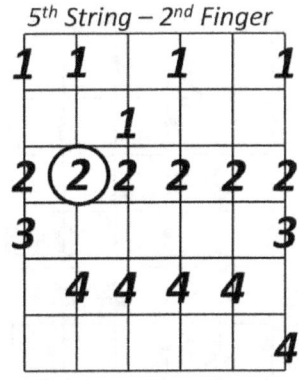
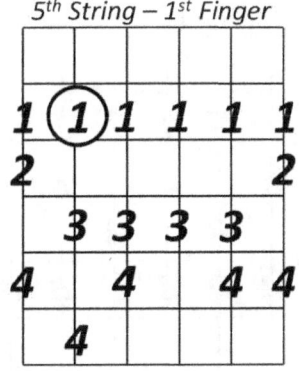
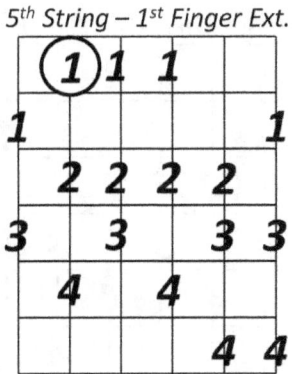

(See pages 56–57 to view the spelling of the mixolydian ♭6 modes)

The 6th/"Aeolian ♭5" Mode of the Melodic Minor Scale

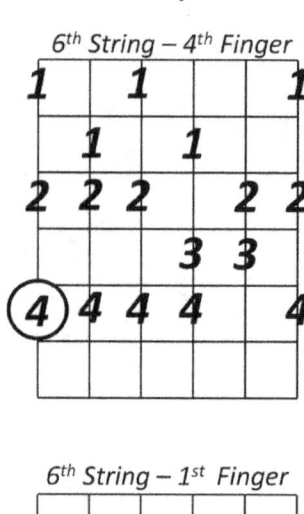
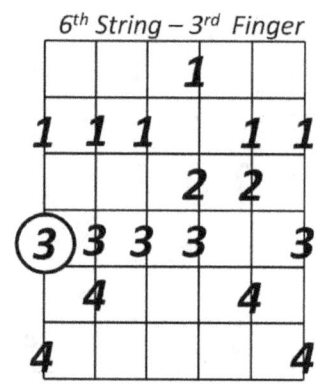
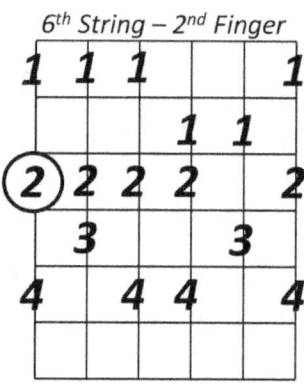
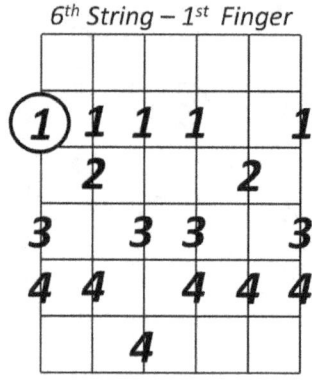
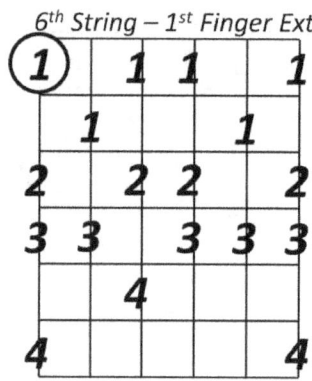
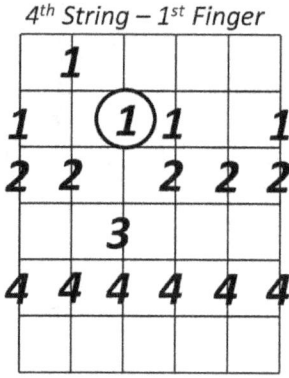
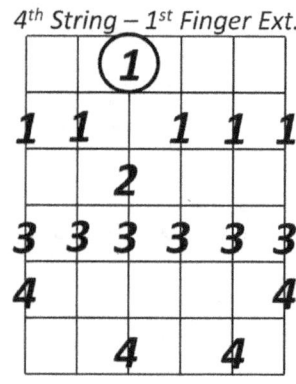
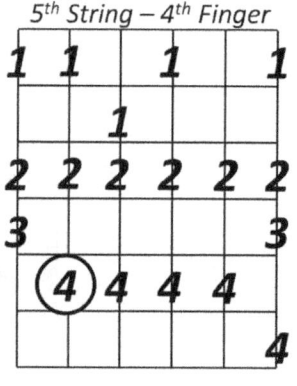
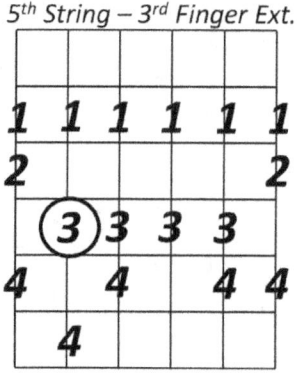
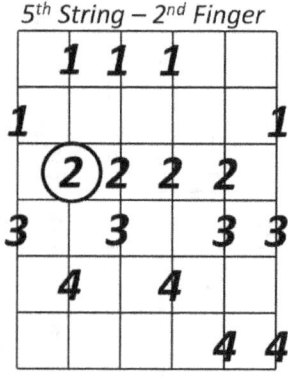
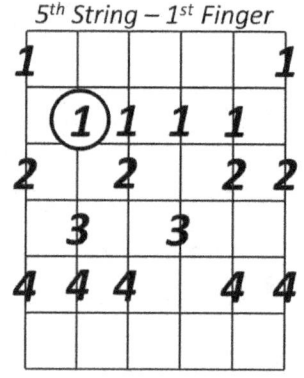
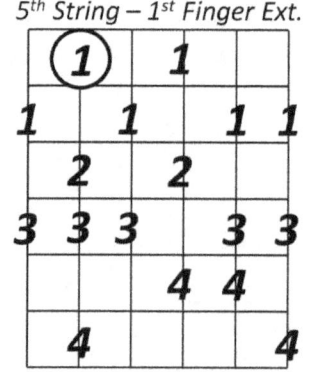

(See pages 58–59 to view the spelling of the aeolian ♭5 modes)

The 7th/"Altered Scale" Mode of the Melodic Minor Scale

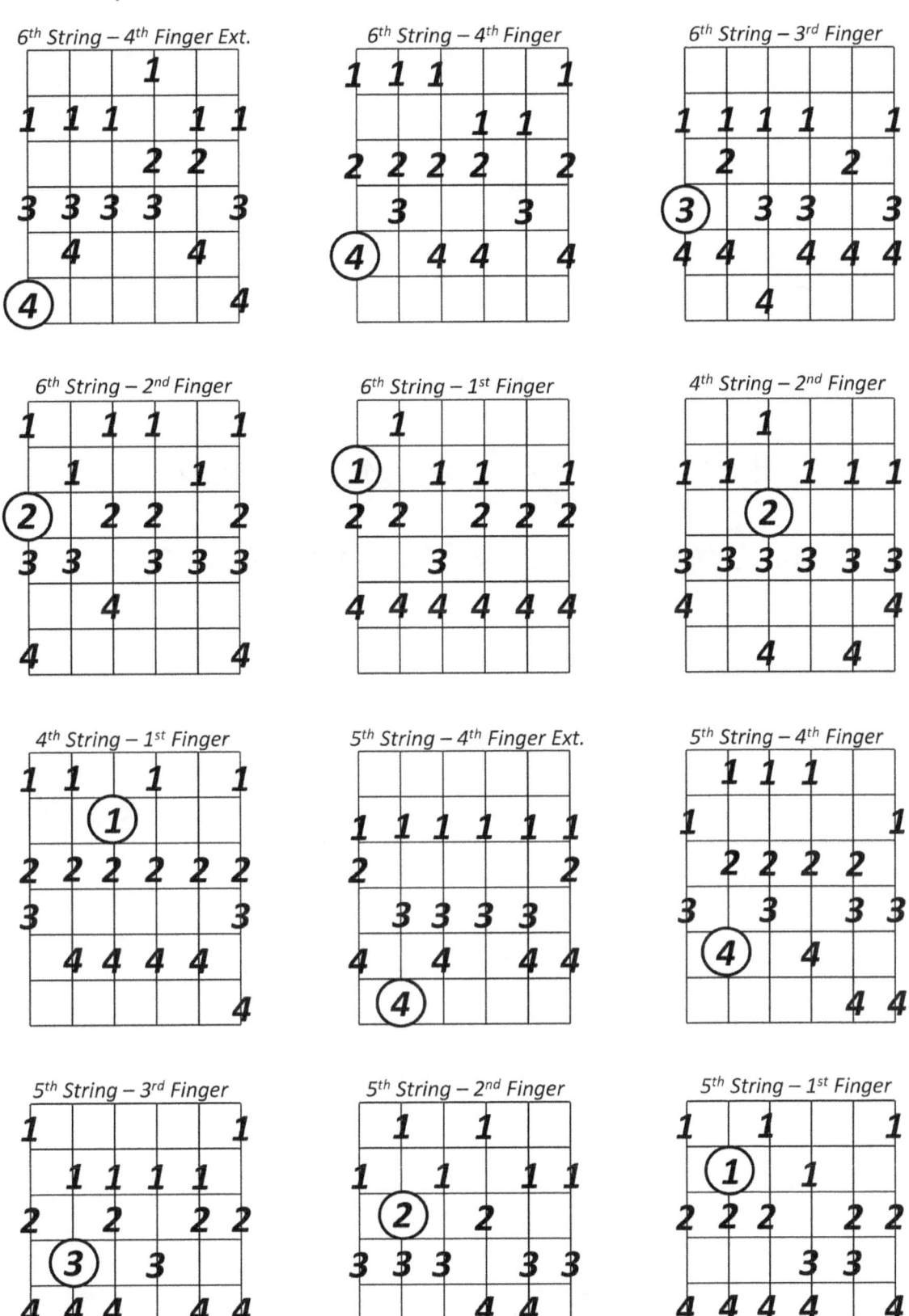

(See pages 60–61 to view the spelling of the super locrian modes)

PART 8
Fingerings for the Modes of the Harmonic Minor Scale

The 1st/"Aeolian #7" Mode of the Harmonic Minor Scale

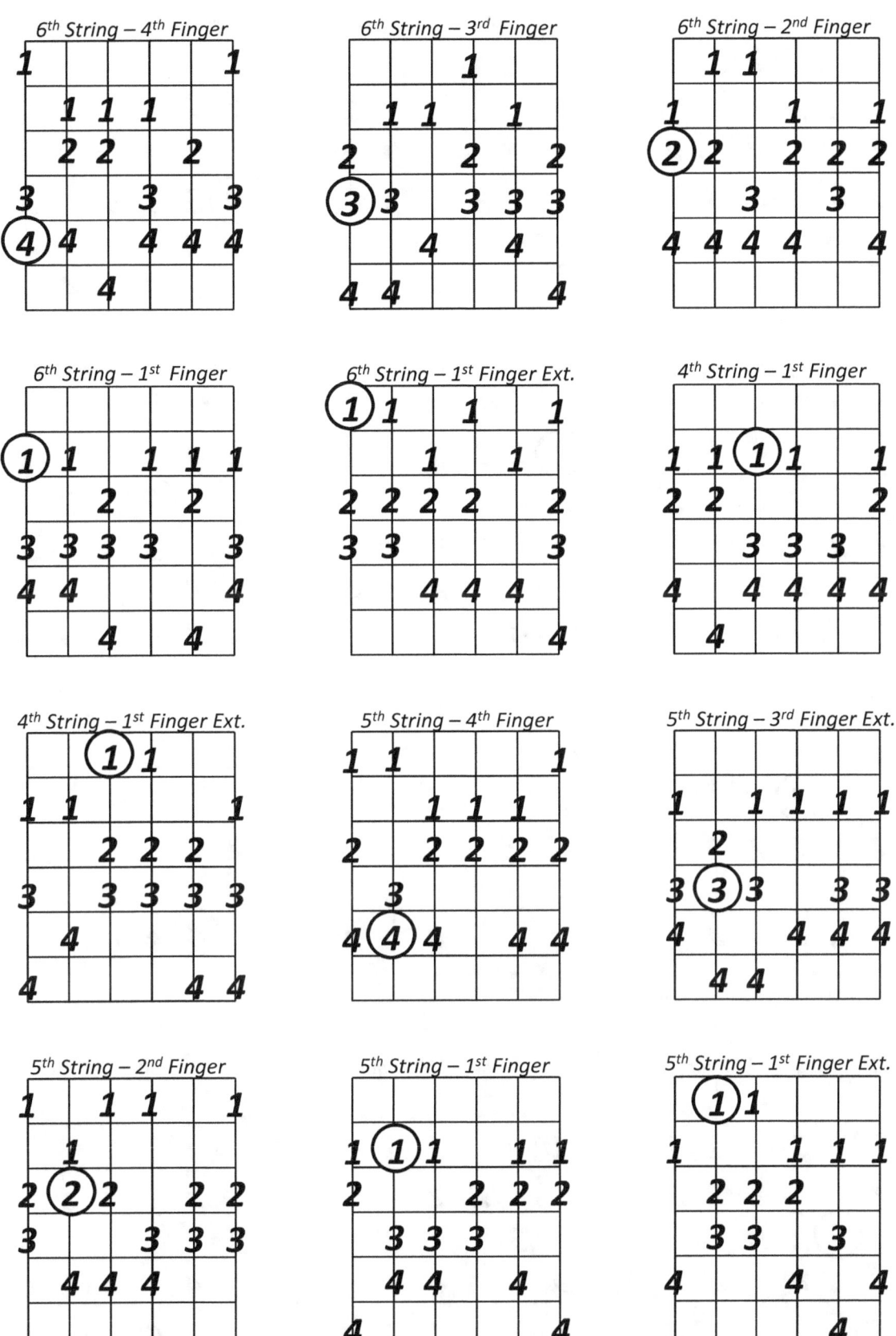

(See pages 72–73 to view the spelling of the aeolian #6 modes)

The 2nd/"Locrian #6" Mode of the Harmonic Minor Scale

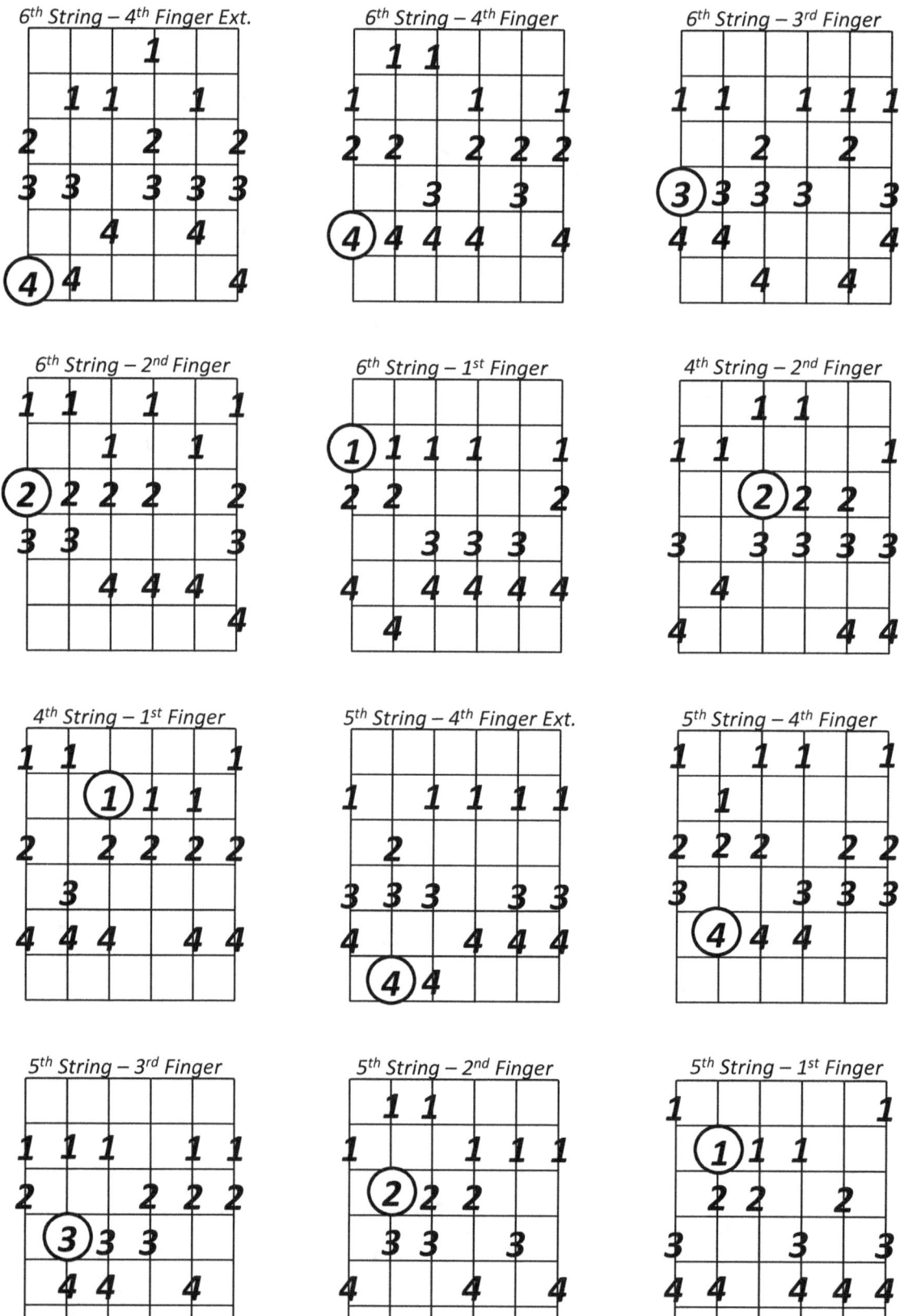

(See pages 74–75 to view the spelling of the locrian #6 modes)

The 3rd /"Ionian #5" Mode of the Harmonic Minor Scale

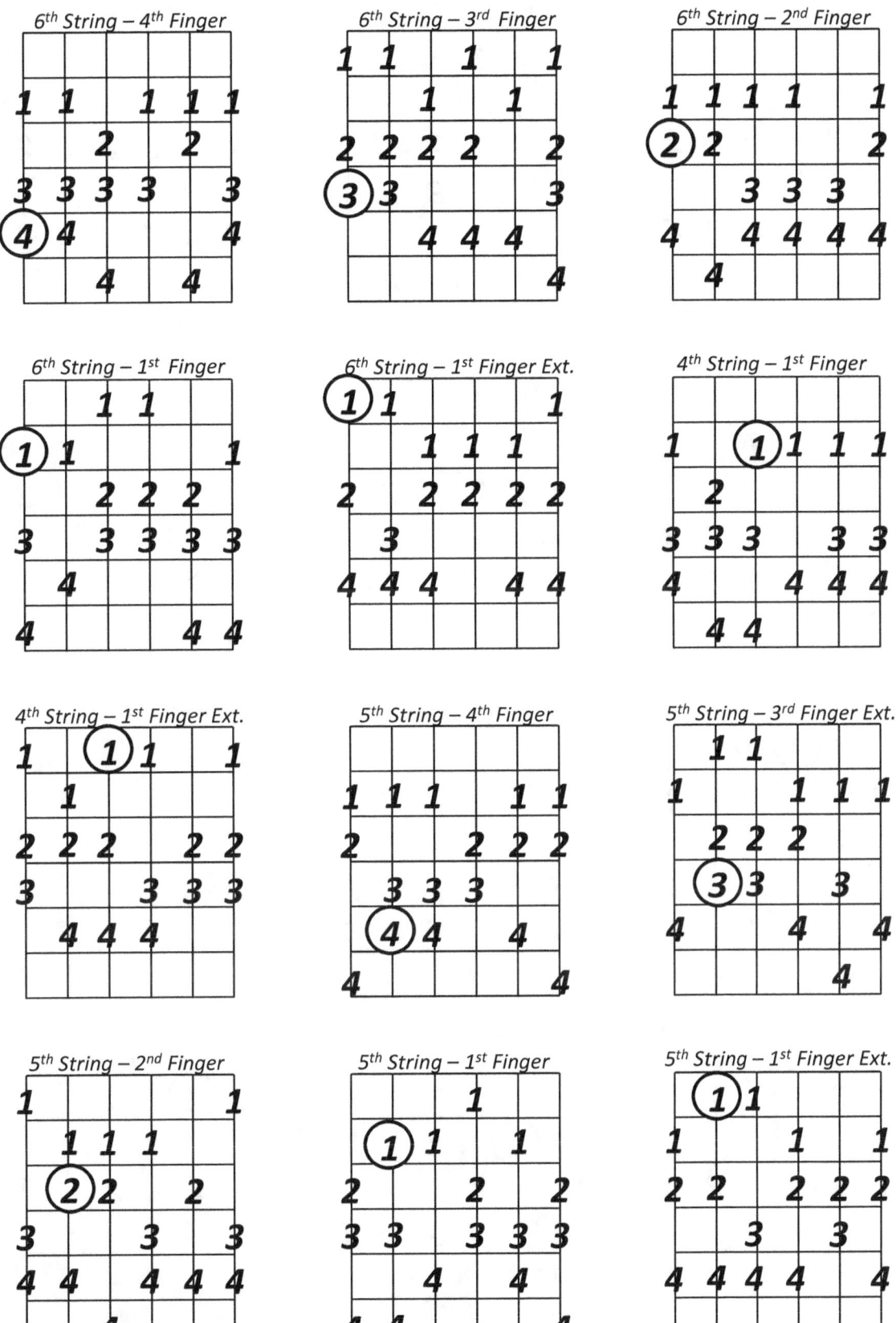

(See pages 76–77 to view the spelling of the ionian #5 modes)

The 4th/"Dorian #4" Mode of the Harmonic Minor Scale

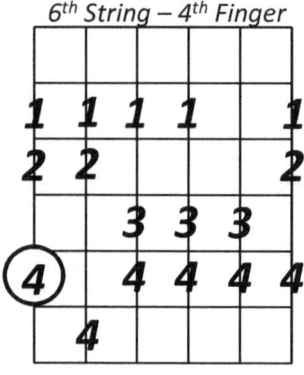
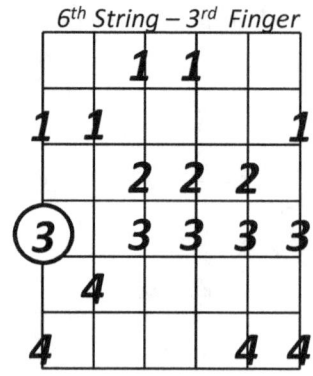
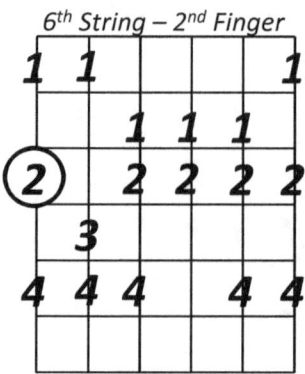
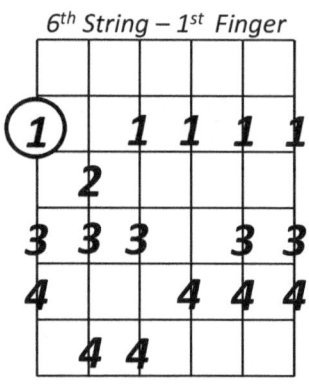
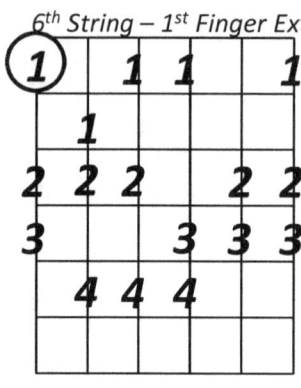
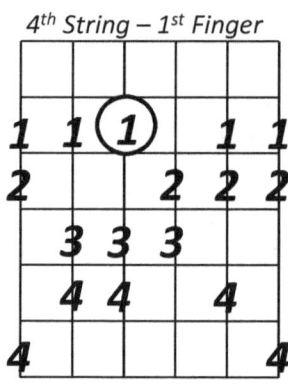
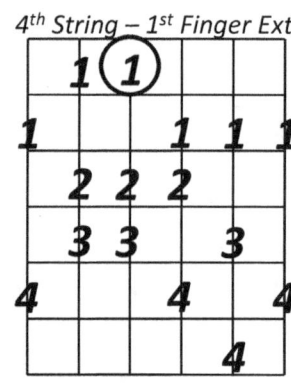
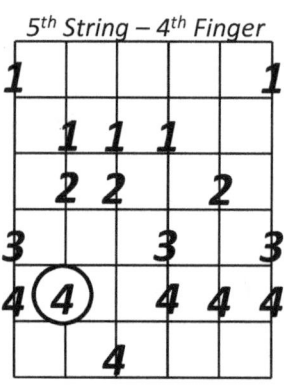
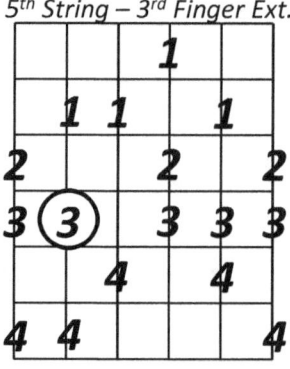
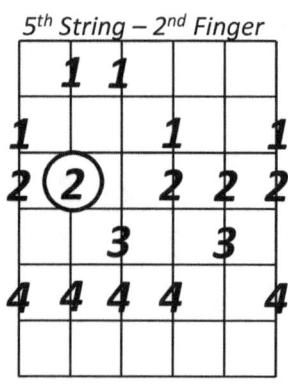
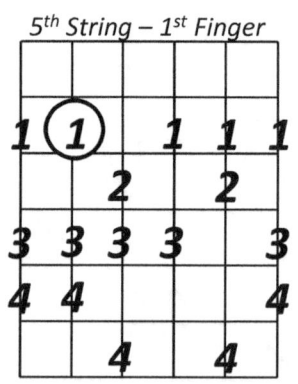
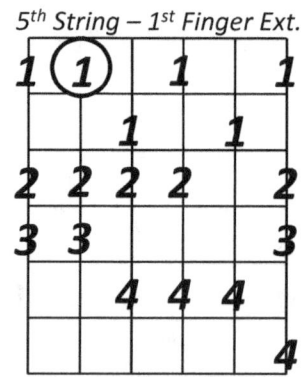

(See pages 78–79 to view the spelling of the dorian #4 modes)

The 5th/"Phrygian Dominant" Mode of the Harmonic Minor Scale

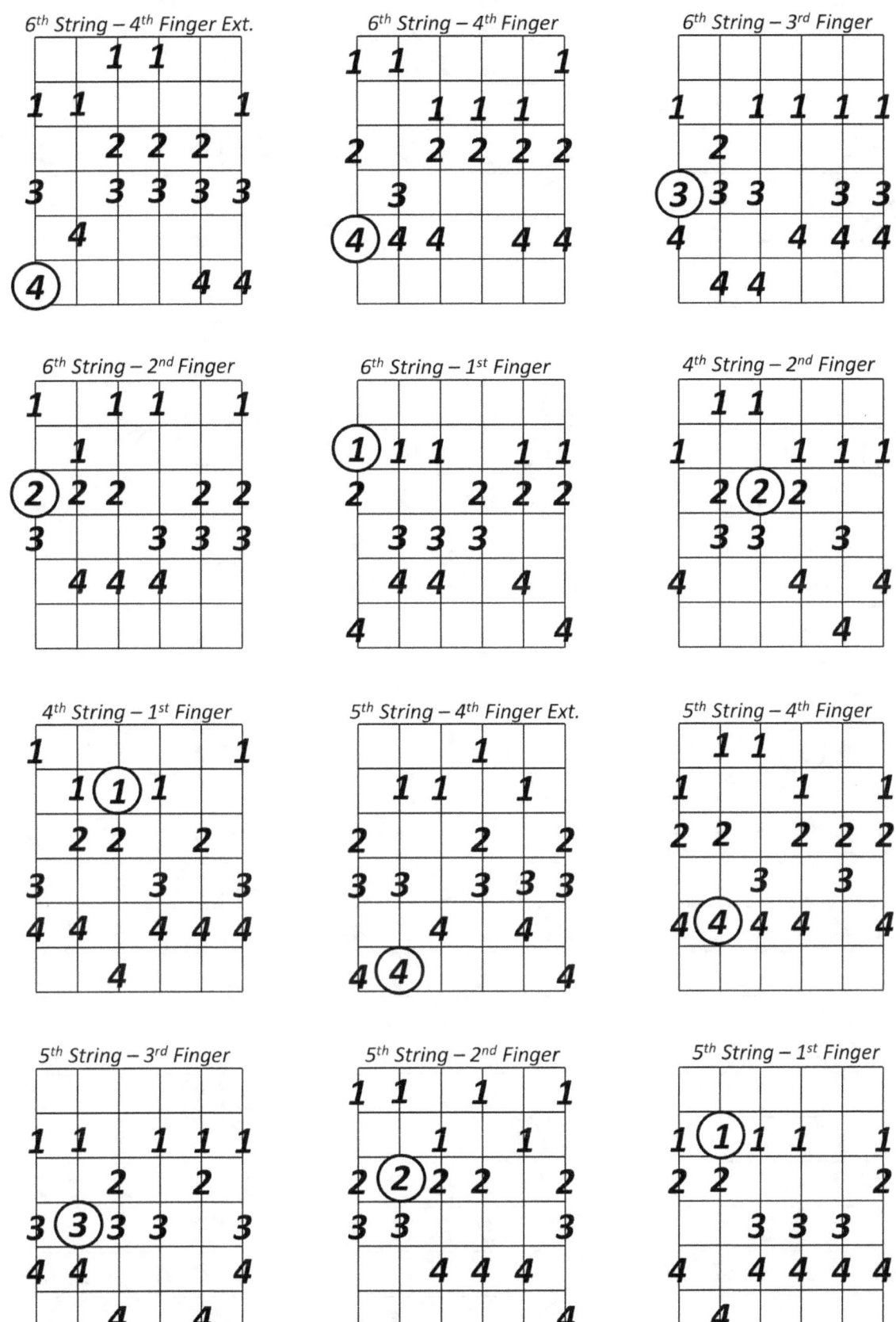

(See pages 80–81 to view the spelling of the phrygian dominant modes)

The 6th/"Lydian #2" Mode of the Harmonic Minor Scale

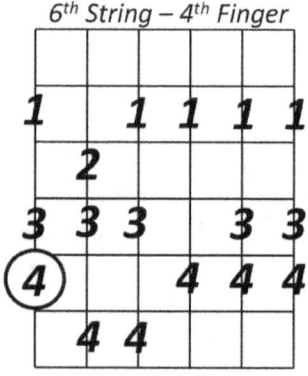
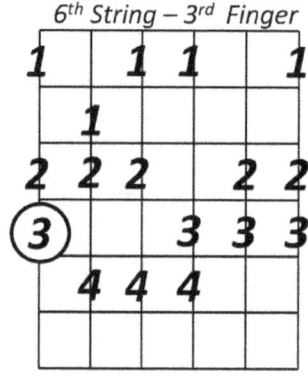
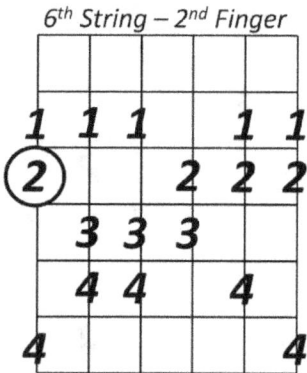
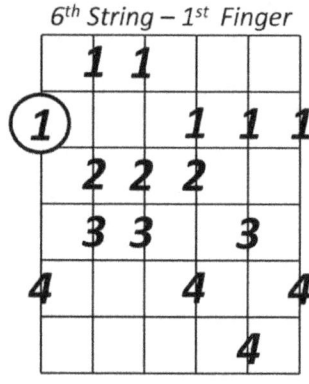
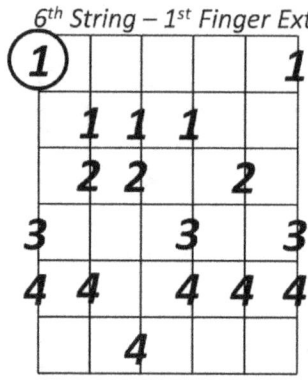
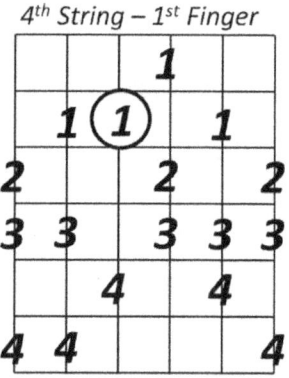
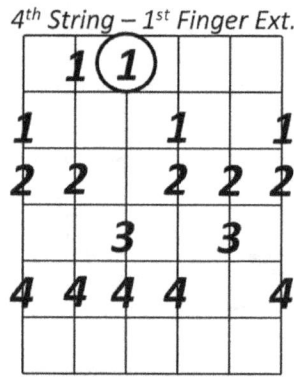
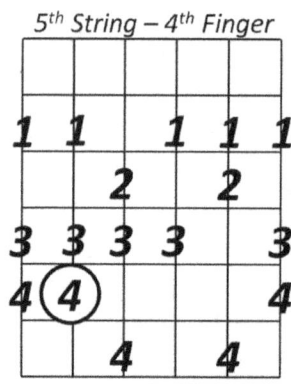
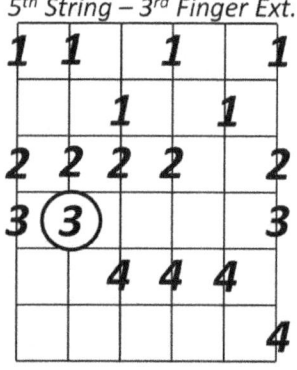
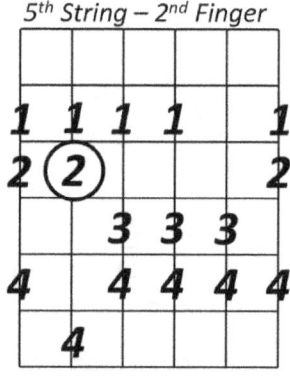
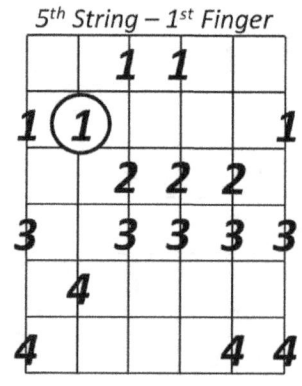
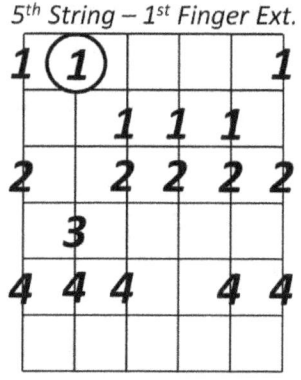

(See pages 82–83 to view the spelling of the lydian #2 modes)

The 7th/"Super Locrian ♭♭7" Mode of the Harmonic Minor Scale

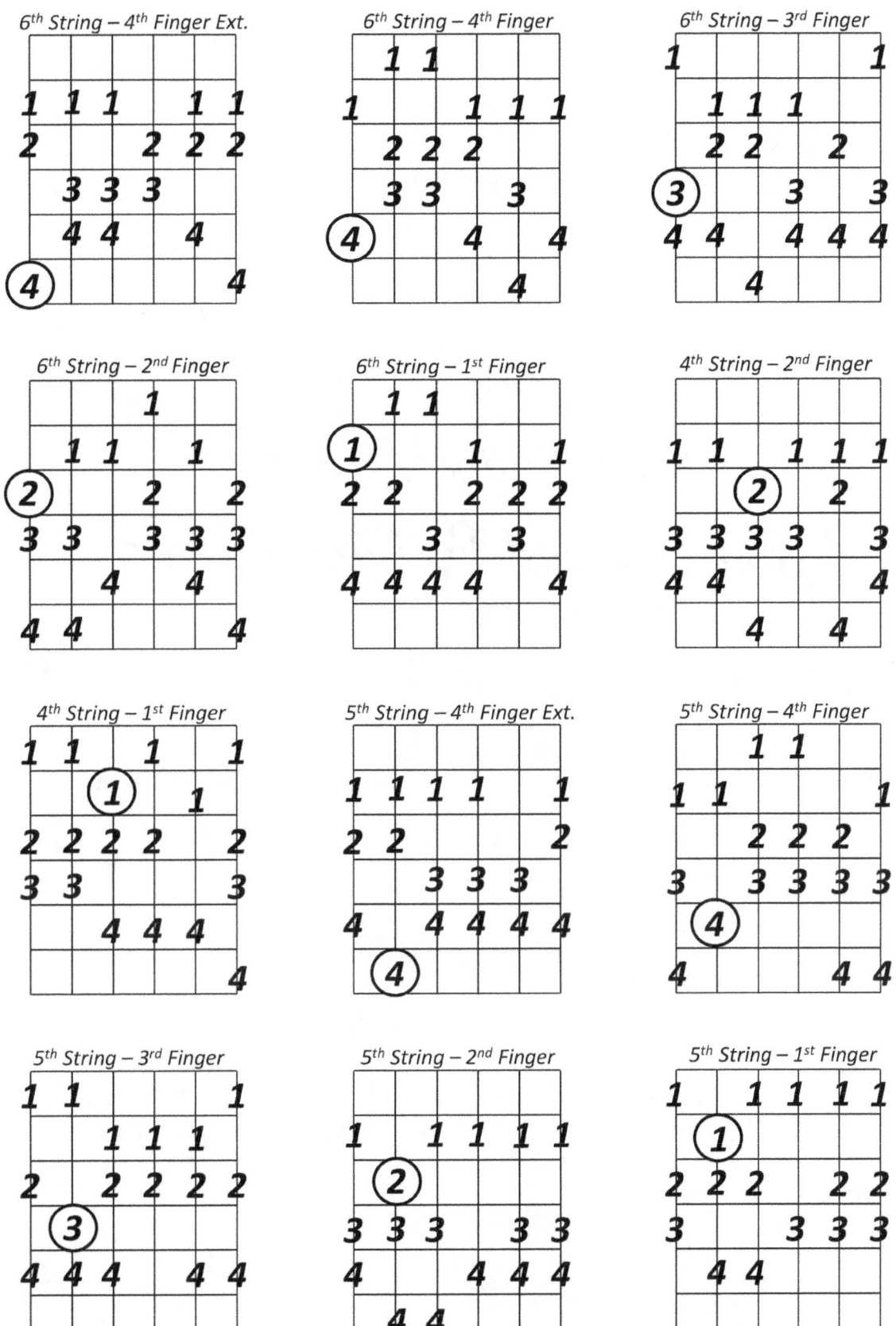

(See pages 84–85 to view the spelling of the super locrian ♭♭7 modes)

PART 9
Fingerings for the Symmetric and Pentatonic Scales

(Notice there are only 3 distinct patterns)

The Half Step/Whole Step Scale

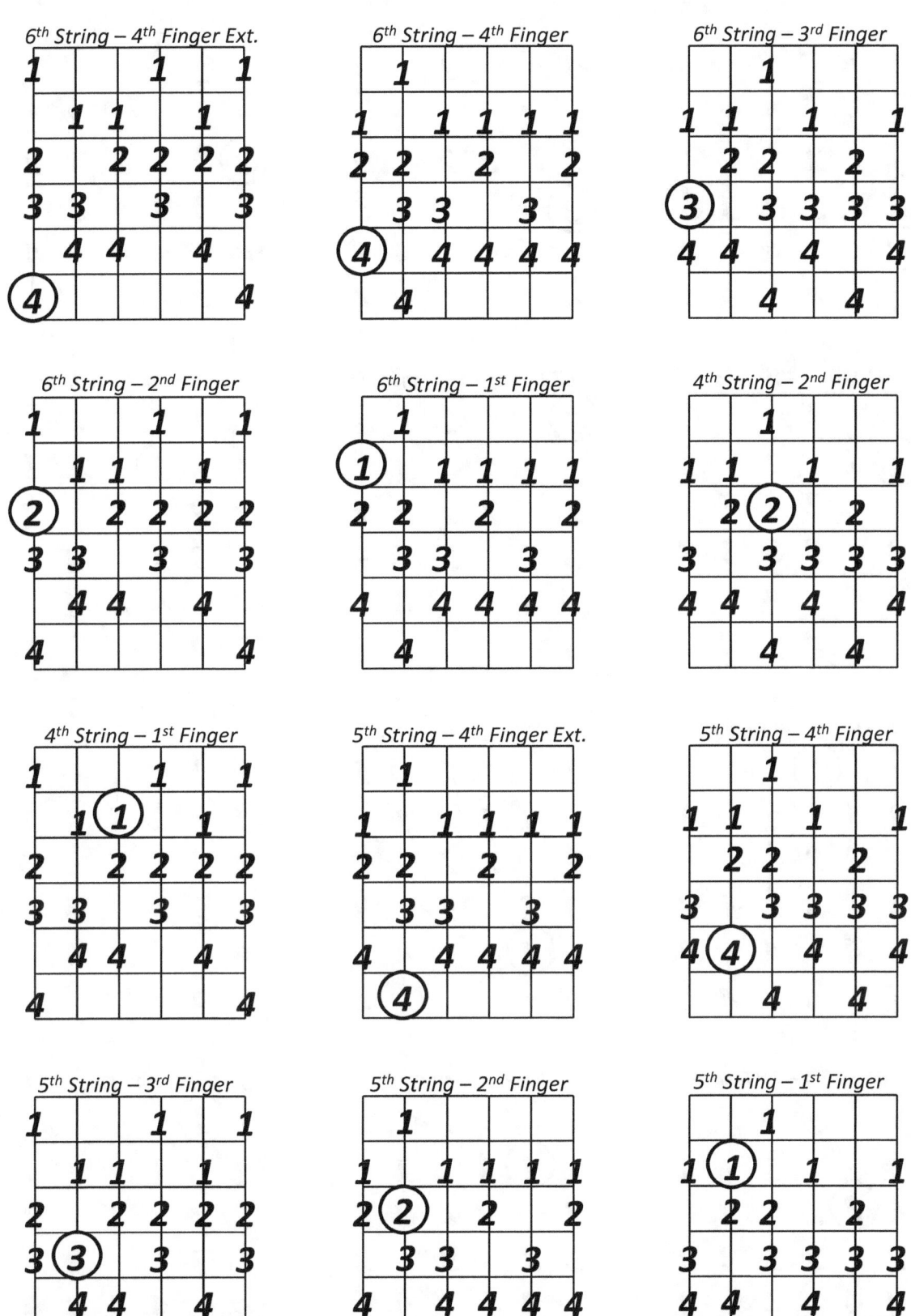

(See pages 88–89 to view the spelling of this scale)

The Whole Step/Half Step Scale

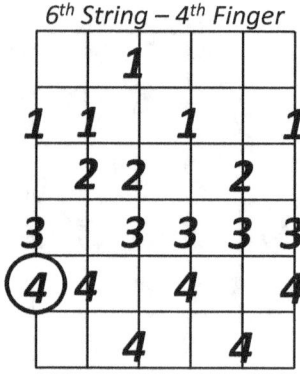
6th String – 4th Finger

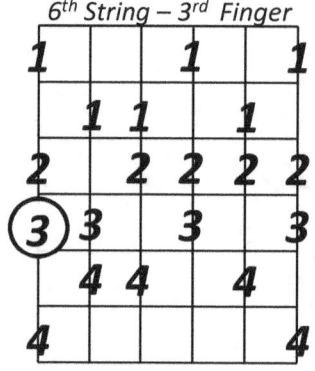
6th String – 3rd Finger

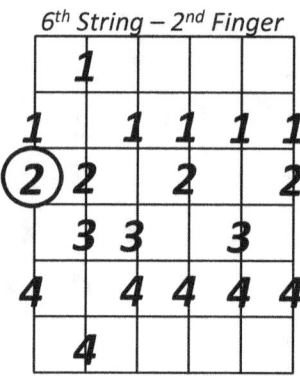
6th String – 2nd Finger

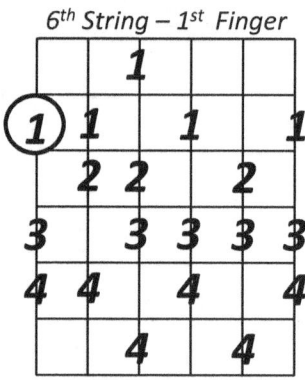
6th String – 1st Finger

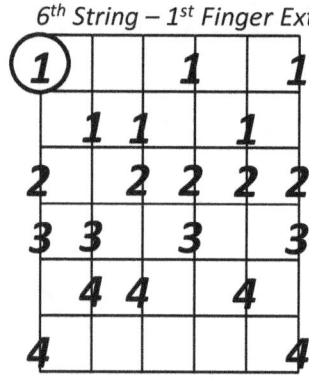
6th String – 1st Finger Ext.

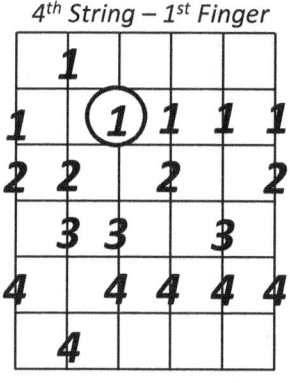
4th String – 1st Finger

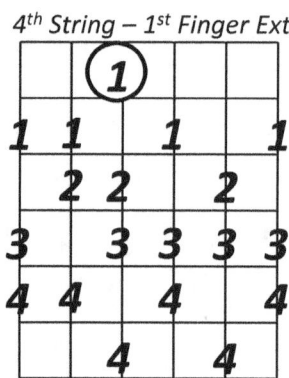
4th String – 1st Finger Ext.

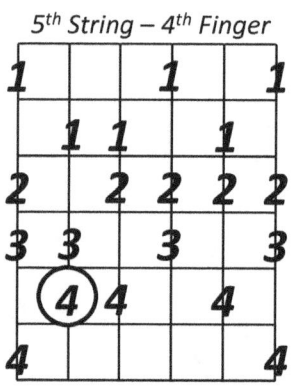
5th String – 4th Finger

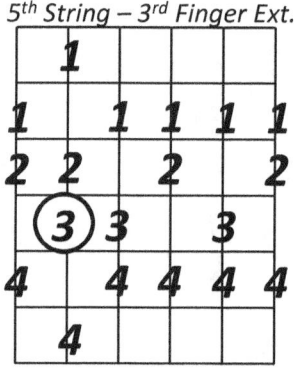
5th String – 3rd Finger Ext.

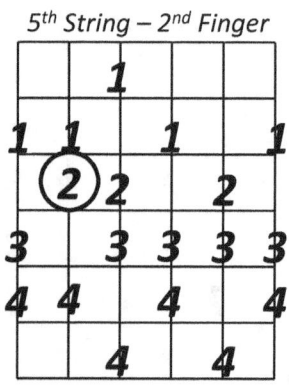
5th String – 2nd Finger

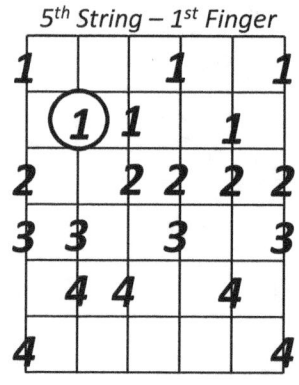
5th String – 1st Finger

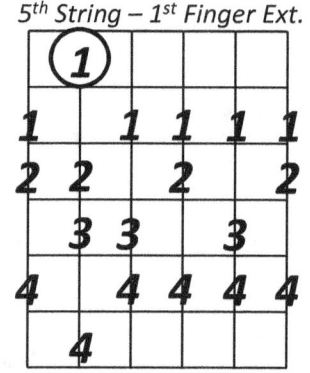
5th String – 1st Finger Ext.

(See pages 90–91 to view the spelling of this scale)

The Whole Tone Scale

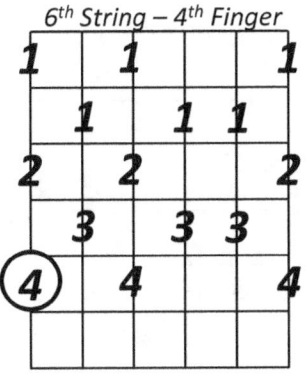
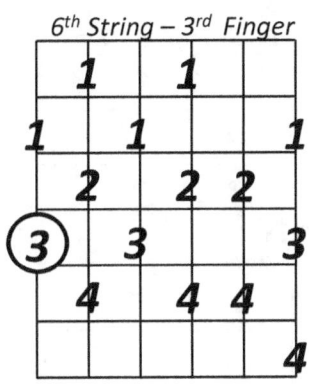
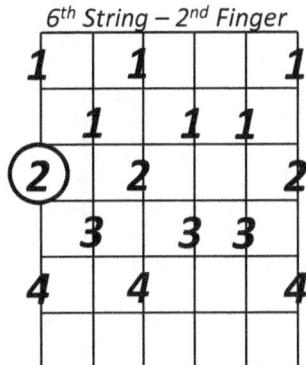
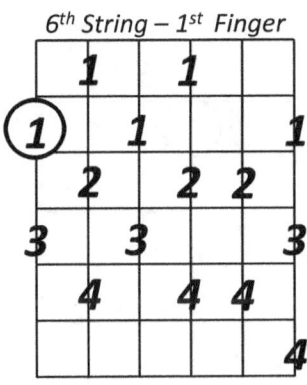
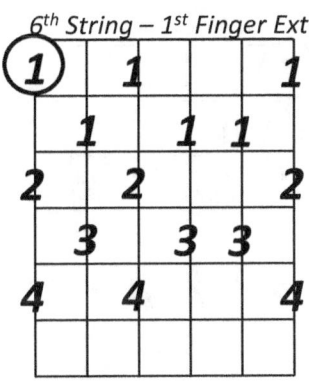
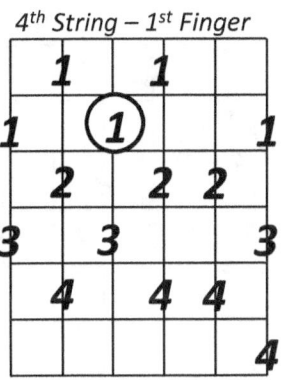
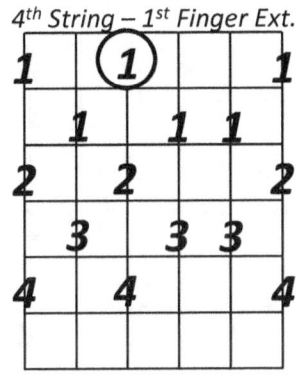
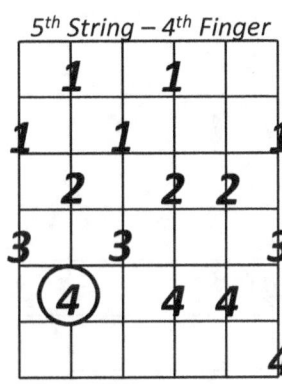
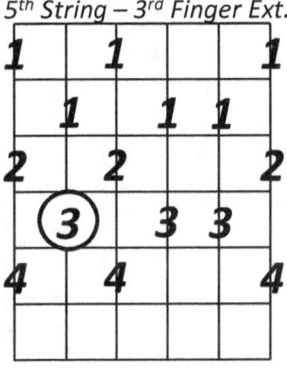
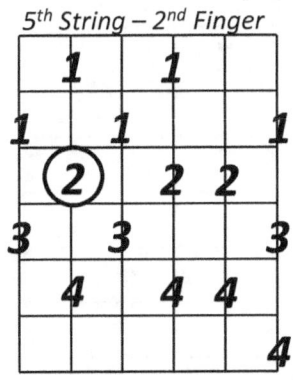
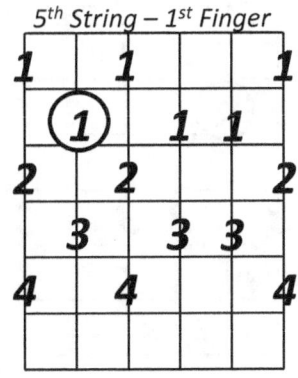
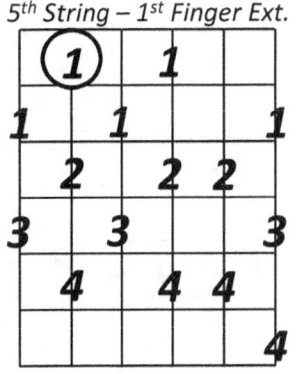

(See pages 92–93 to view the spelling of this scale)

The Major Pentatonic Scale

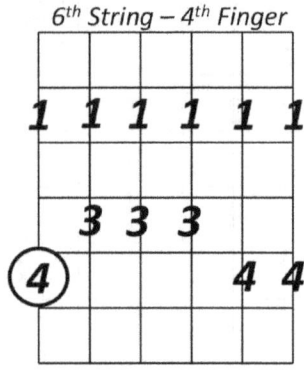
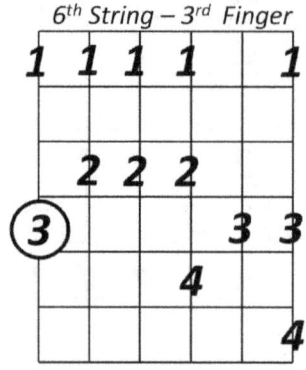
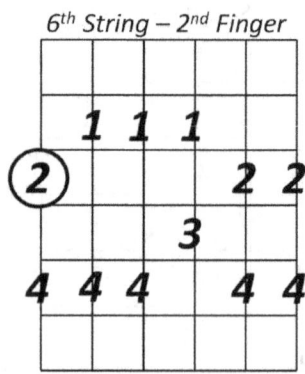
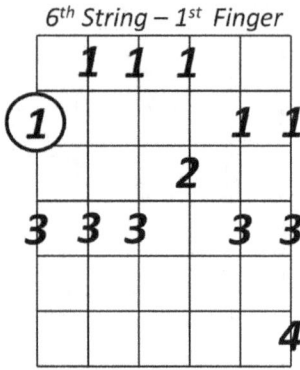
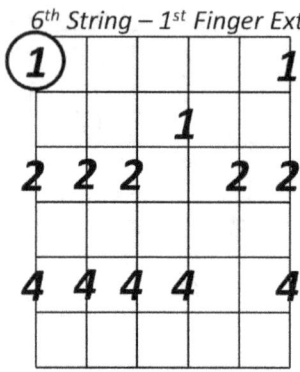
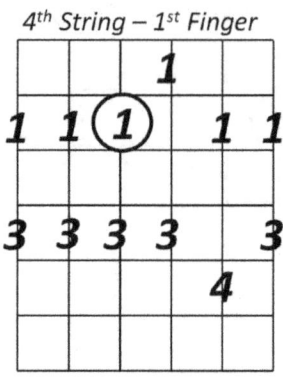
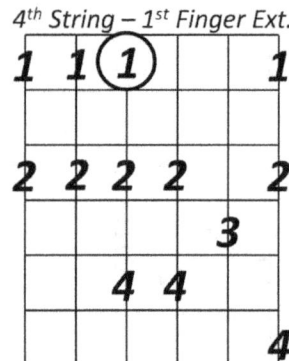
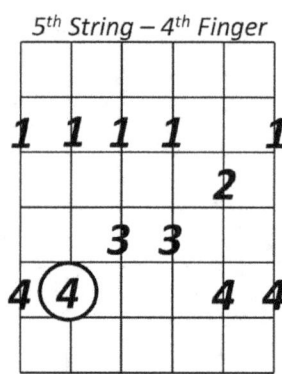
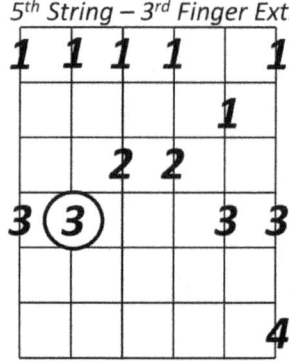
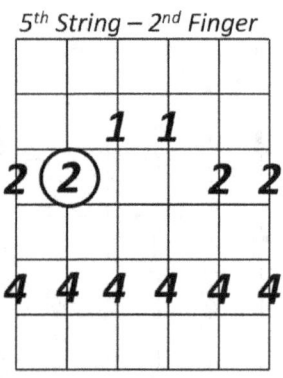
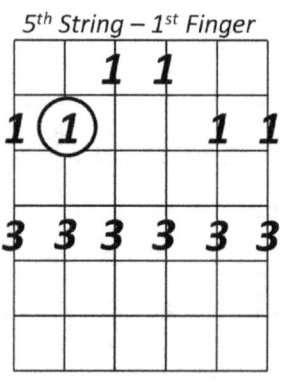
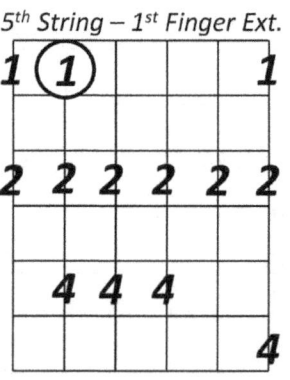

(See pages 94–95 to view the spelling of this scale)

The Minor Pentatonic Scale

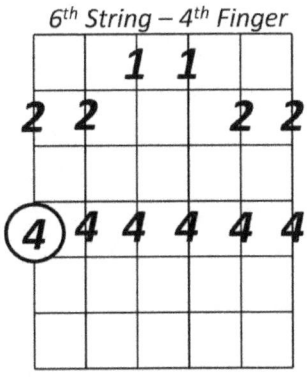
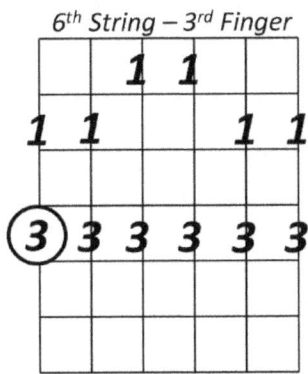
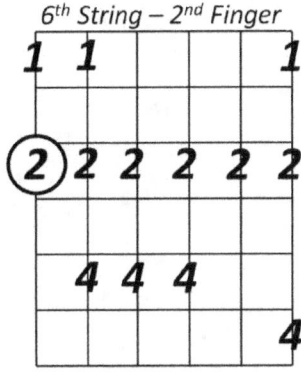
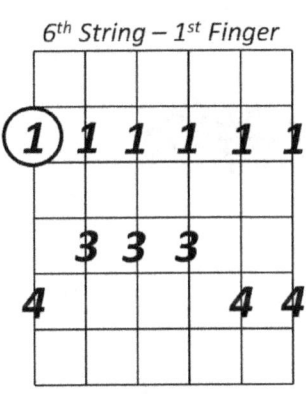
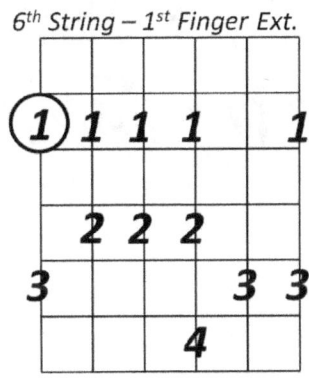
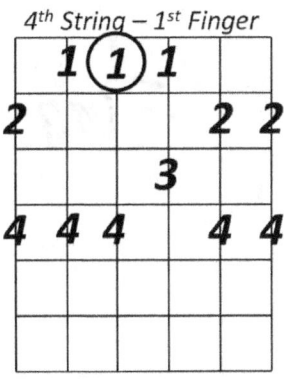
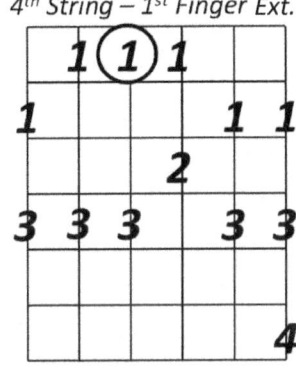
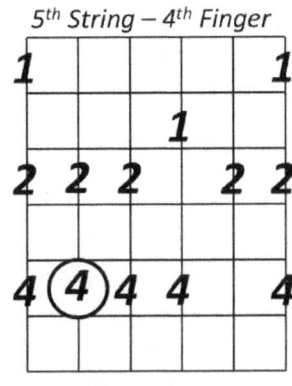
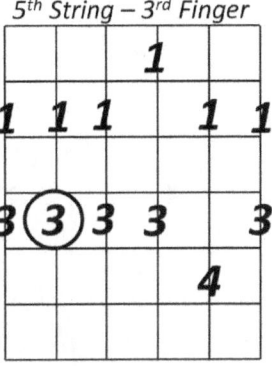
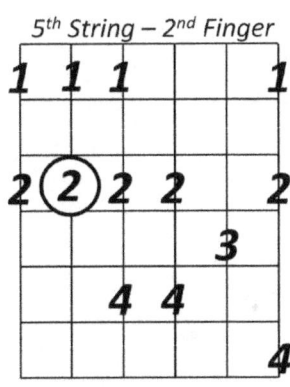
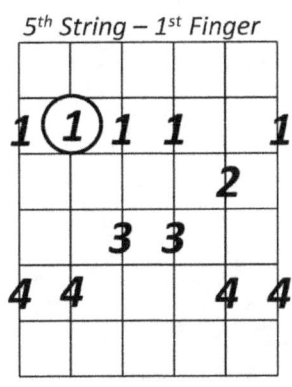
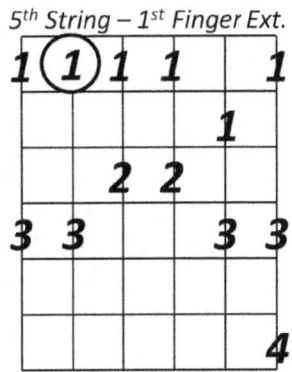

(See pages 96–97 to view the spelling of this scale)

PART 10
Fingerings for the Arpeggios

The Major 7th Arpeggio

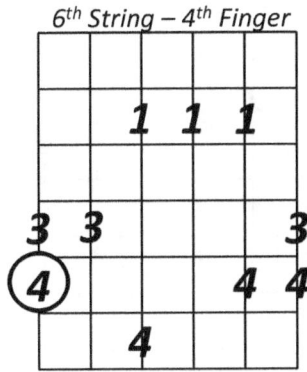
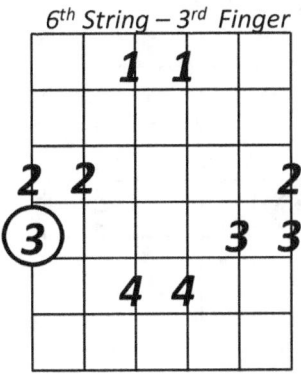
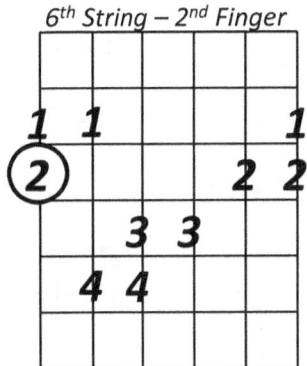
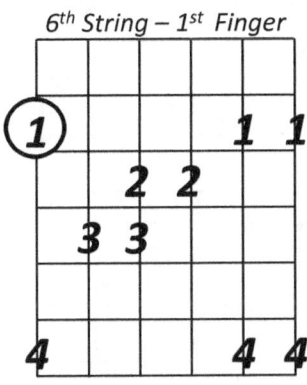
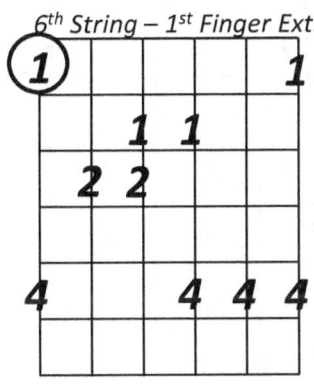
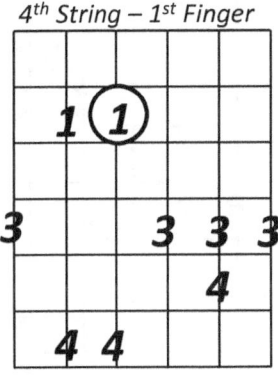
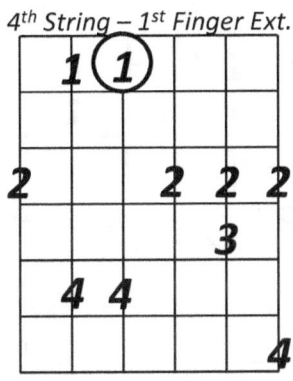
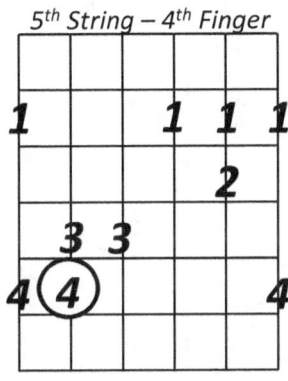
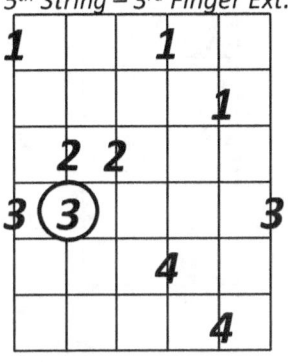
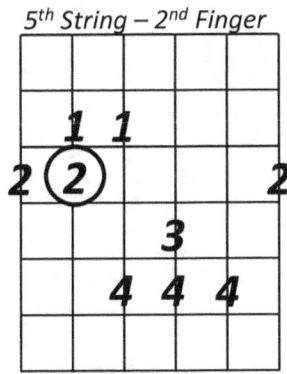
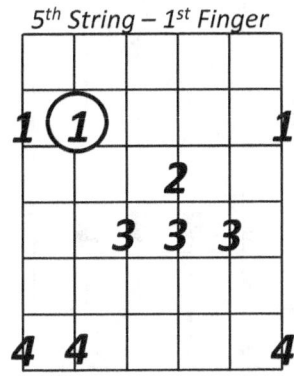
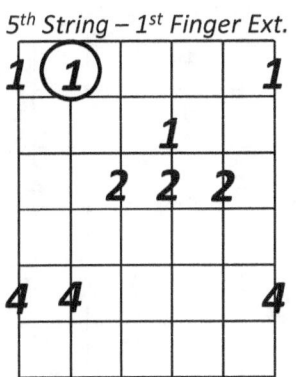

(See pages 104–105 to view the spelling of this arpeggio)

The Major 6th Arpeggio

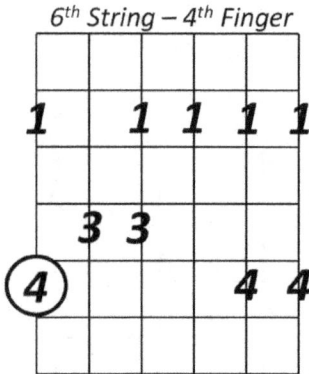
6th String – 4th Finger

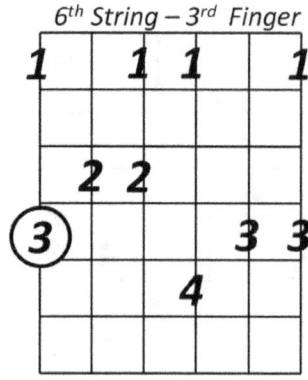
6th String – 3rd Finger

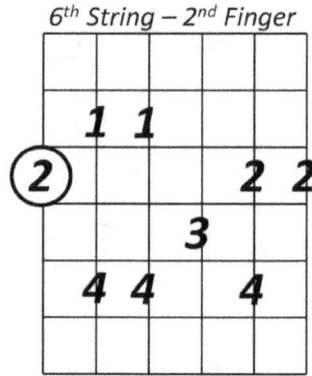
6th String – 2nd Finger

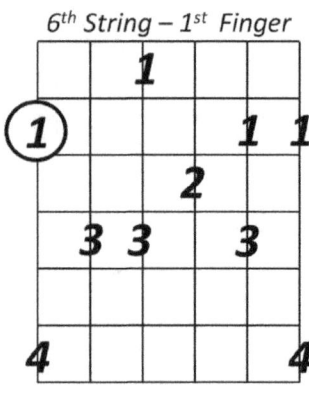
6th String – 1st Finger

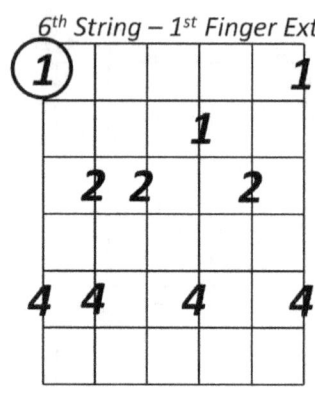
6th String – 1st Finger Ext.

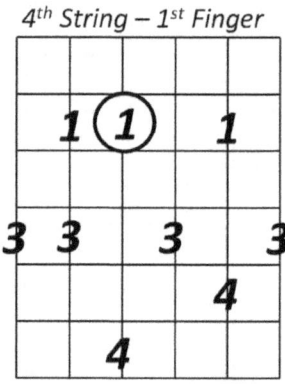
4th String – 1st Finger

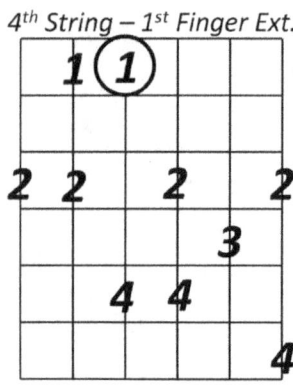
4th String – 1st Finger Ext.

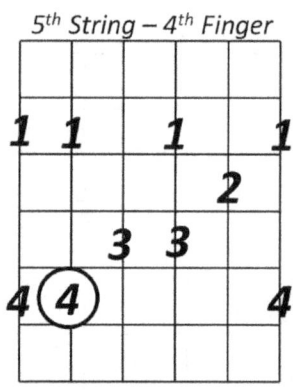
5th String – 4th Finger

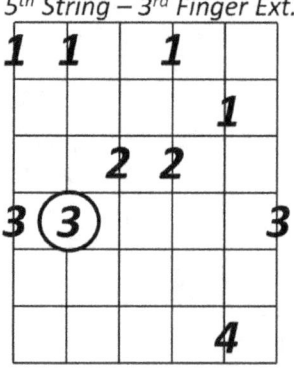
5th String – 3rd Finger Ext.

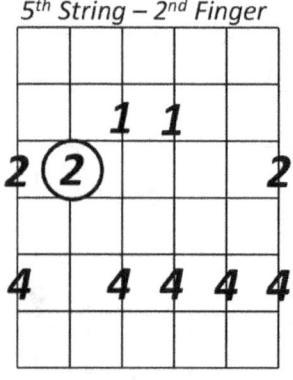
5th String – 2nd Finger

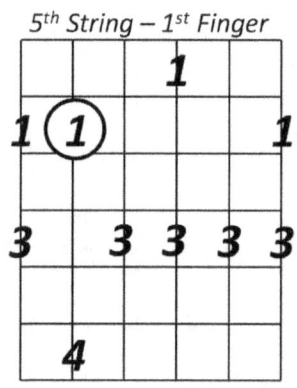
5th String – 1st Finger

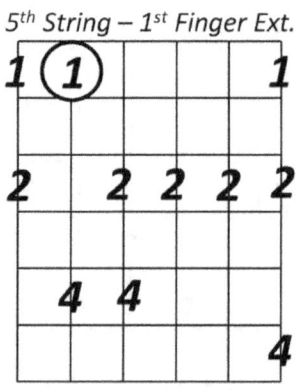
5th String – 1st Finger Ext.

(See pages 106–107 to view the spelling of this arpeggio)

The Dominant 7th Arpeggio

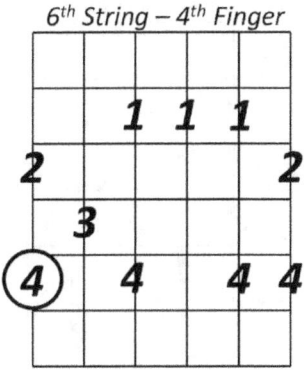
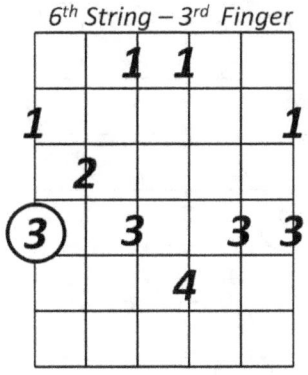
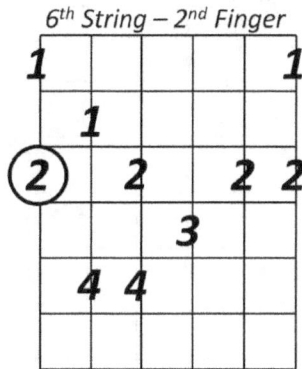
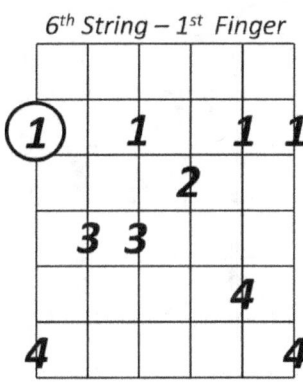
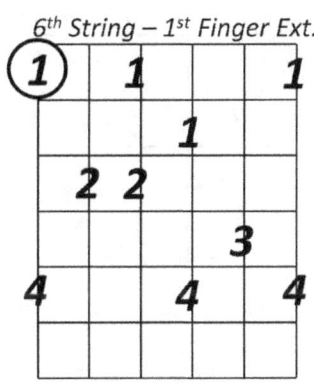
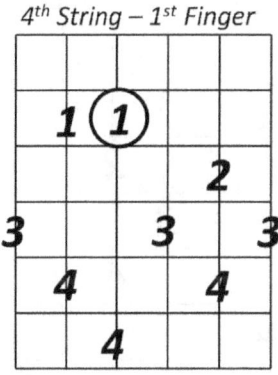
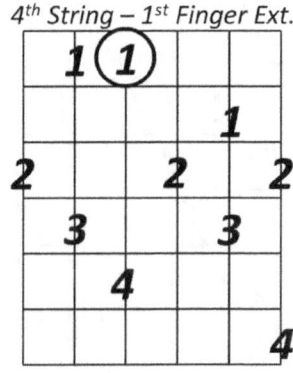
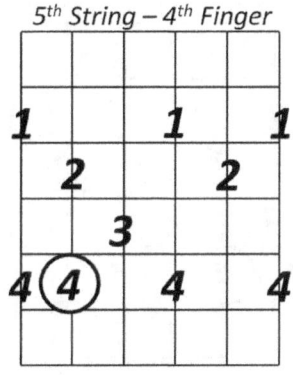
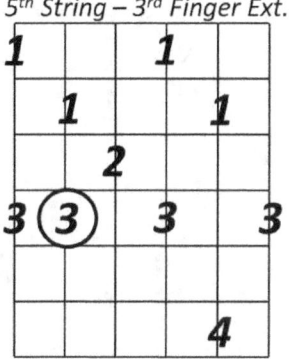
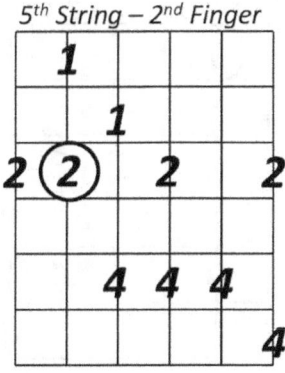
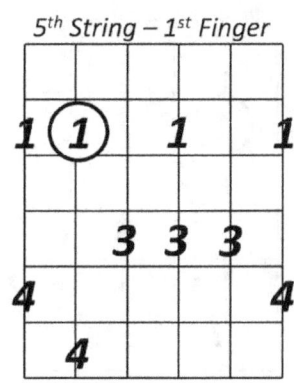
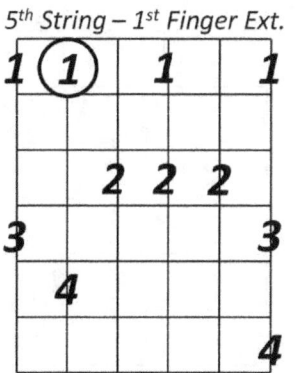

(See pages 108–109 to view the spelling of this arpeggio)

The Dominant 7(♭5) Arpeggio

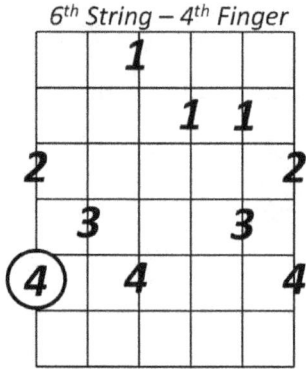
6th String – 4th Finger

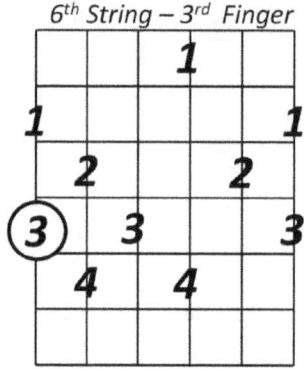
6th String – 3rd Finger

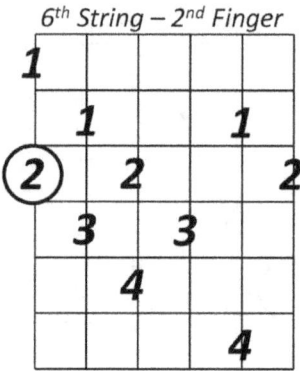
6th String – 2nd Finger

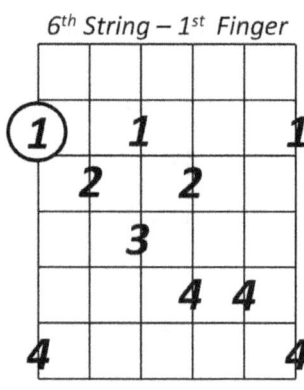
6th String – 1st Finger

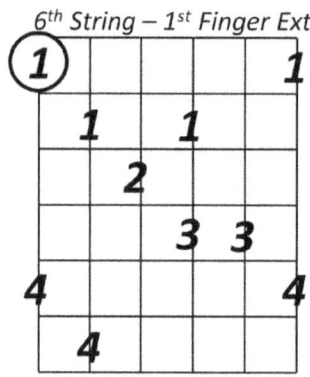
6th String – 1st Finger Ext.

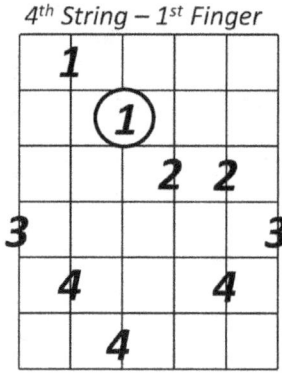
4th String – 1st Finger

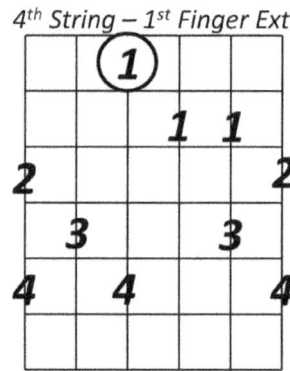
4th String – 1st Finger Ext.

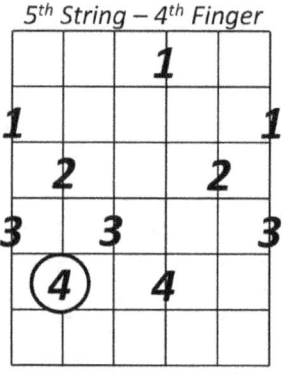
5th String – 4th Finger

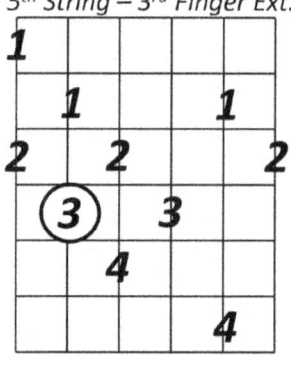
5th String – 3rd Finger Ext.

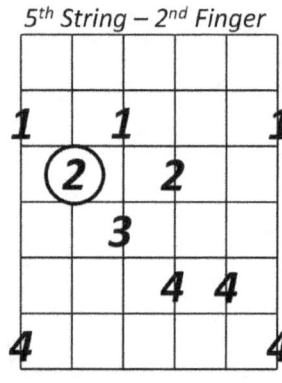
5th String – 2nd Finger

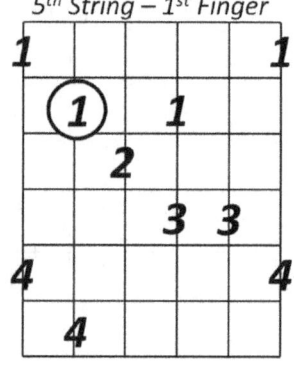
5th String – 1st Finger

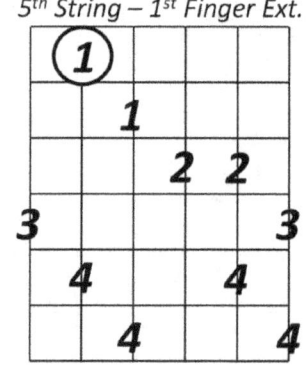
5th String – 1st Finger Ext.

(See pages 110–111 to view the spelling of this arpeggio)

The Dominant 7(#5) Arpeggio

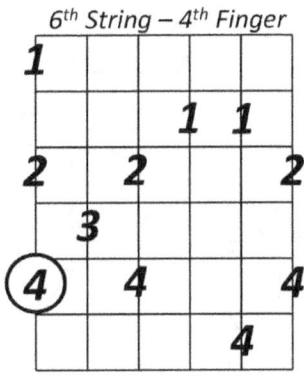
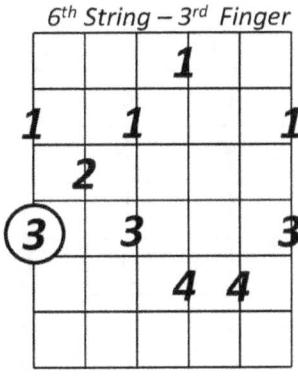
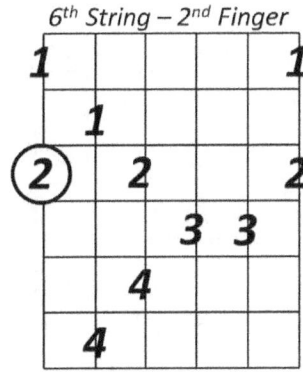
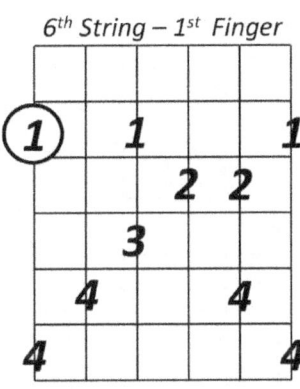
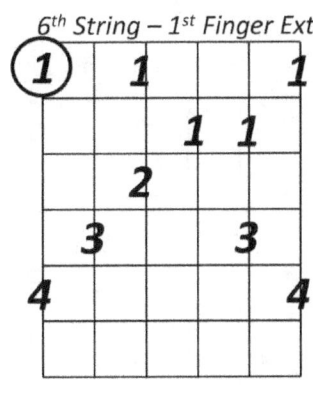
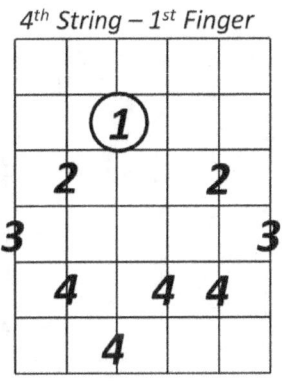
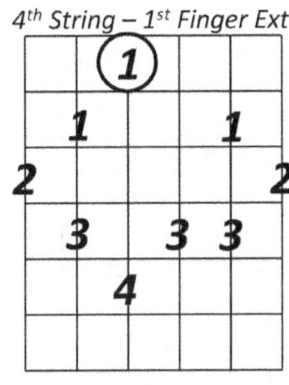
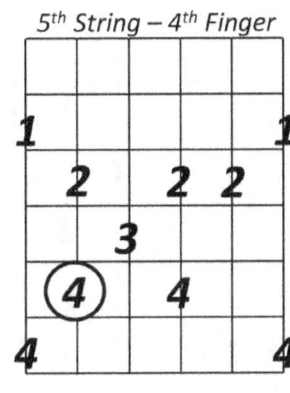
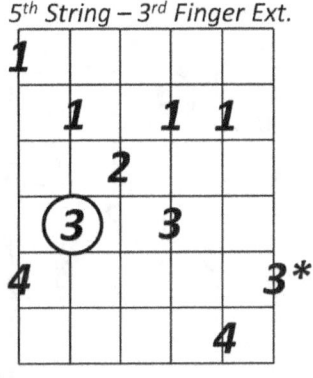
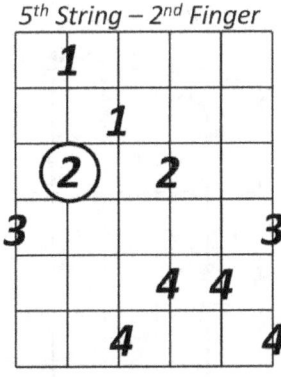
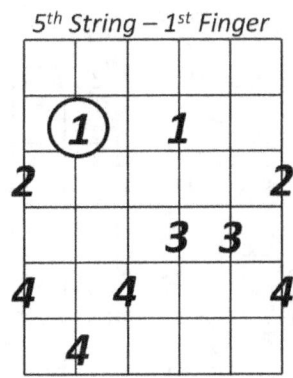
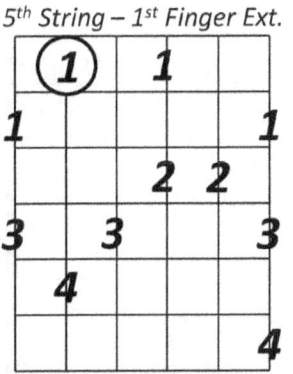

(See pages 112–113 to view the spelling of this arpeggio)

* Shifted 3rd finger is an exception

The Minor 7th Arpeggio

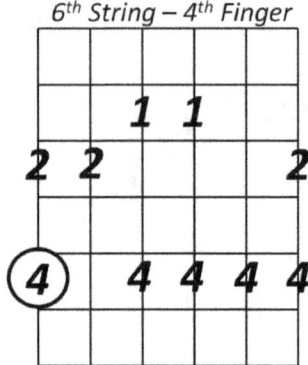
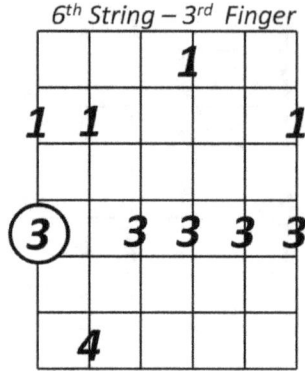
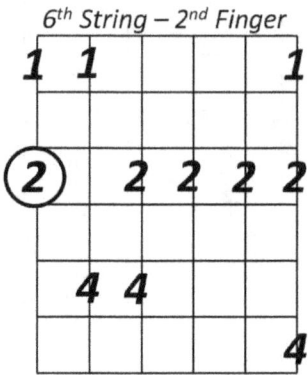
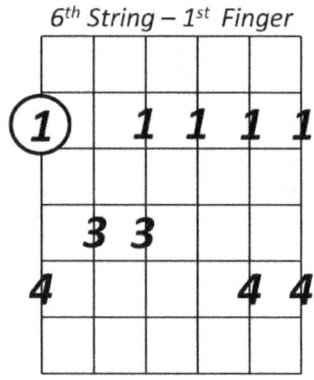
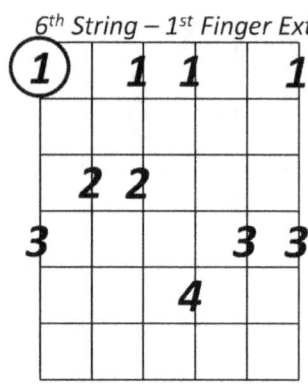
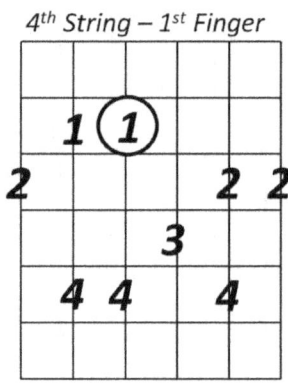
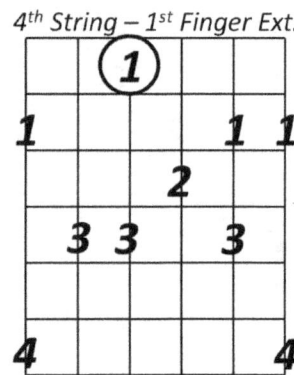
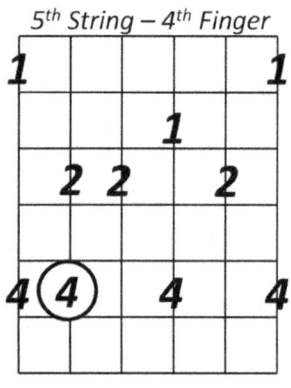
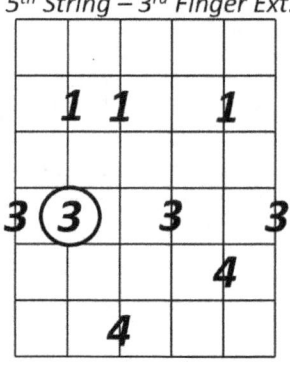
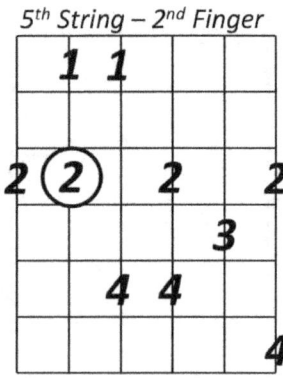
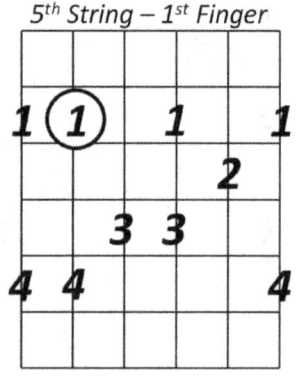
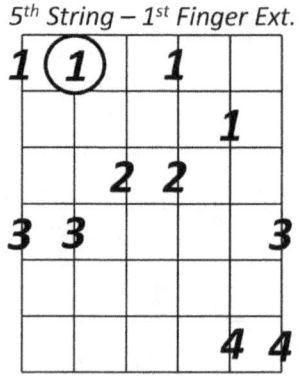

(See pages 114–115 to view the spelling of this arpeggio)

The Minor 7♭5 (Half-Diminished) Arpeggio

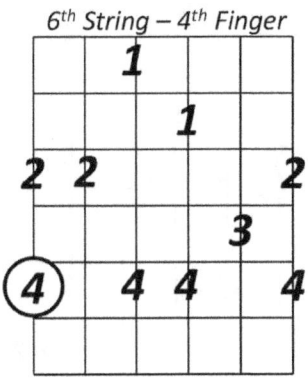
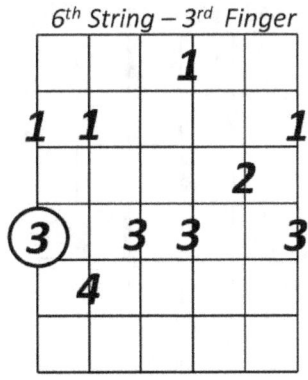
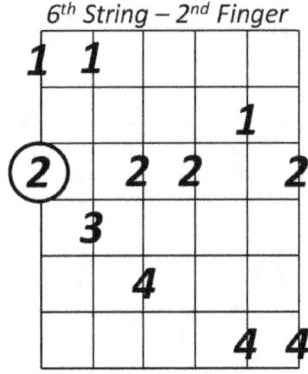
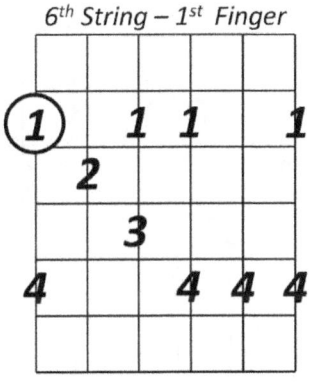
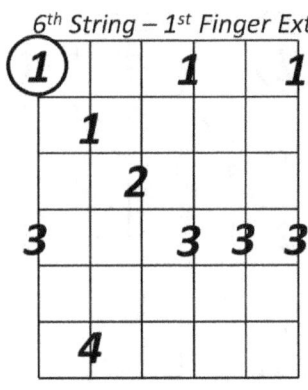
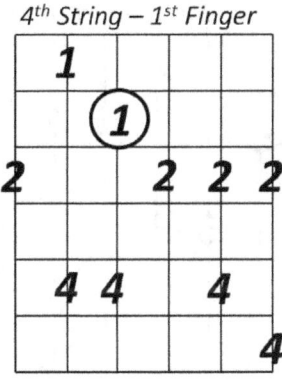
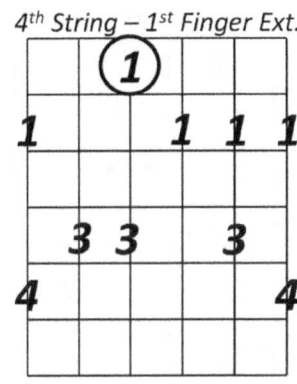
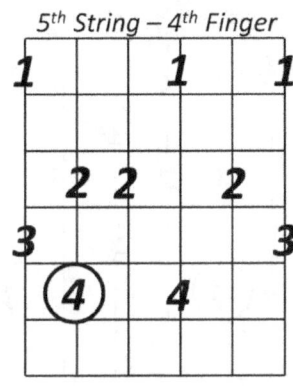
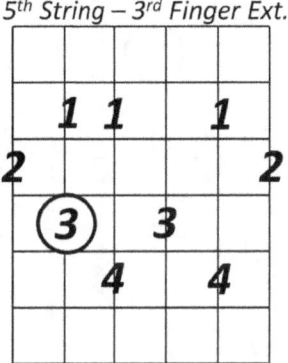
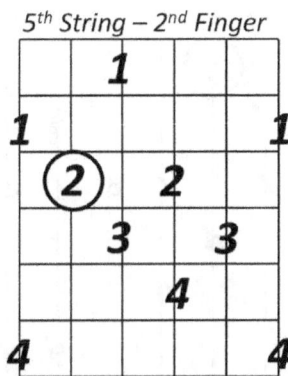
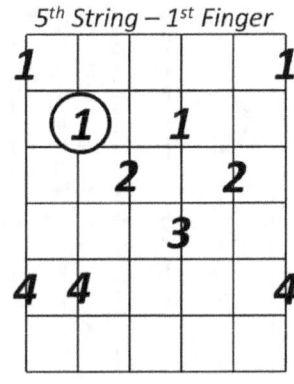
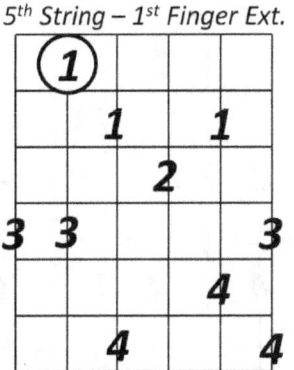

(See pages 116–117 to view the spelling of this arpeggio)

The Minor 6th Arpeggio

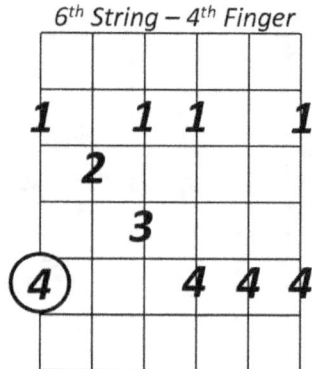
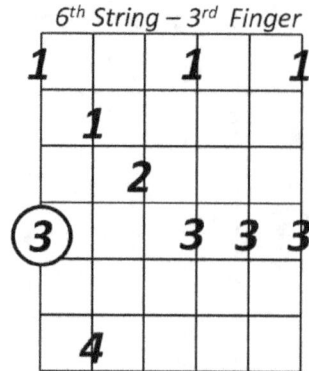
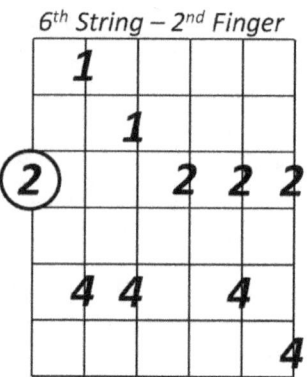
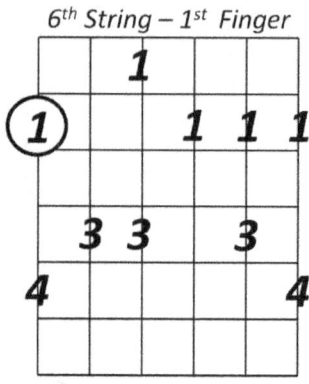
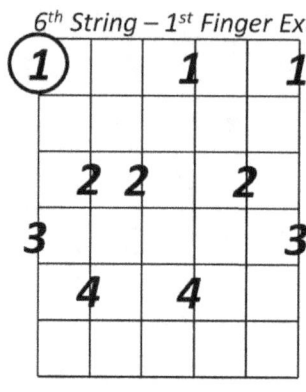
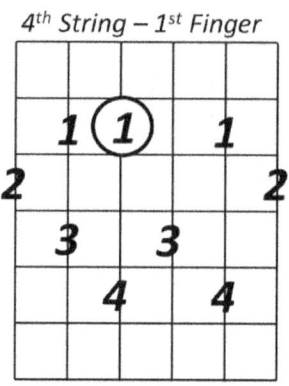
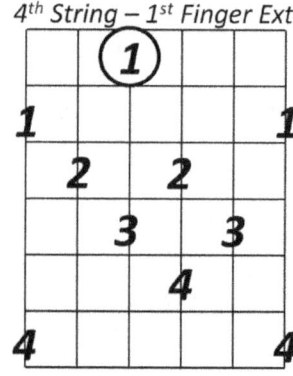
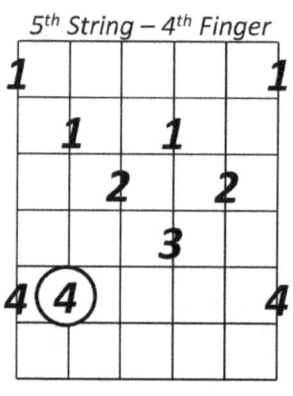
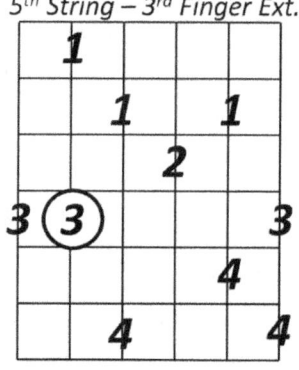
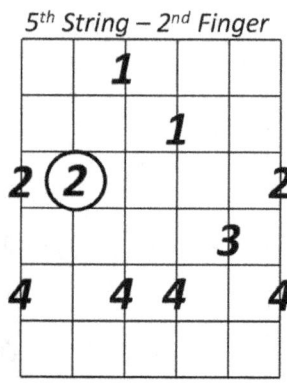
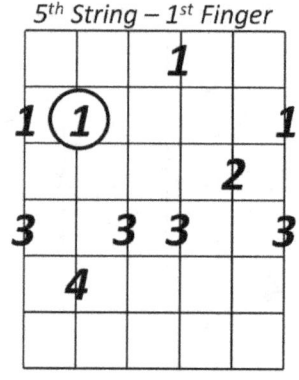
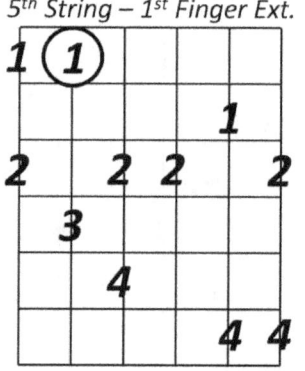

(See pages 118–119 to view the spelling of this arpeggio)

The Minor ♭6th Arpeggio

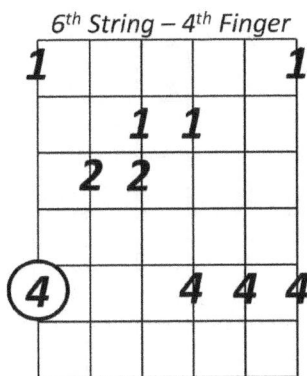
6th String – 4th Finger

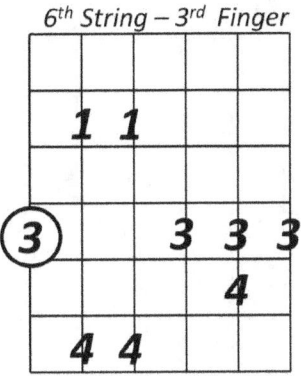
6th String – 3rd Finger

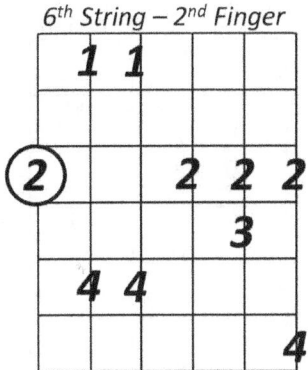
6th String – 2nd Finger

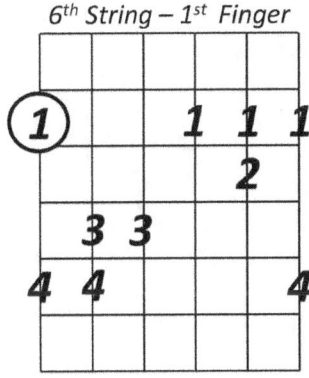
6th String – 1st Finger

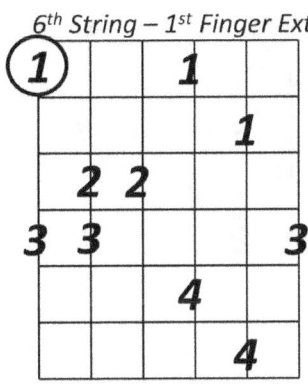
6th String – 1st Finger Ext.

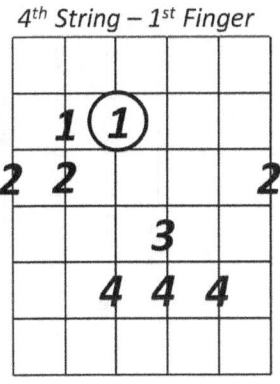
4th String – 1st Finger

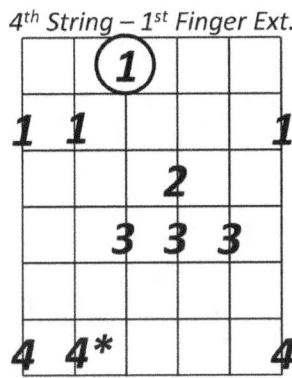
4th String – 1st Finger Ext.

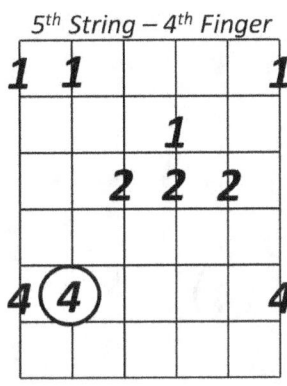
5th String – 4th Finger

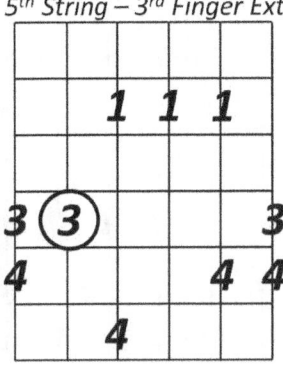
5th String – 3rd Finger Ext.

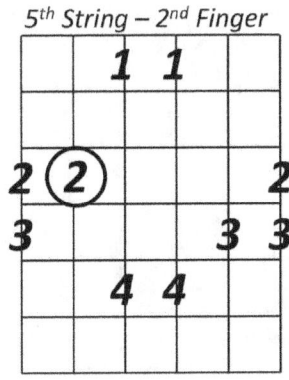
5th String – 2nd Finger

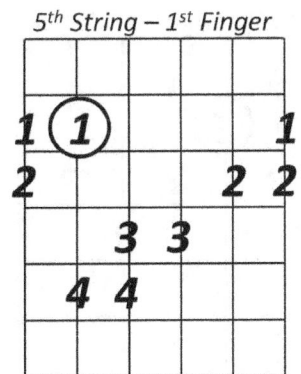
5th String – 1st Finger

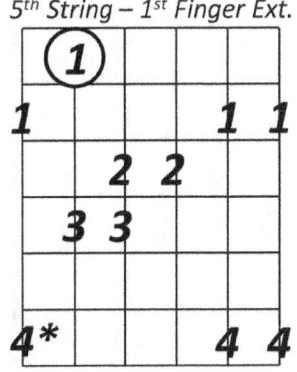
5th String – 1st Finger Ext.

(See pages 120–121 to view the spelling of this arpeggio)

* Play extended 4th finger instead of extended 1st finger when descending

The Minor ♭6♭5 Arpeggio

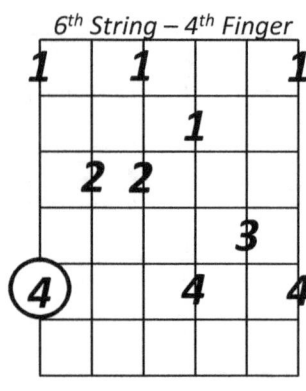
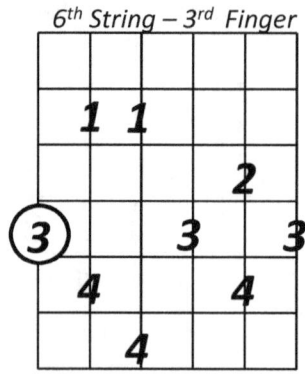
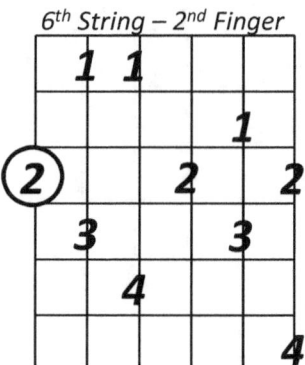
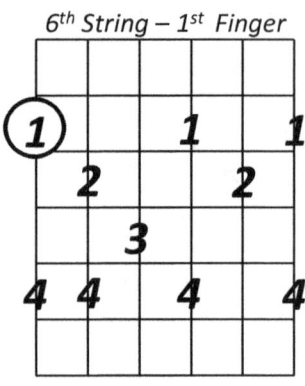
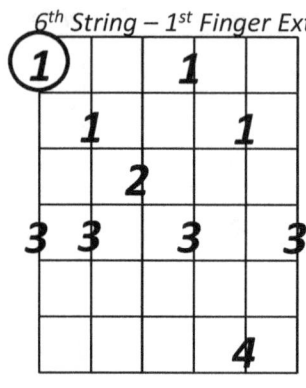
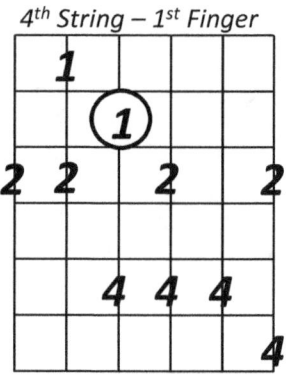
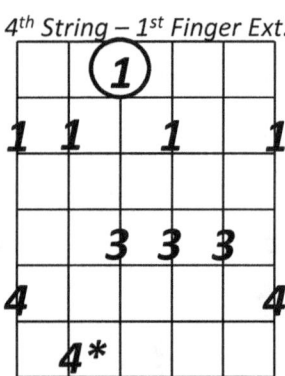
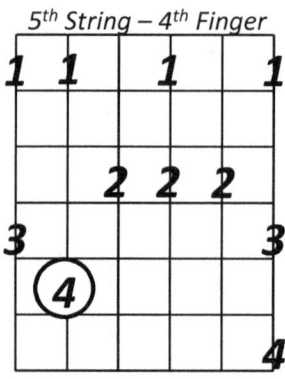
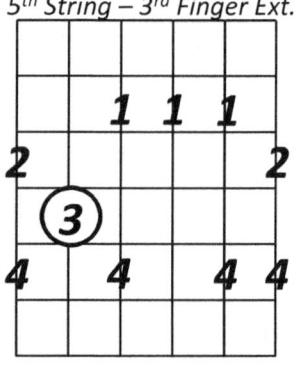
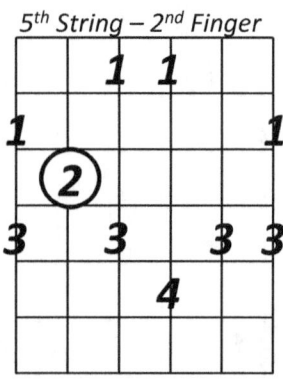
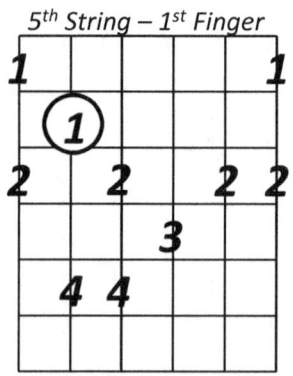
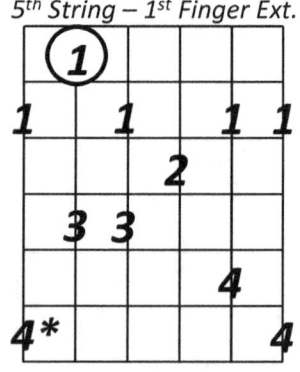

(See pages 122–123 to view the spelling of this arpeggio)

* Play extended 4th finger instead of extended 1st finger when descending

The Minor (Maj7) Arpeggio

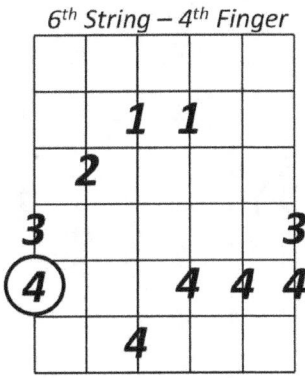
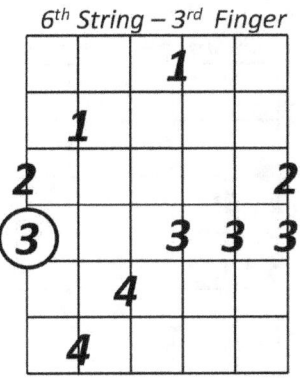
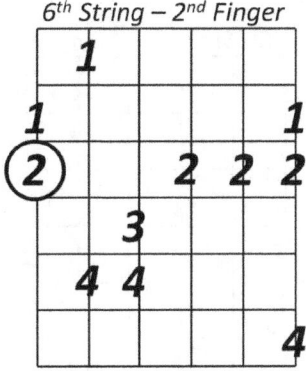
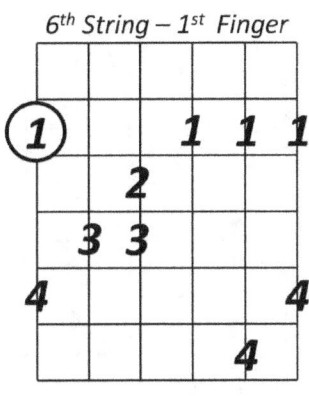
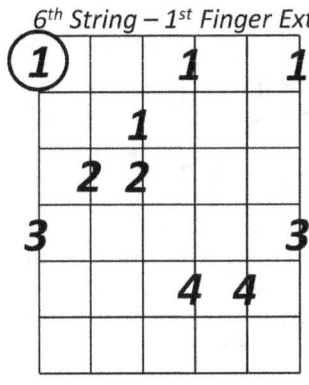
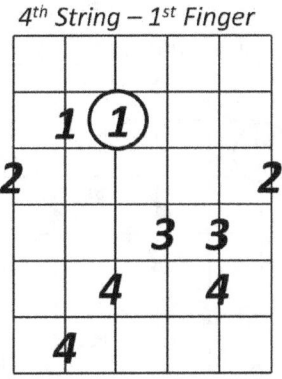
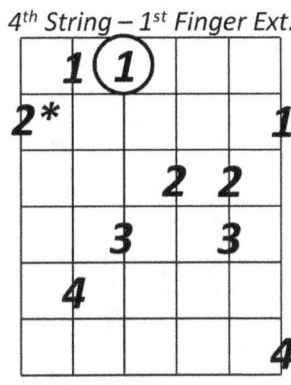
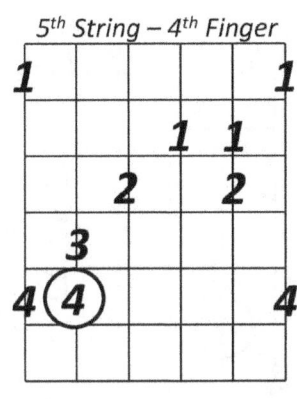
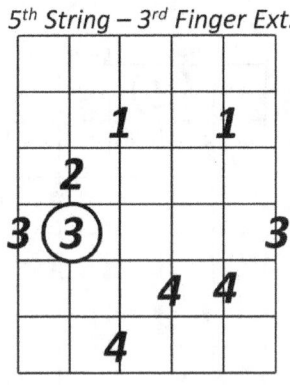
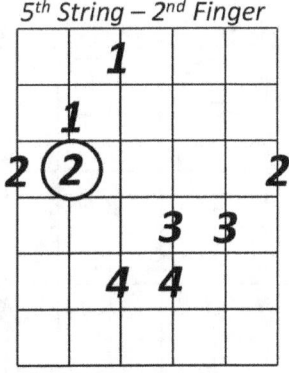
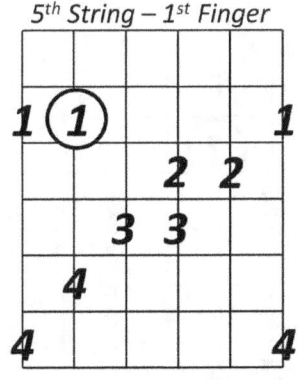
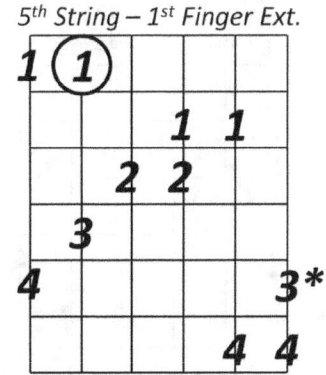

(See pages 124–125 to view the spelling of this arpeggio)

* Shifted 2nd finger is an exception

The Major 7th(#5) Arpeggio

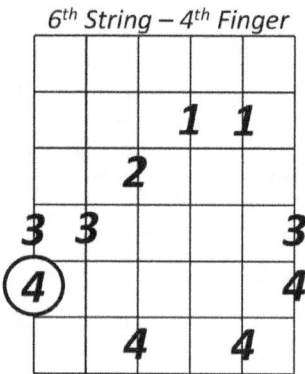
6th String – 4th Finger

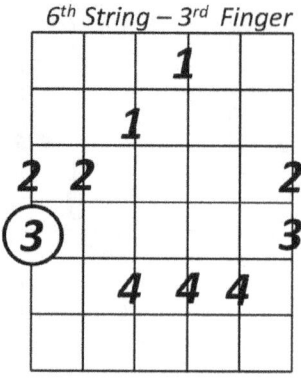
6th String – 3rd Finger

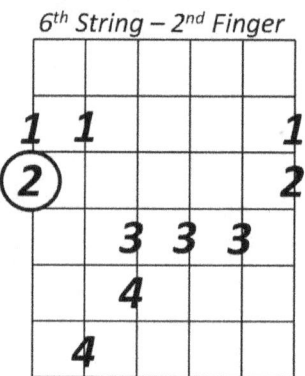
6th String – 2nd Finger

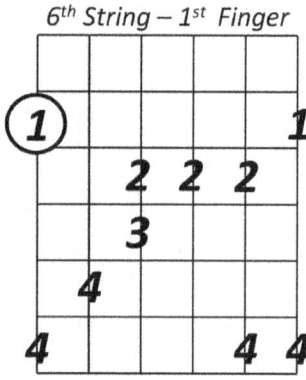
6th String – 1st Finger

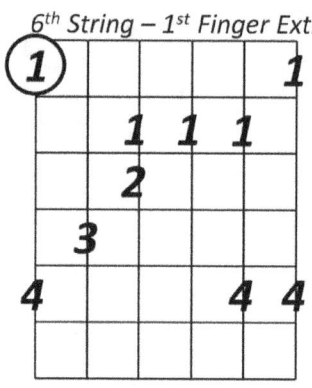
6th String – 1st Finger Ext.

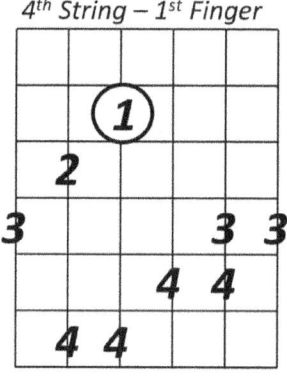
4th String – 1st Finger

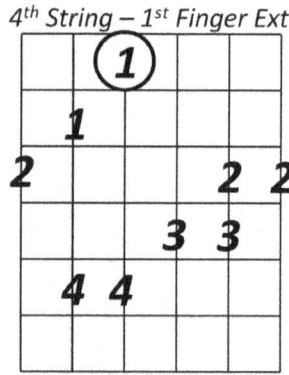
4th String – 1st Finger Ext.

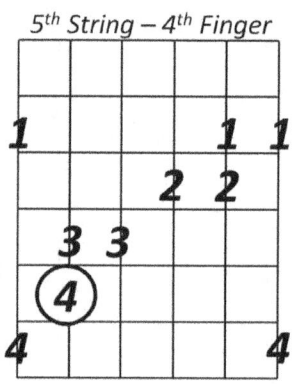
5th String – 4th Finger

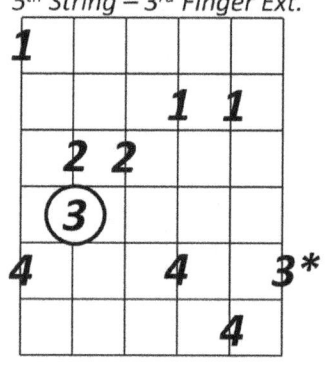
5th String – 3rd Finger Ext.

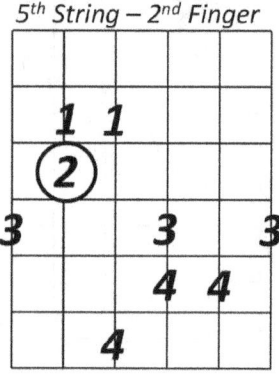
5th String – 2nd Finger

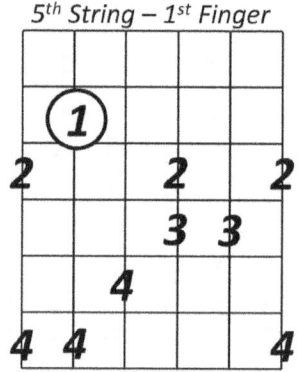
5th String – 1st Finger

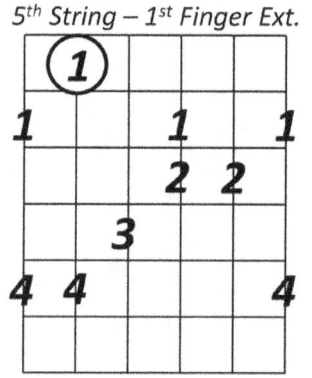
5th String – 1st Finger Ext.

(See pages 126–127 to view the spelling of this arpeggio)

* Shifted 3rd finger is an exception

The Diminished 7th Arpeggio

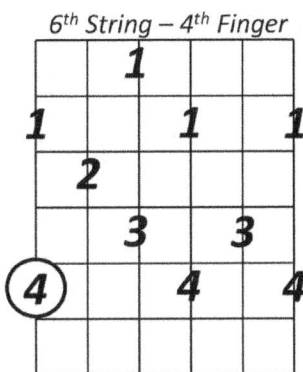
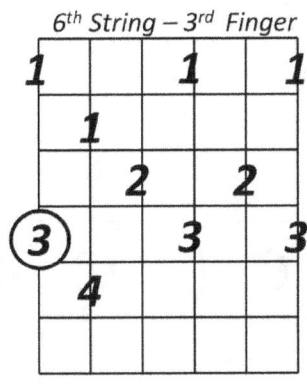
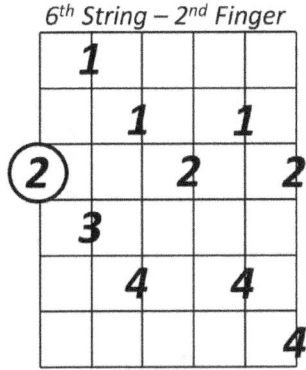
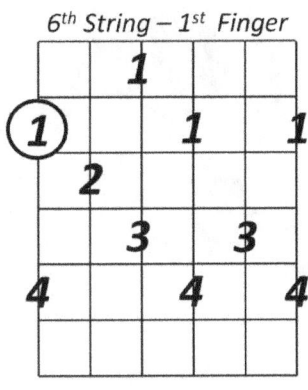
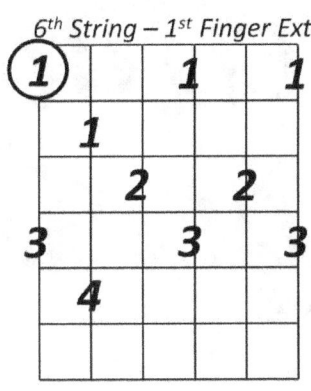
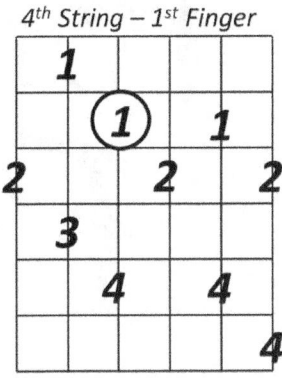
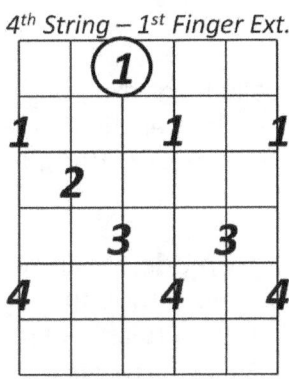
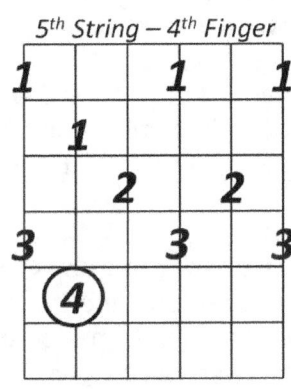
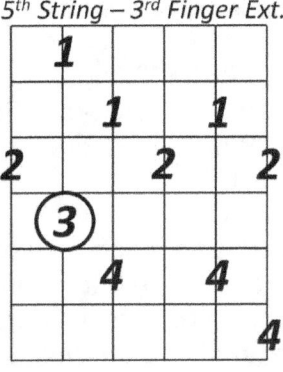
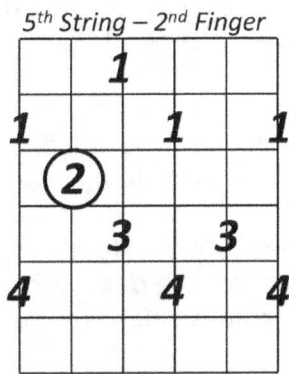
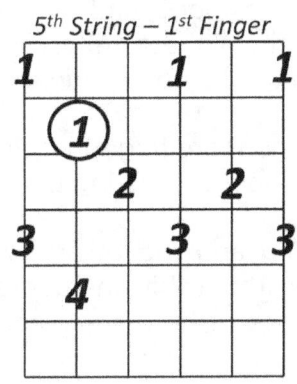
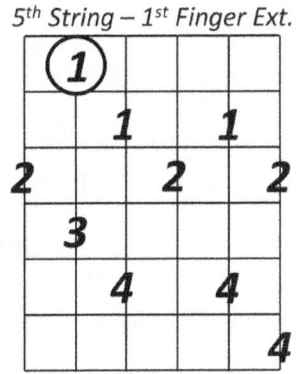

(See pages 128–129 to view the spelling of this arpeggio)

SECTION 3

Forgetting the Fingerings

This section of the book guides you in an approach to blend the fingerings presented in Section 2 into a complete whole—of which the parts are no longer seen.

Obviously, the 12 fingering patterns learned in Section 2 are not actually forgotten, but rather by doing the exercises in Section 3 you will reach a point where you no longer think in terms of patterns, but rather see possibilities ALL OVER THE FRETBOARD—on every string, on every fret.

The goal is to practice this until the fretboard roadmaps for every scale, mode, and arpeggio—in every key—are burned into your subconscious and no longer occupy your thoughts when playing. Rather, your mind is free to think of melodies while your fingers take care of navigating the possibilities with almost no thought given to fingerings.

By fusing the 12 fingerings of each scale, mode, and arpeggio into a map which covers the entire fretboard—from the 1st fret to the highest fret on every string—a profound depth of freedom in improvisation and arranging will be experienced.

Once these roadmaps are mastered, no more fingering rules apply—instead you will find yourself playing with new and spontaneous fingering patterns which you create as needed.

In school we learned grammar, spelling, and vocabulary. But at some point we stopped thinking about that and just SPOKE without thinking about speaking. Yet the depth of study and learning impacts the effectiveness of our communication. The same is true with music.

PART 11
Blending the 12 Patterns into ONE Comprehensive Roadmap

Here are some ways I have approached fusing the fingerings of Section 2 into a singular consolidated roadmap of the fretboard.

1. First, I learned all the fingerings in Section 1 of this book.
2. On any given day, I will pick a key (e.g. the key of G) and play the following:

   The exercise shown on the following pages in this section for each mode of the major, melodic minor, and harmonic scales, as well as the symmetric and pentatonic scales, and the arpeggios.

   The next day, I pick a different key (e.g. C#) and play through the exercises again.

   This exercise takes me about an hour. Of course, it may take you longer when you first begin. It is important to spend only 10% to 20% of your practice time on scales and arpeggios. Be sure to devote the majority of your practice time to learning/composing/arranging SONGS, licks, solos, etc.

3. It is extremely important to keep your hands TOTALLY RELAXED while playing these exercises. This will help prevent injury to the hands and muscle fatigue. Relaxed hands = a relaxed mind. And a relaxed mind comes up with better solos.

Tying together the 12 patterns: Connect as shown below when scale, mode, or arpeggio begins with a <u>whole step</u> interval between the first two notes.

To cover the entire neck with a scale, mode, or arpeggio, play the 12 patterns in the order below, starting with the pattern which allows the first finger to be played on the first fret. For those patterns in which the first two notes are separated by a whole step, use the following approach (see example on following three pages).

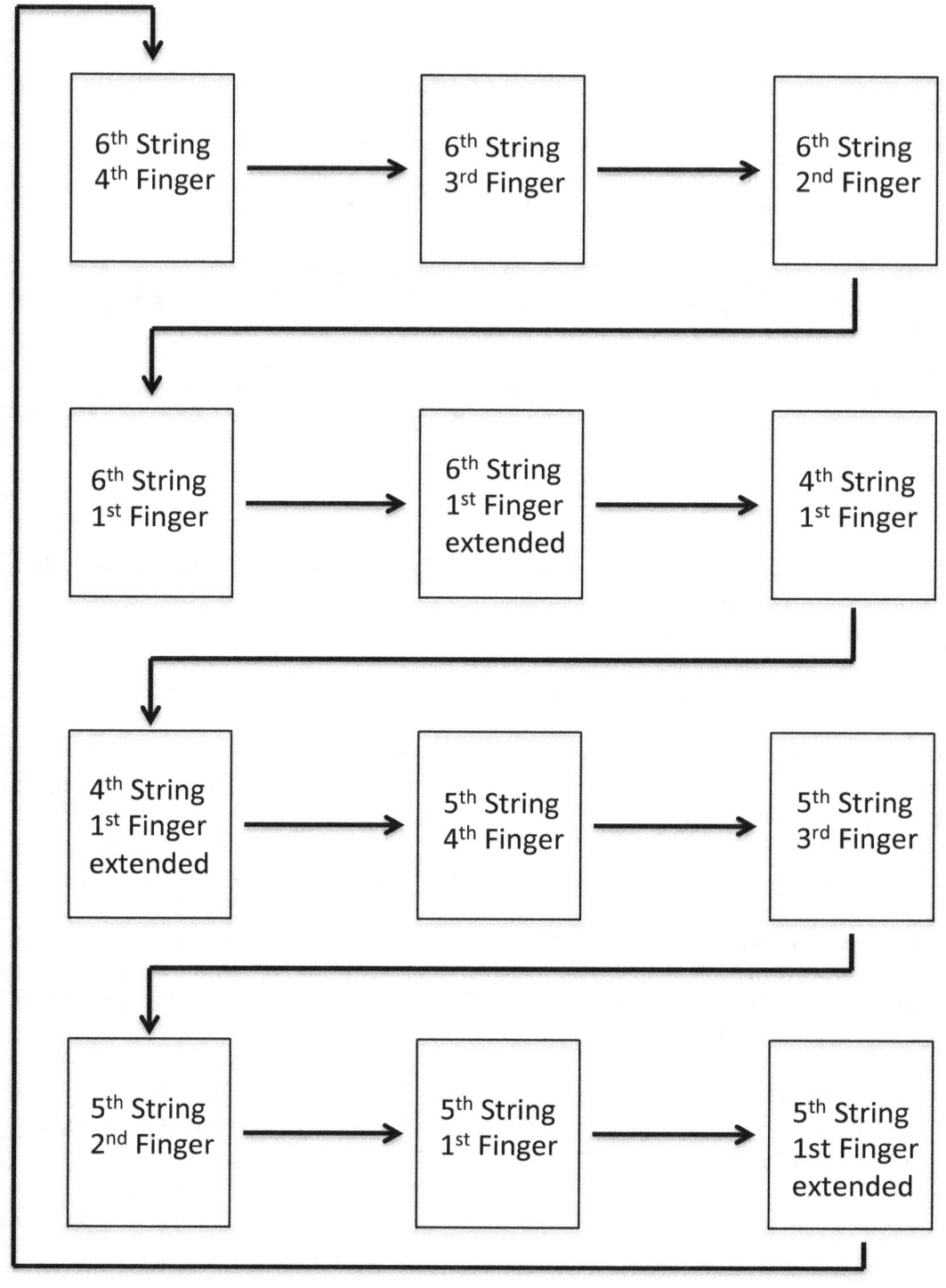

Example of combining 12 patterns when first two notes are a WHOLE STEP apart
(G ionian mode of the major scale is used in this example)

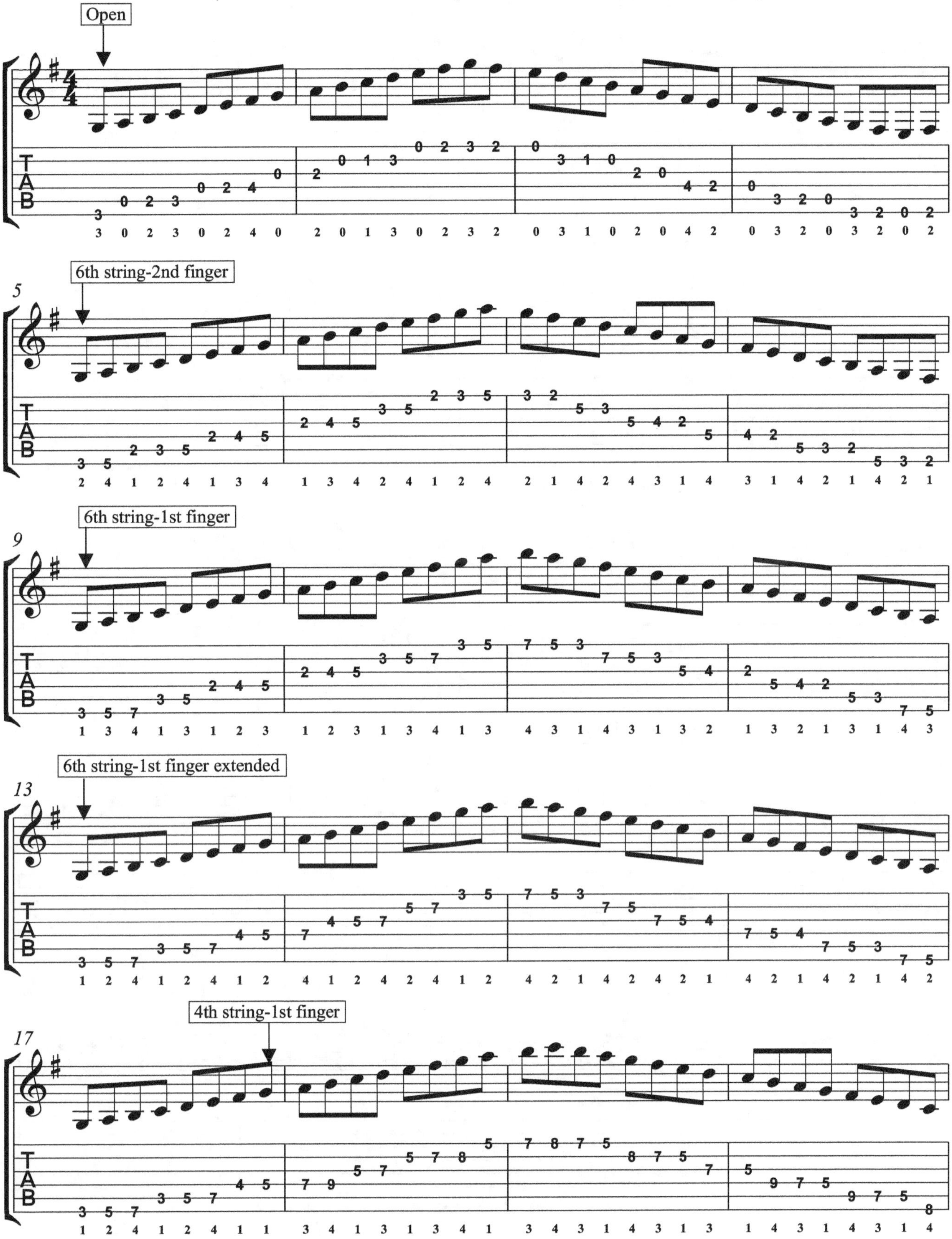

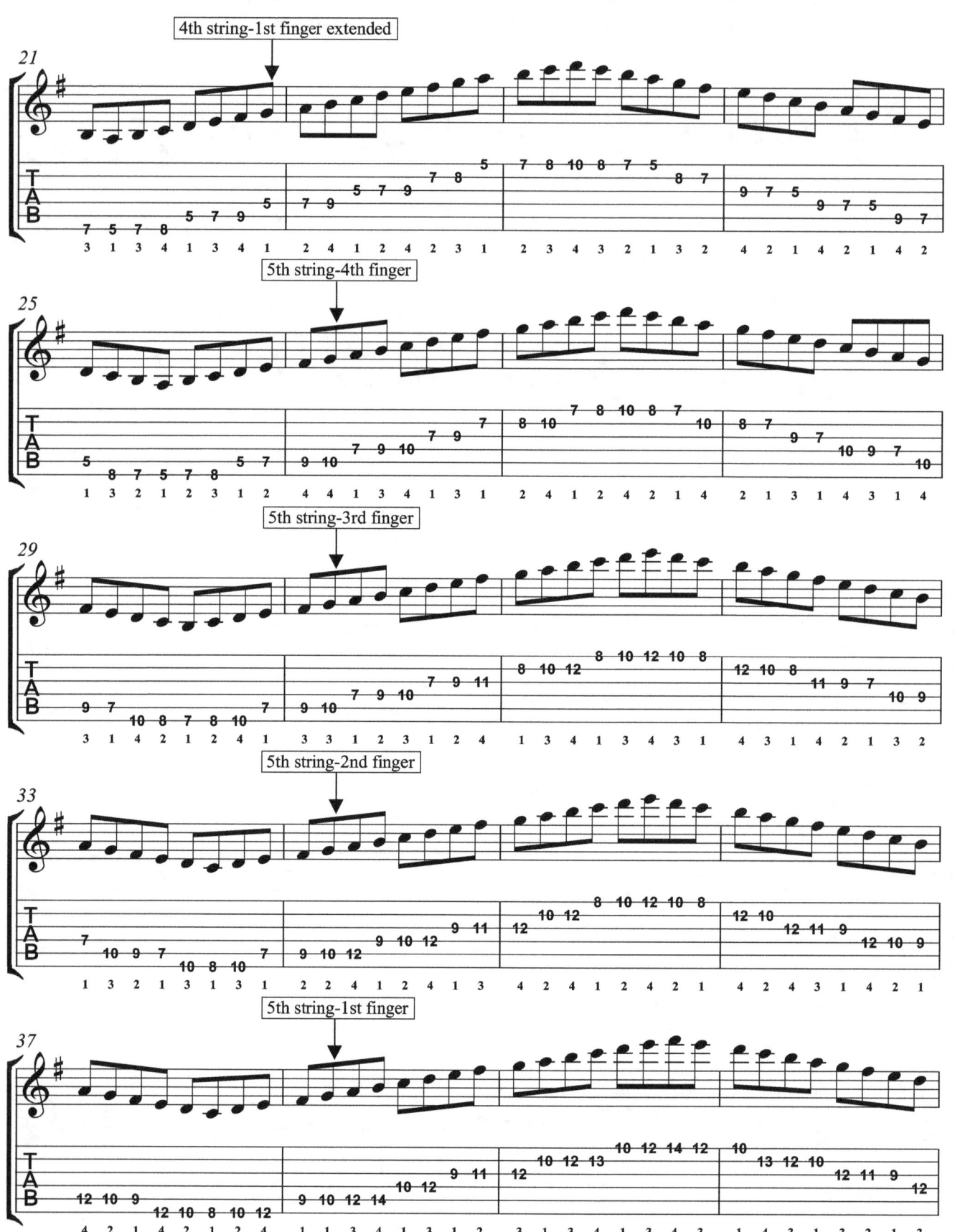

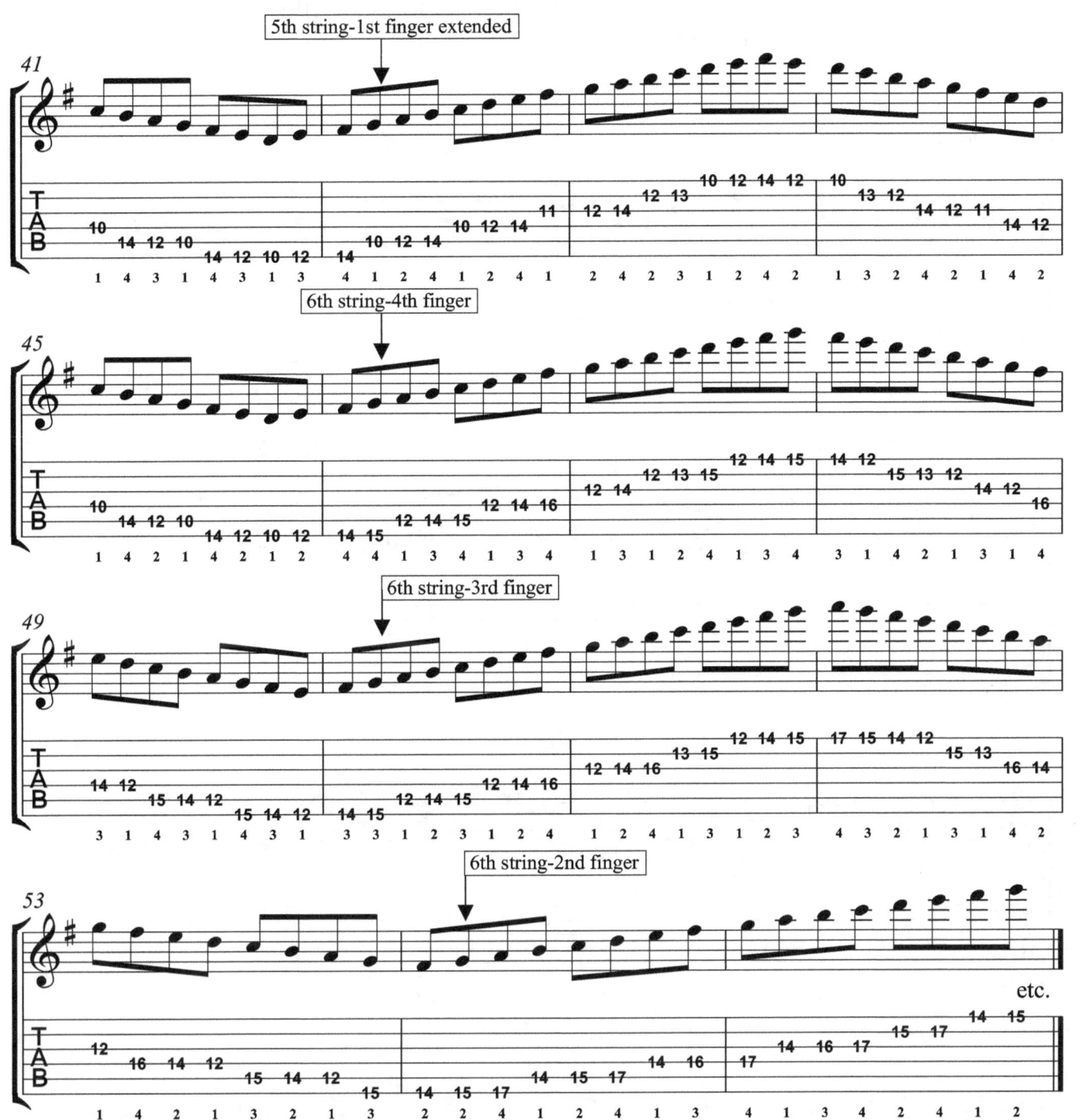

Example of combining 12 patterns for an ARPEGGIO

(G7 arpeggio is used in this example)

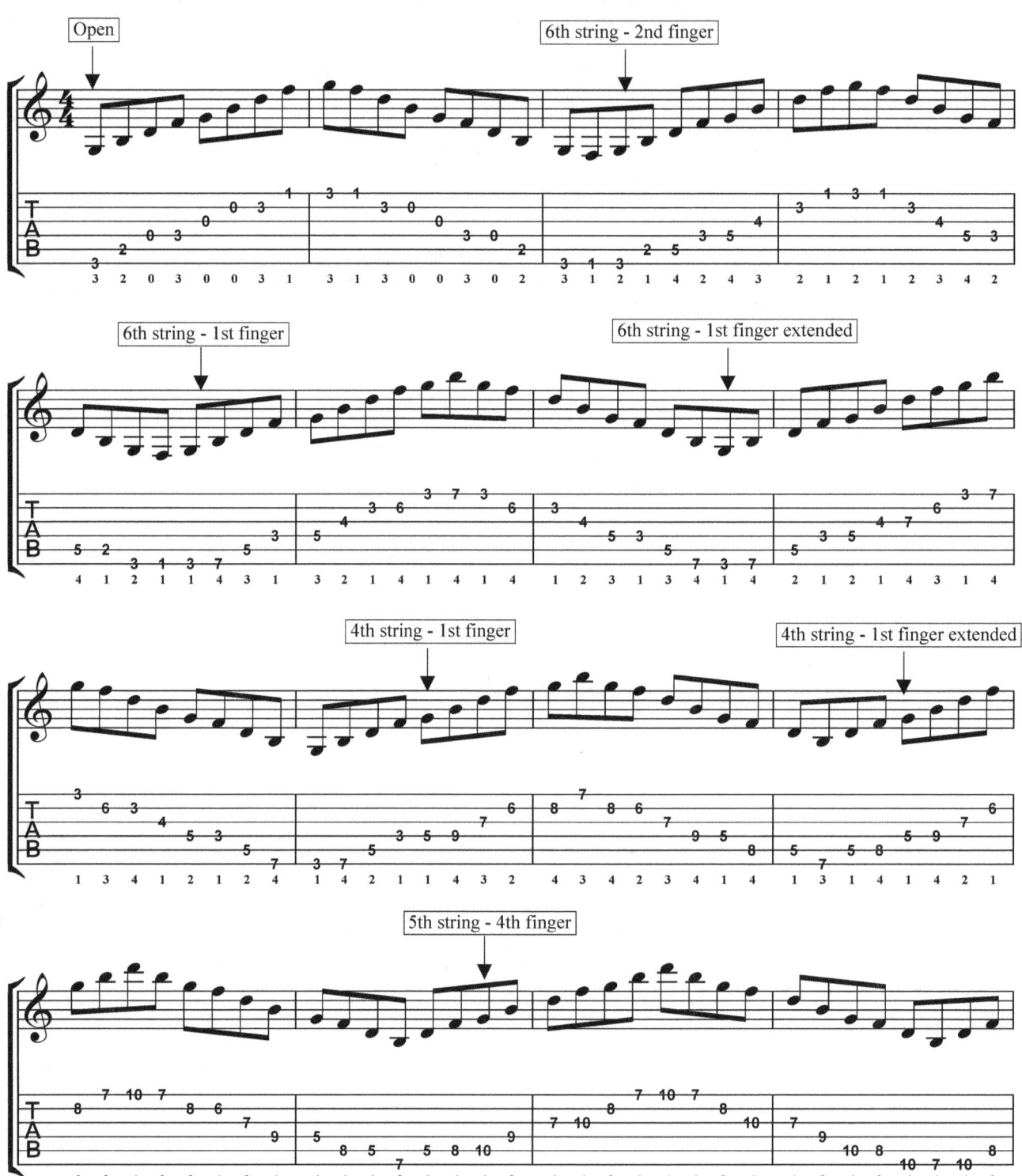

186

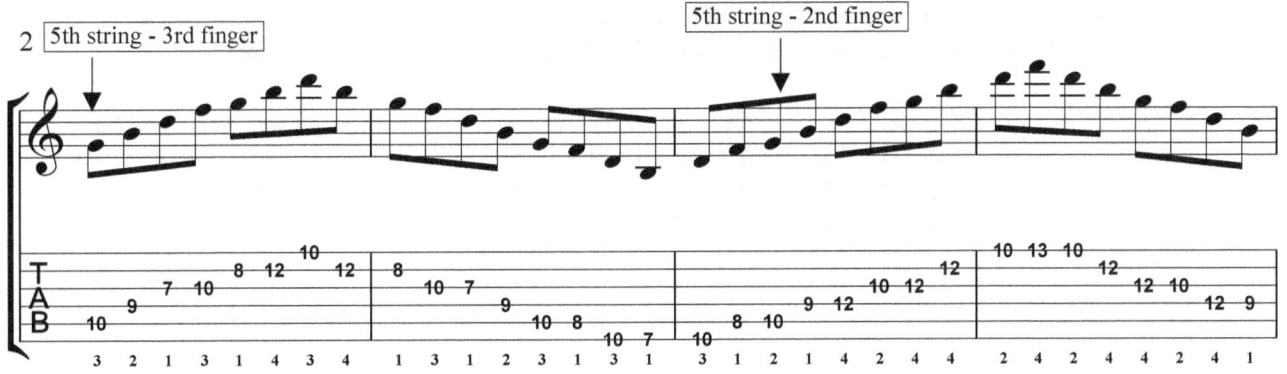
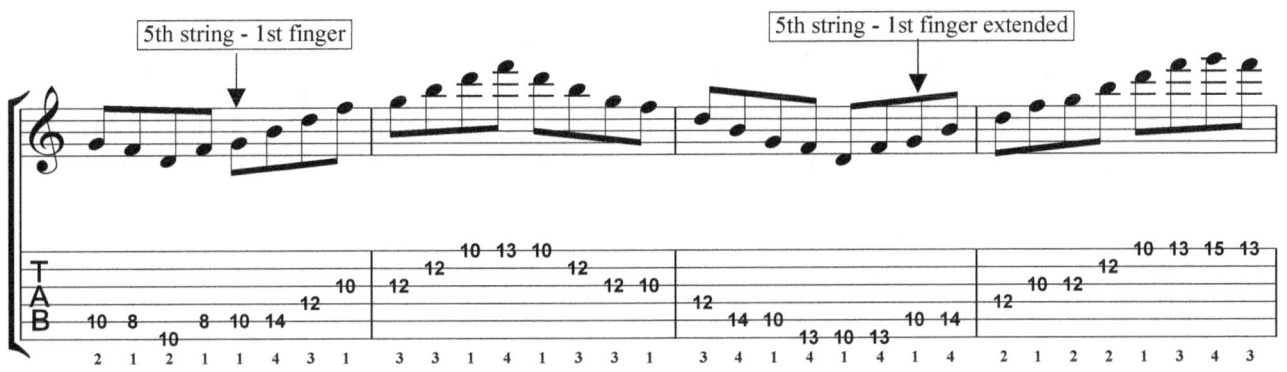
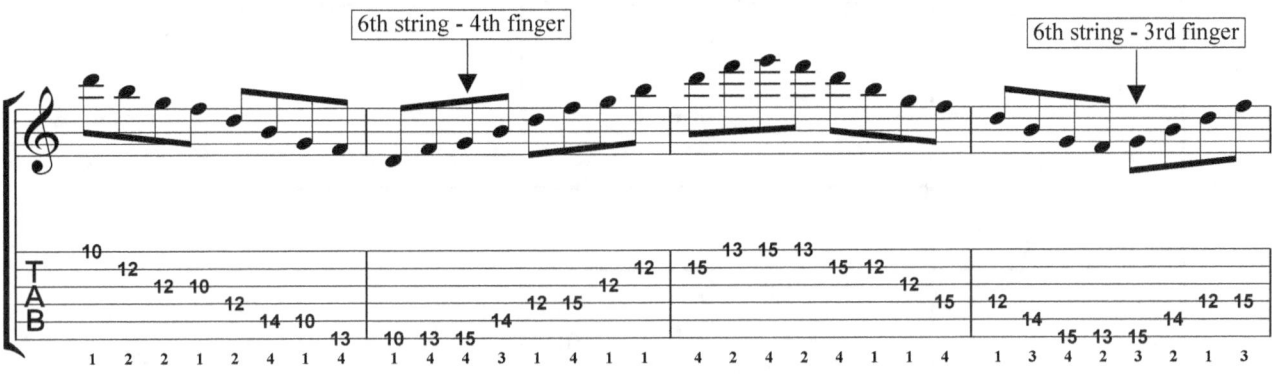
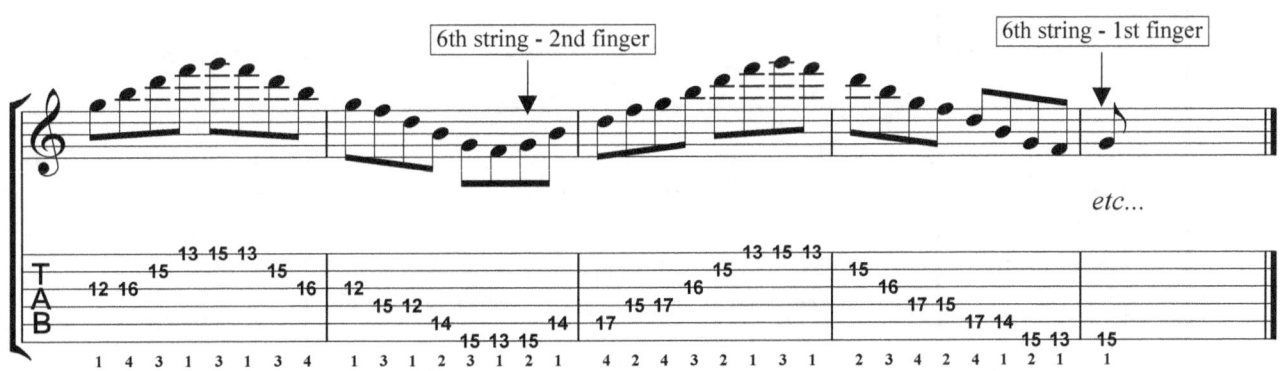

Tying together the 12 patterns: Connect as shown below when scale, mode, or arpeggio begins with a <u>half step</u> interval between the first two notes.

To cover the entire neck with a scale, mode, or arpeggio, play the 12 patterns in the order below, starting with the pattern which allows the first finger to be played on the first fret. For those patterns in which the first two notes are separated by a half step, use the following approach (see example on following three pages).

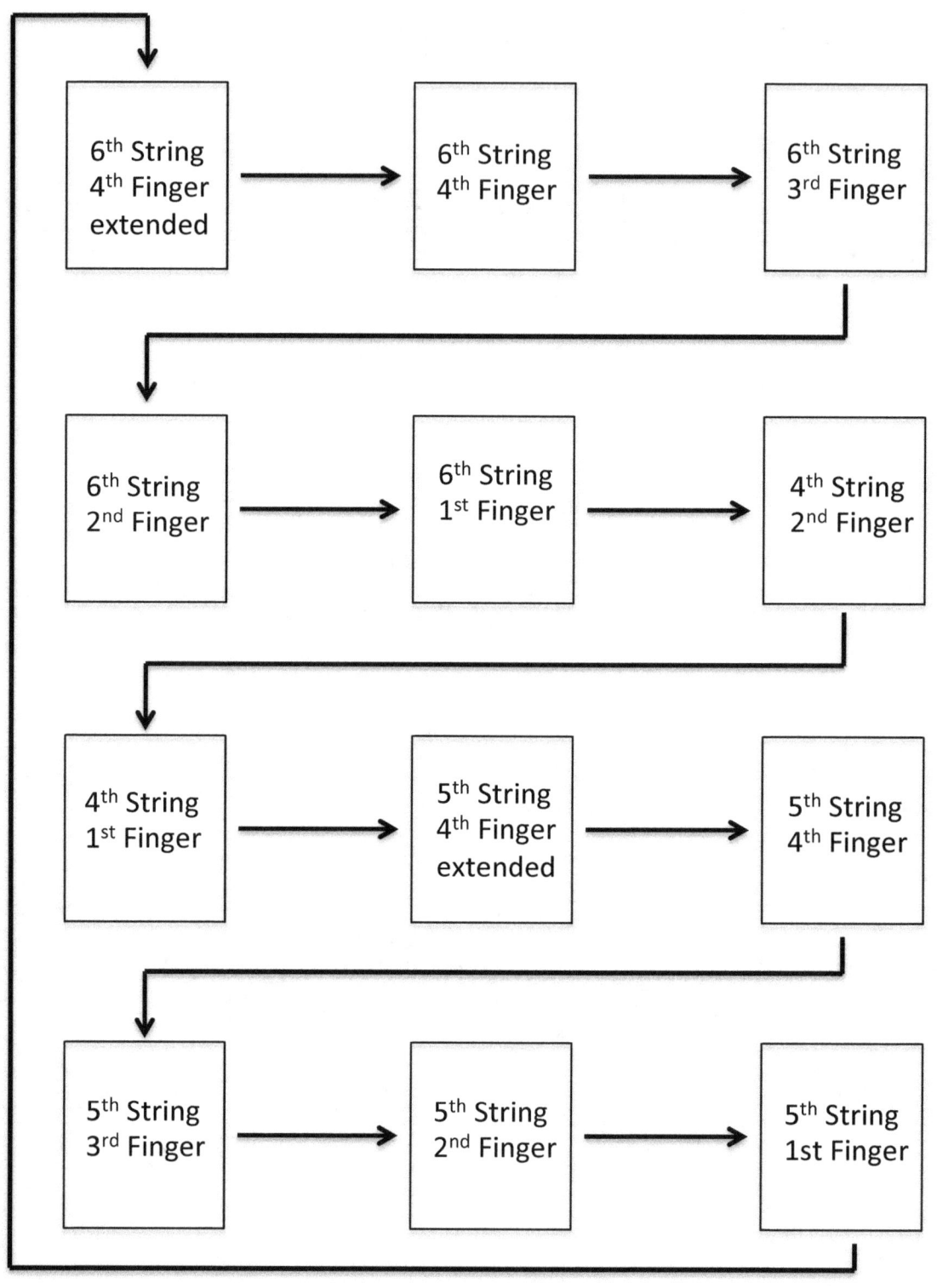

Example of combining 12 patterns when first two notes are a HALF STEP apart
(E super locrian mode of the melodic minor is used in this example)

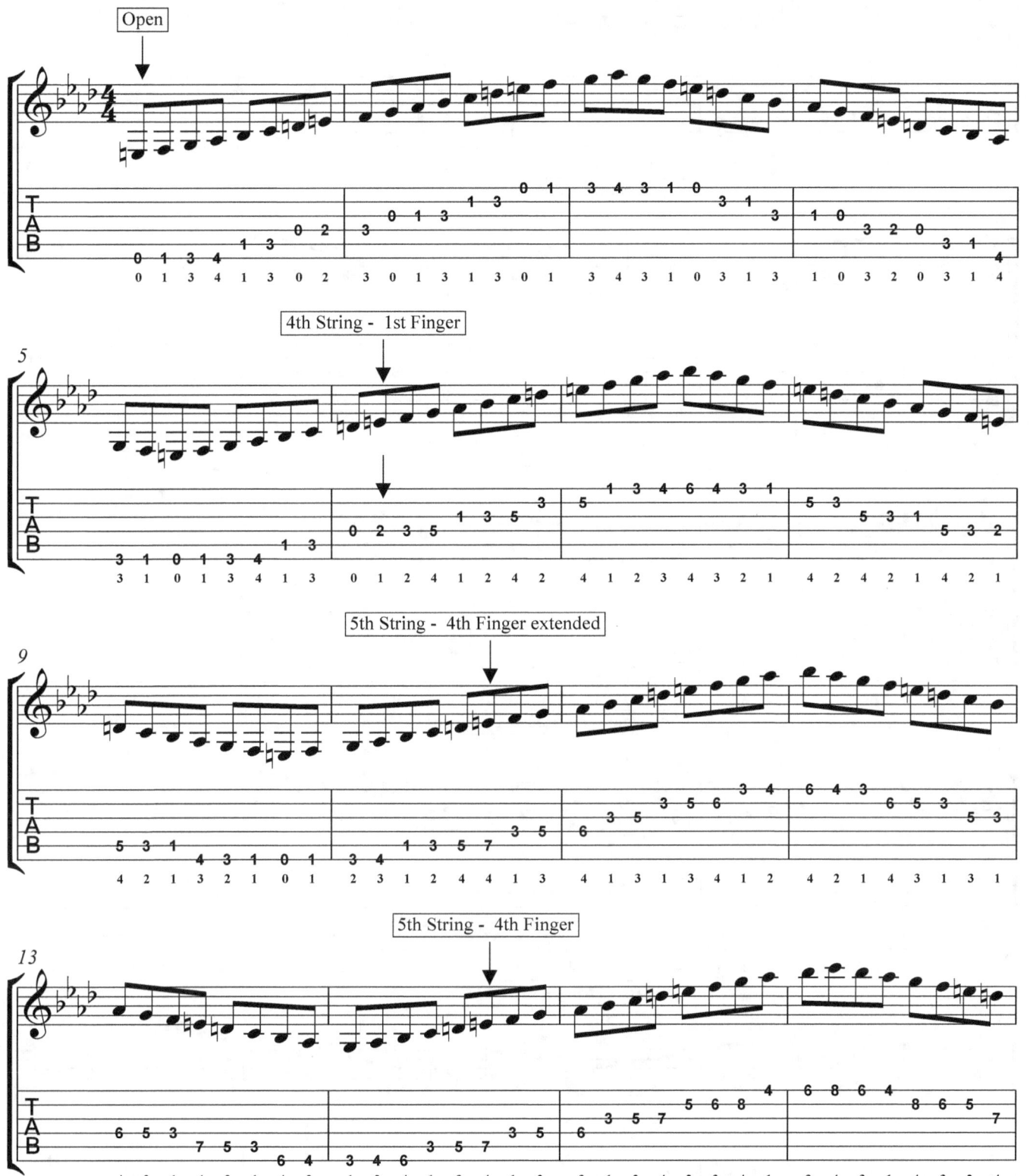

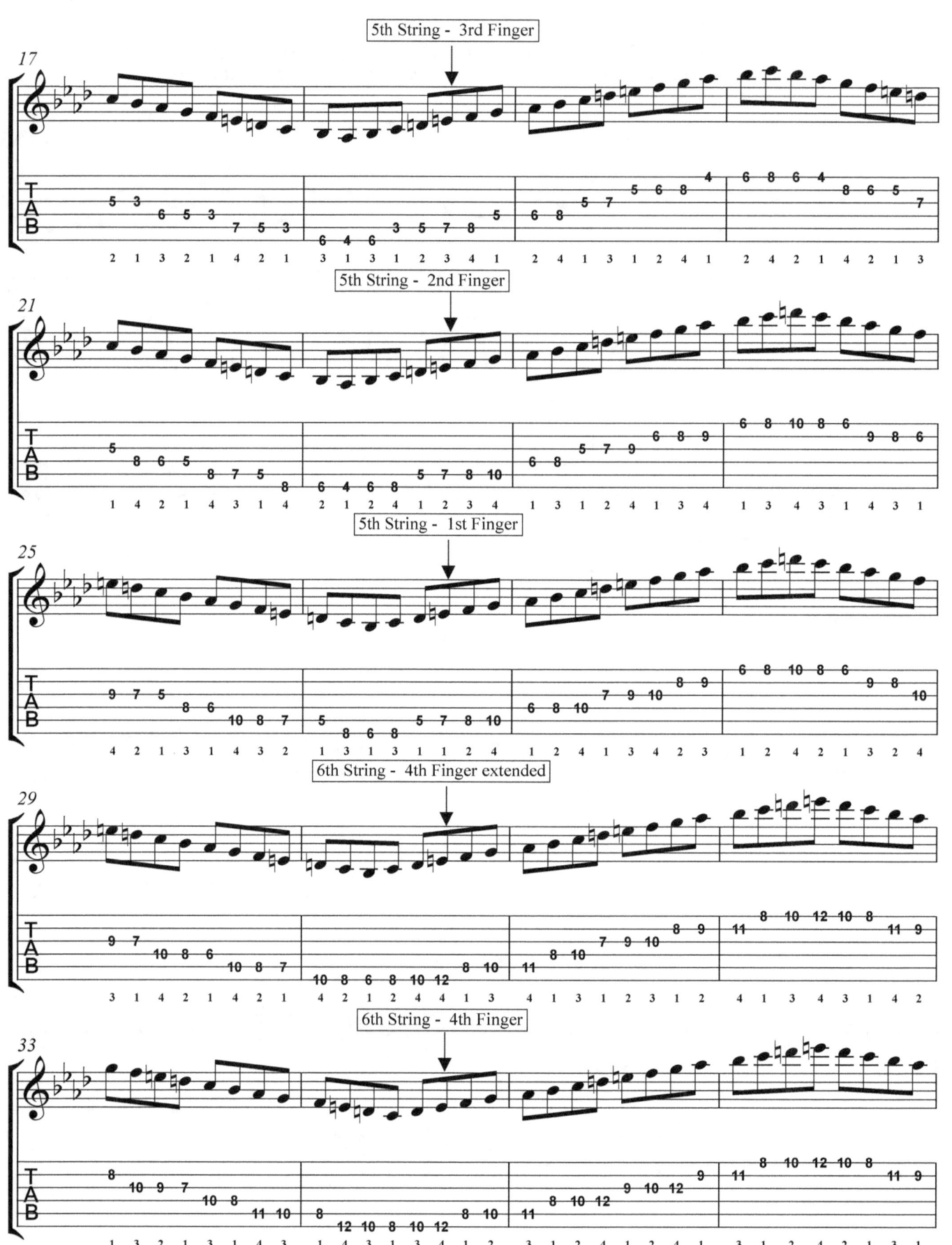

The following pages provide examples of playing scales and arpeggios vertically up and down the fretboard.

Mix this concept with the 12 patterns, to create an infinite number of possibilities for playing scales, modes, and arpeggios across the entire fretboard.

3 Octave Scales

G Major

G Natural Minor

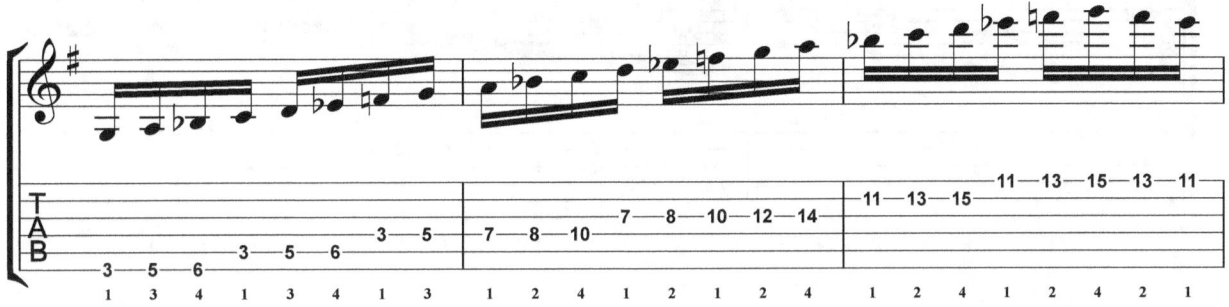

G Harmonic Minor

G Melodic Minor

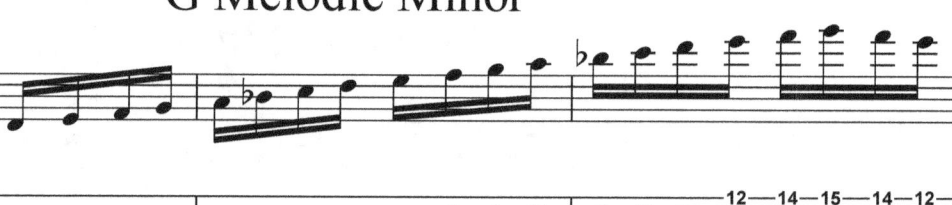

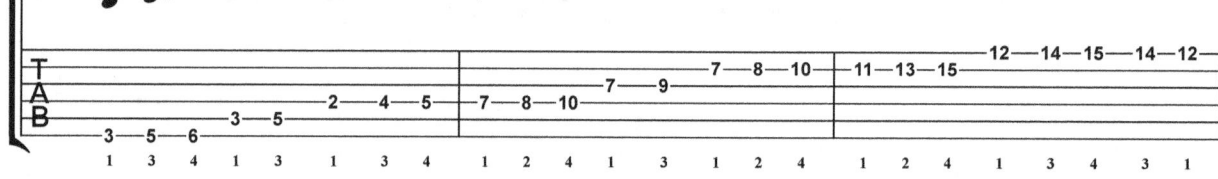

G Half Step-Whole Step

G Whole Step-Half Step

G Whole Tone

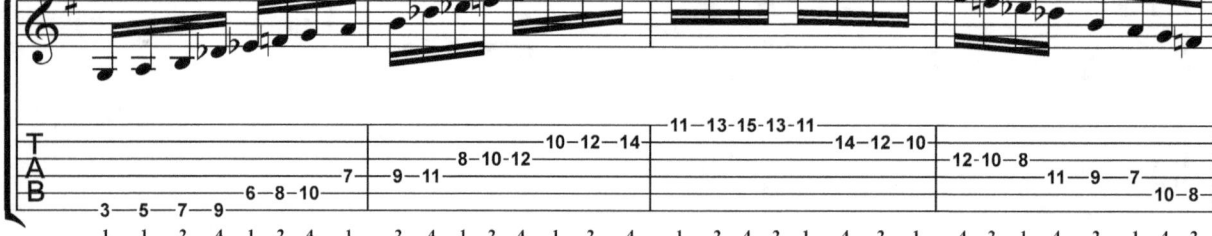

G Chromatic

3 Octave Major Arpeggios

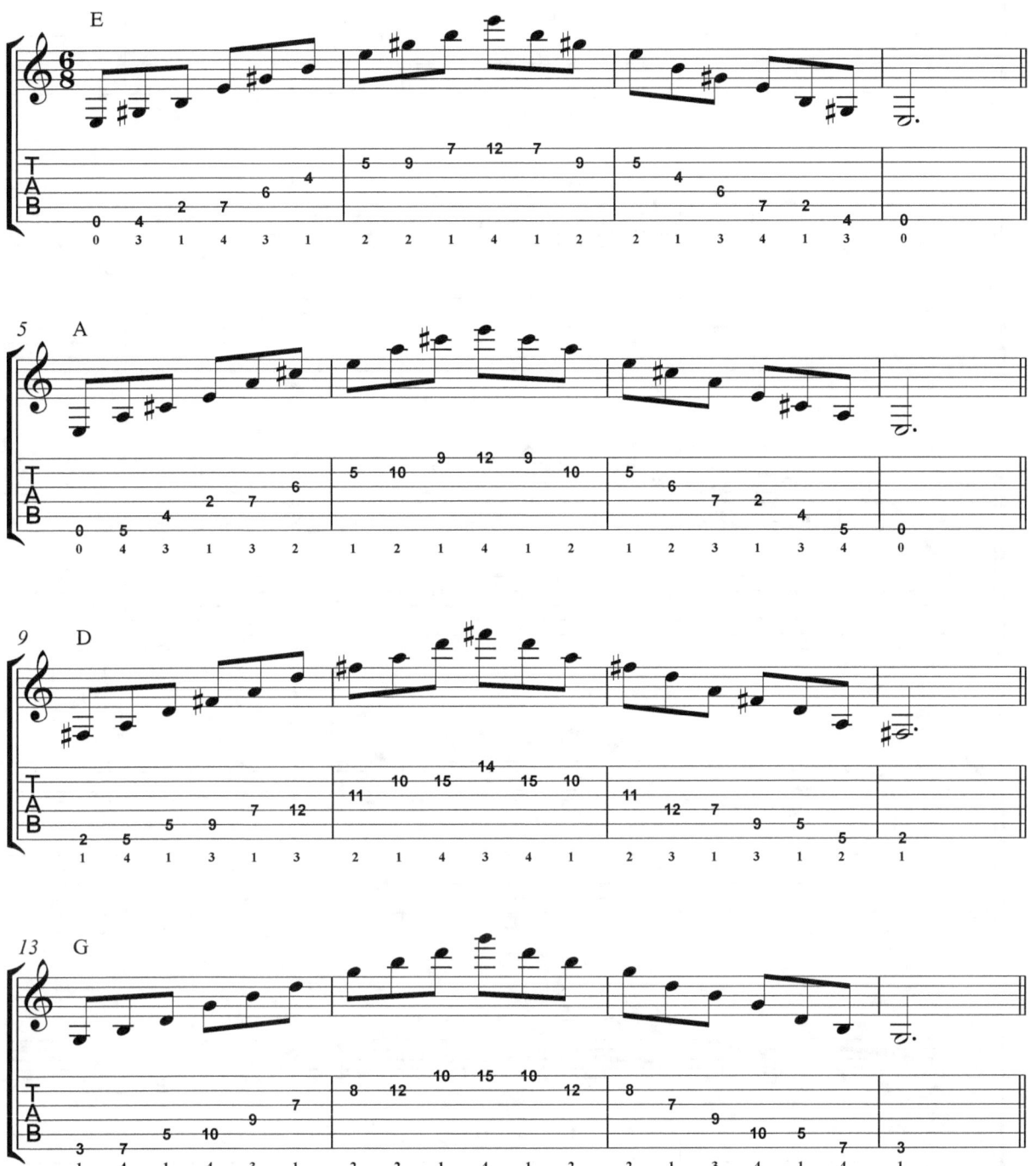

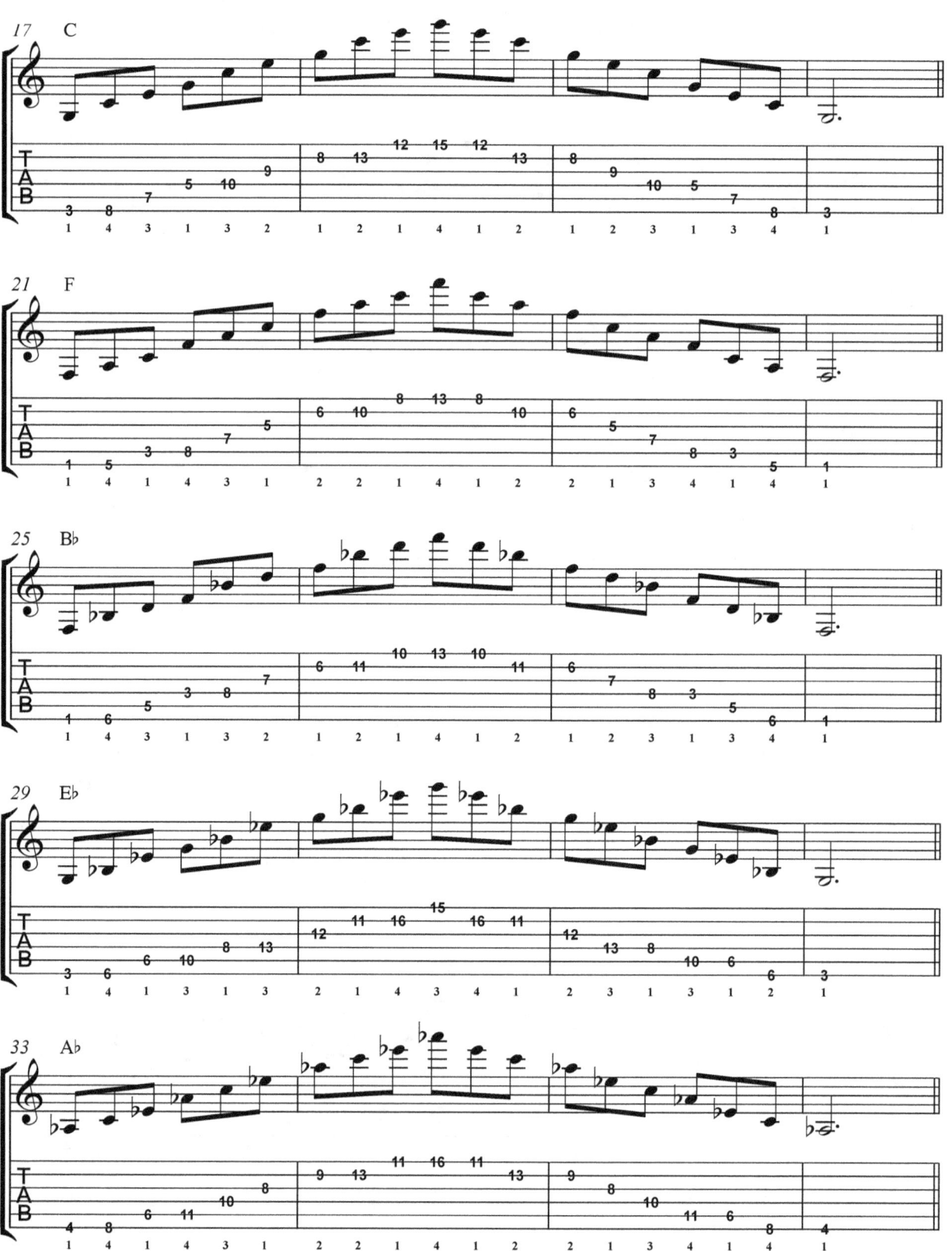

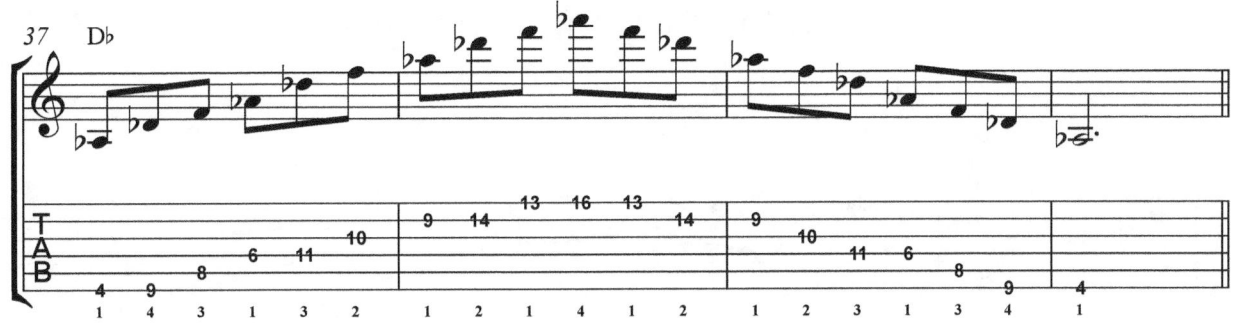

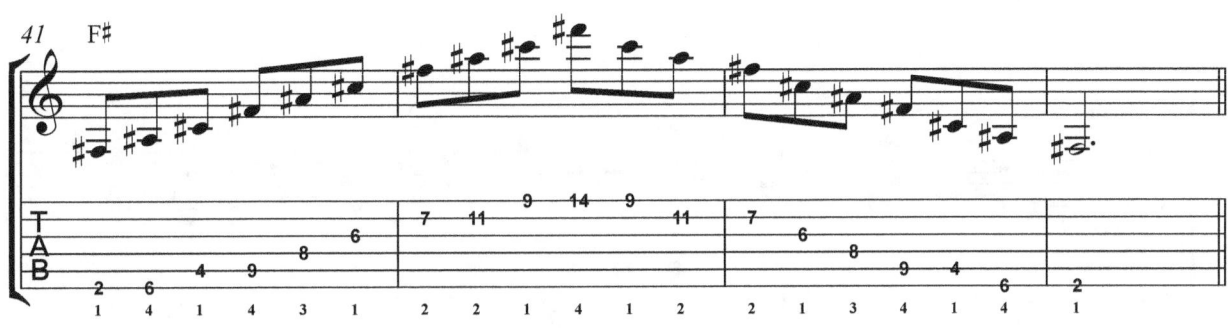

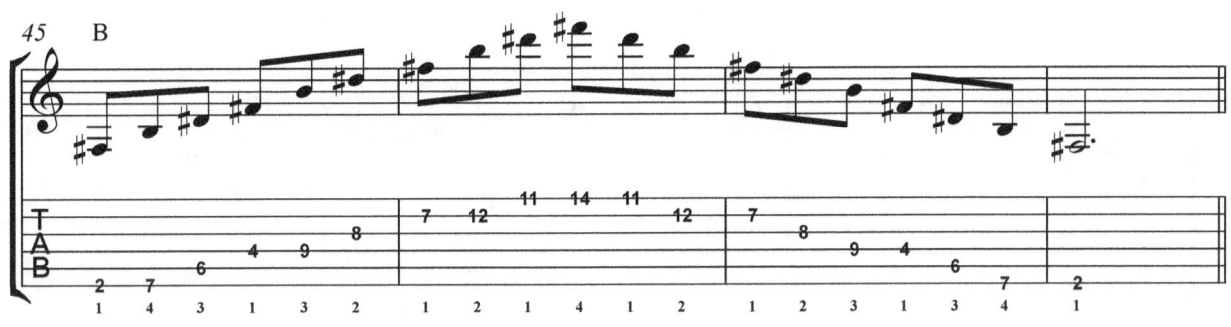

199

3 Octave Minor Arpeggios

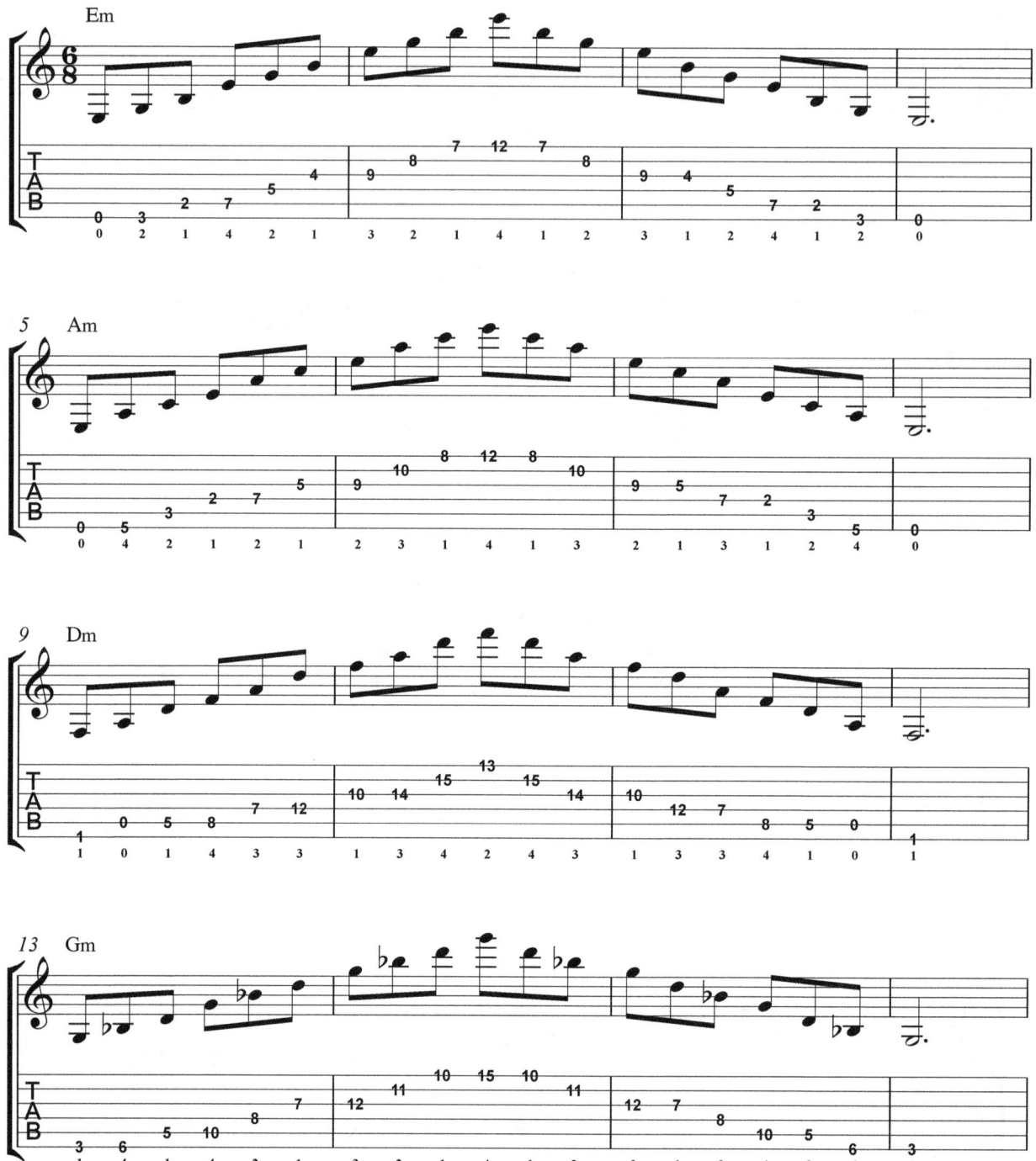

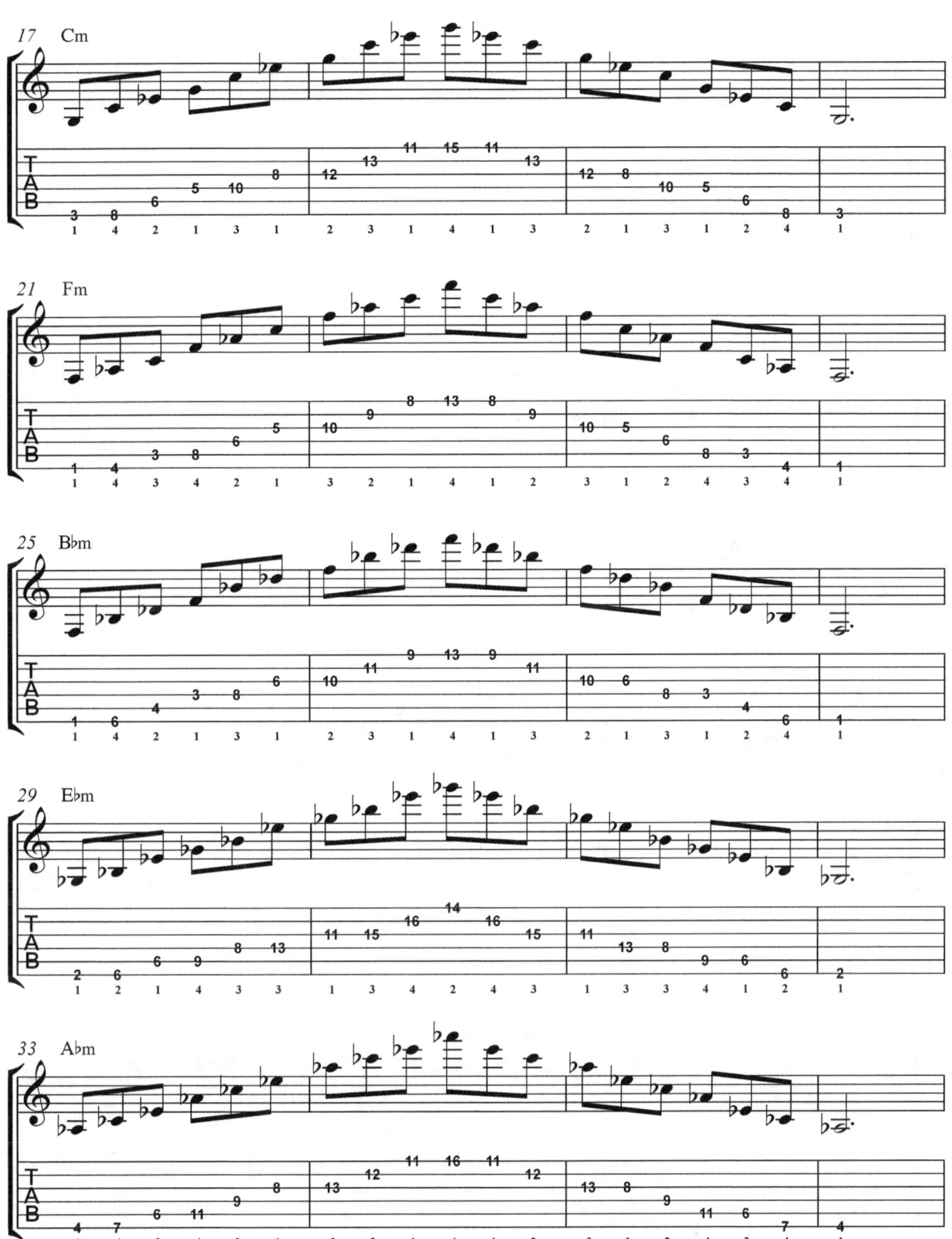

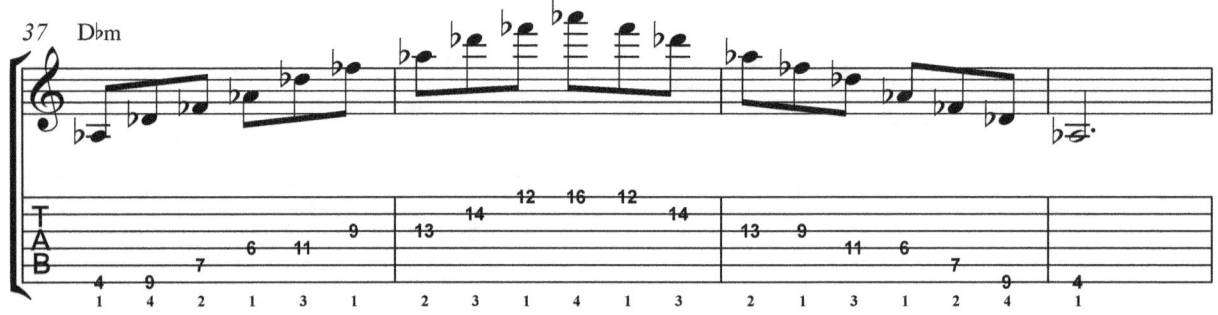
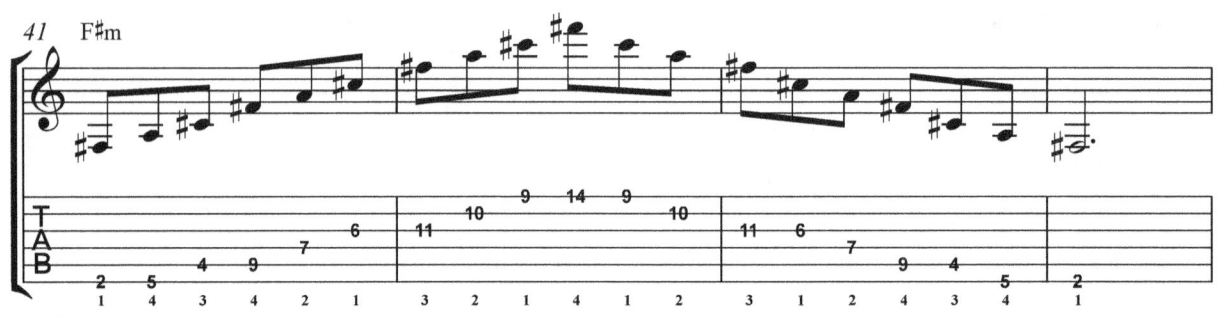
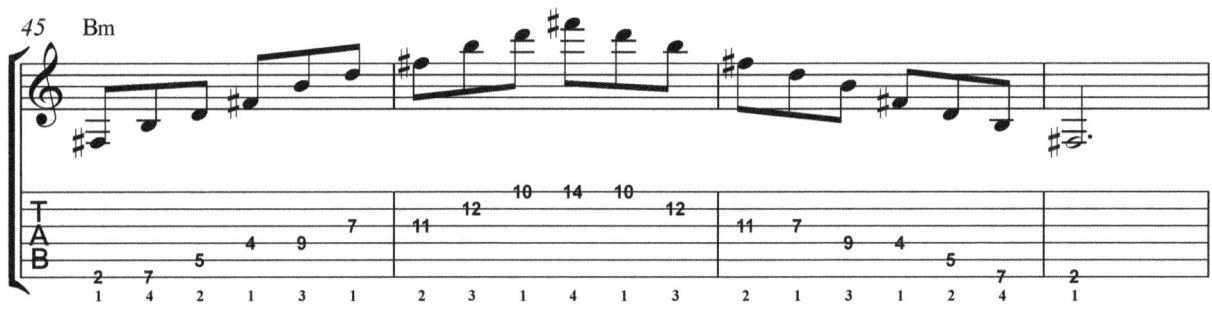
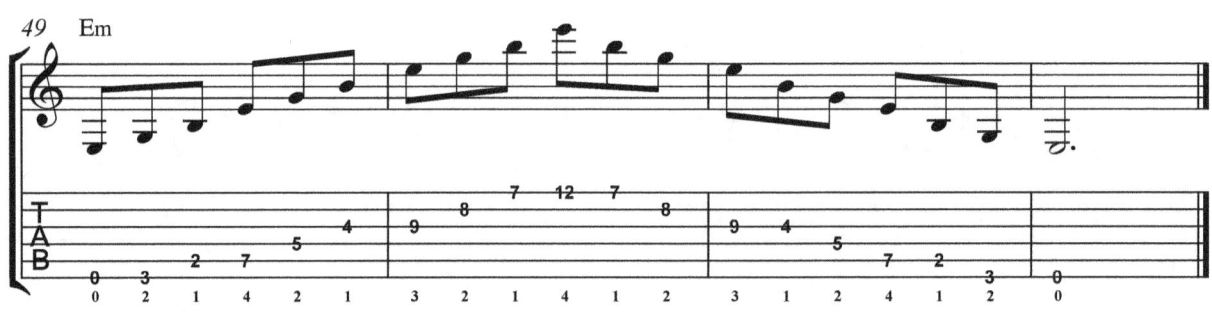

APPENDIX

Guitar Fretboard

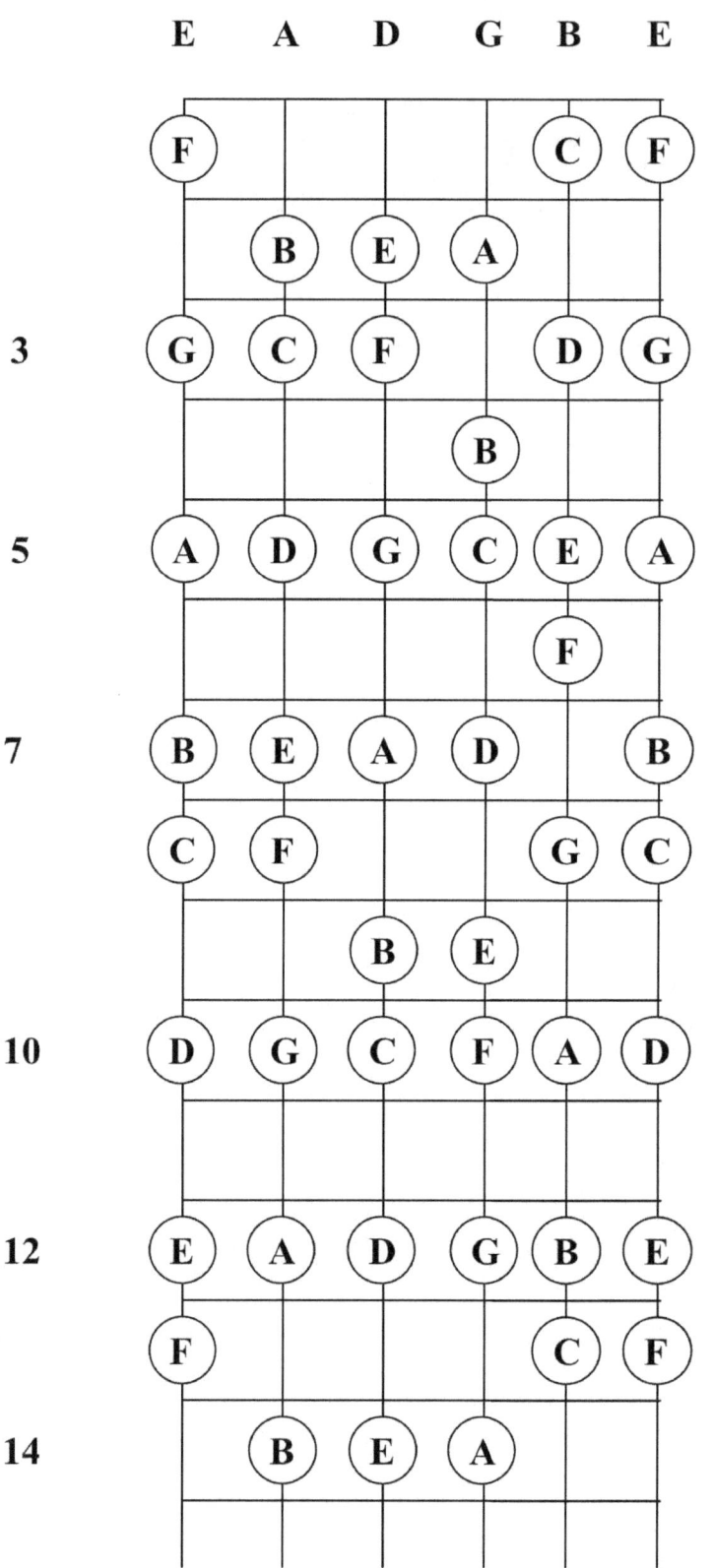

The Notes on Each String of the Guitar

Diatonic 7th Chords: Major Scale

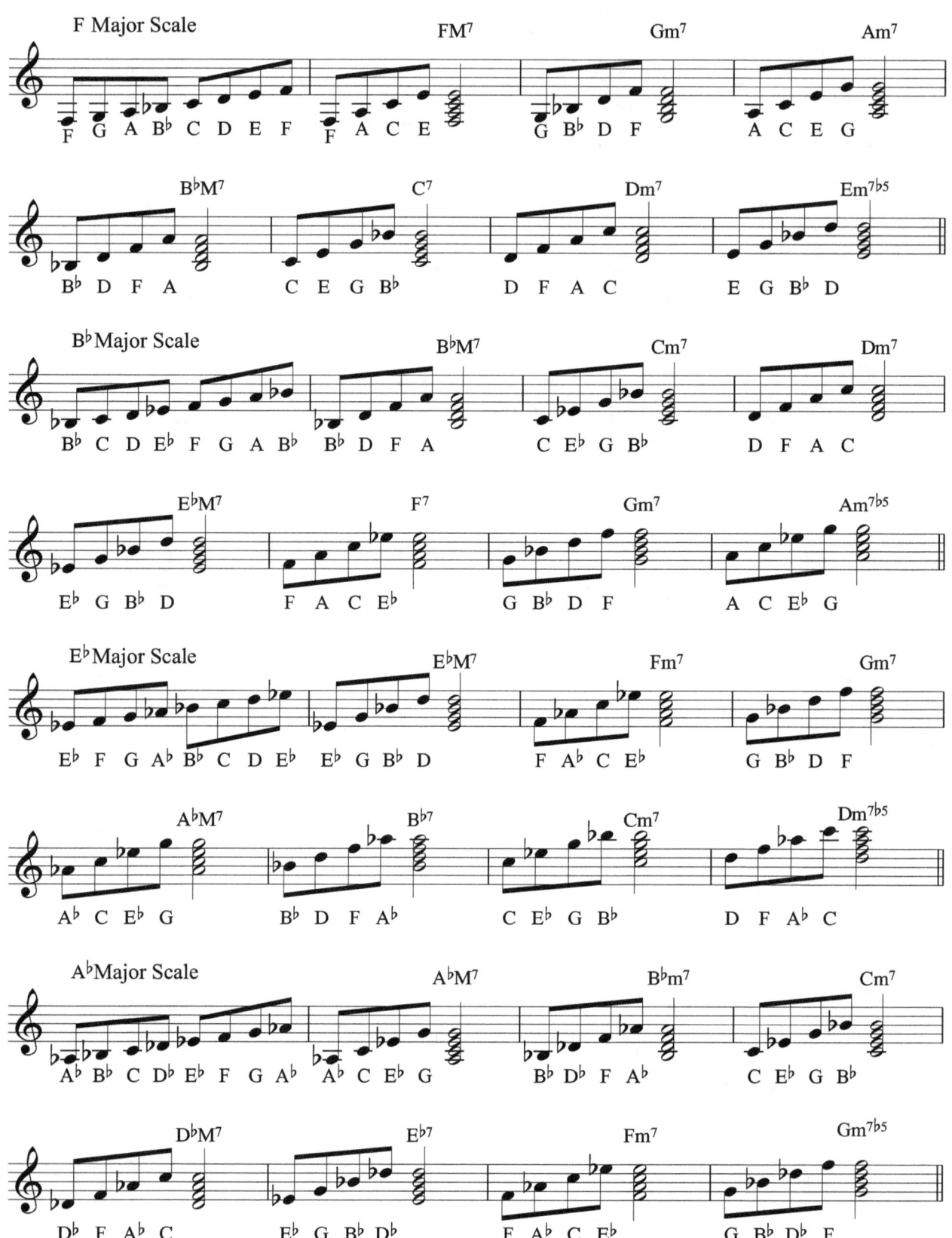

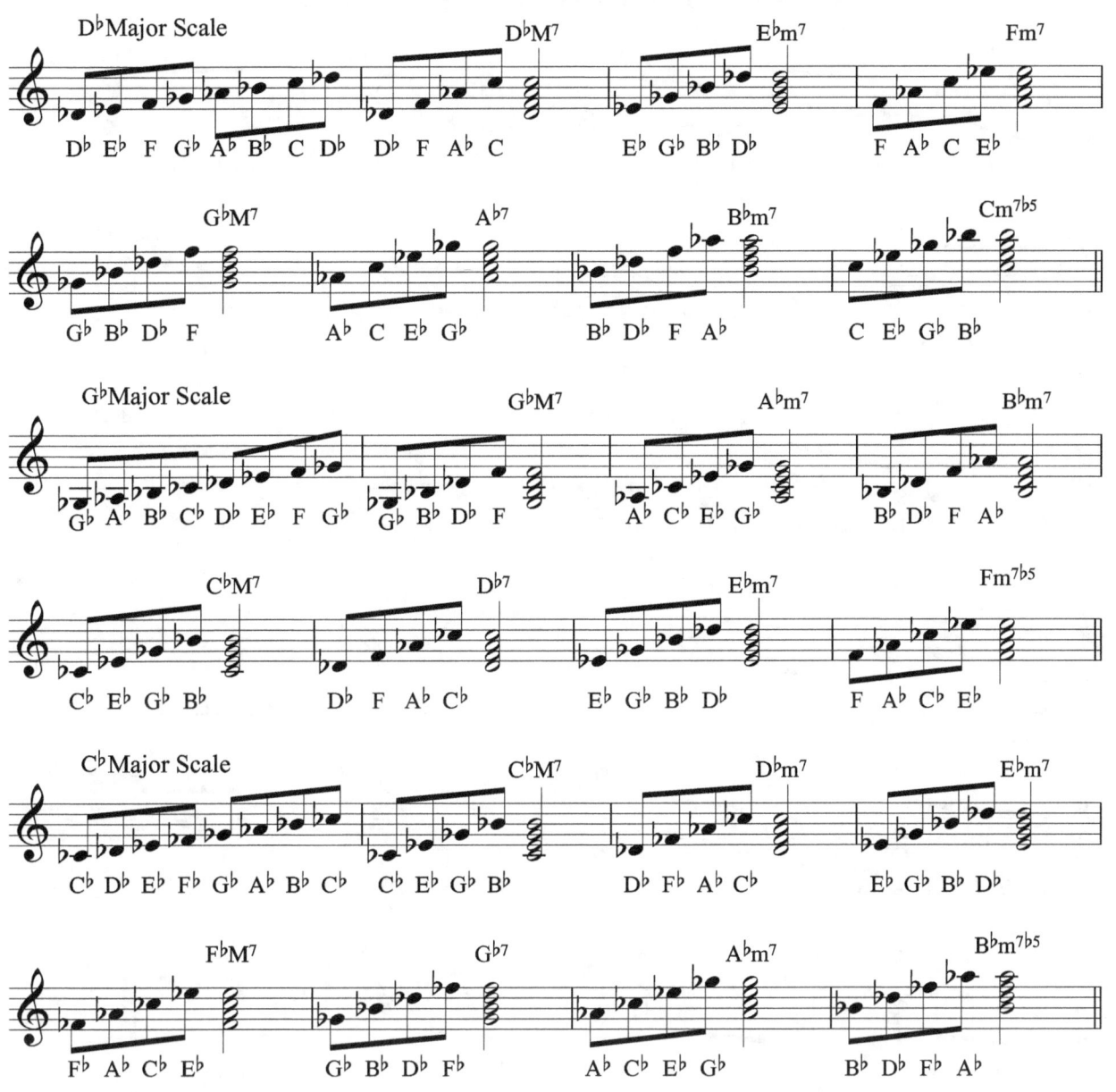

Diatonic 6th Chords: Major Scale

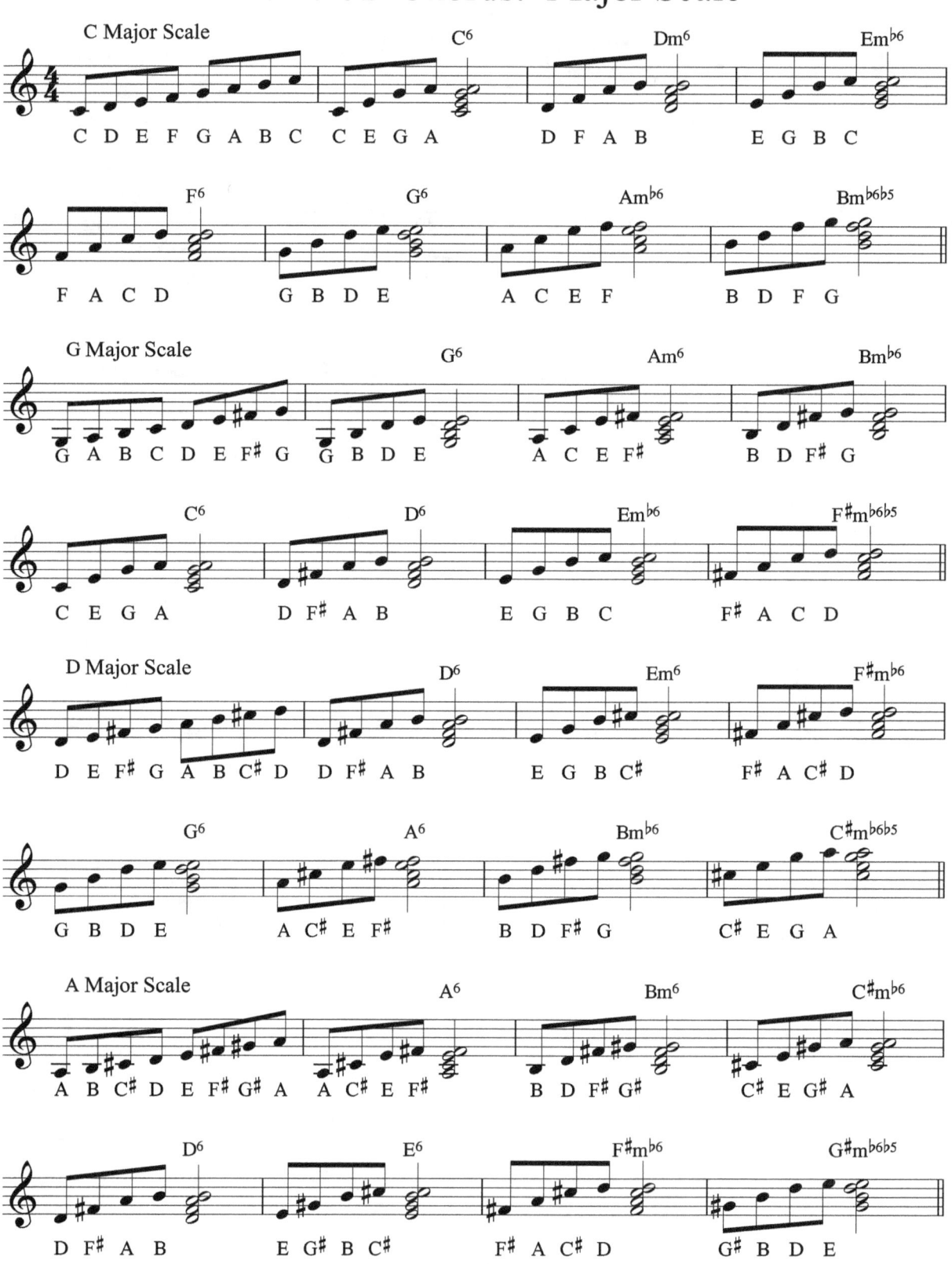

Diatonic 7th Chords: Melodic Minor Scale

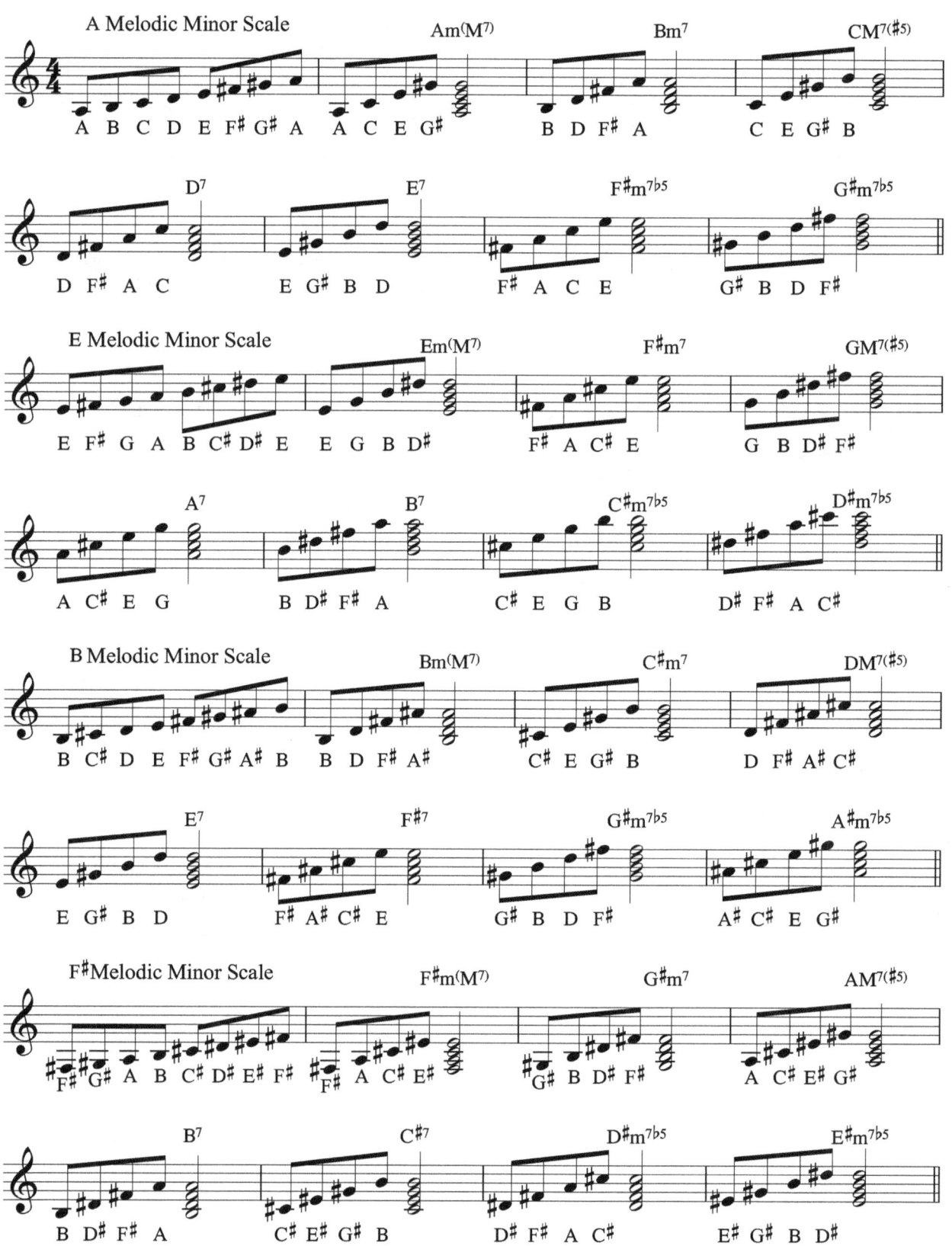

214

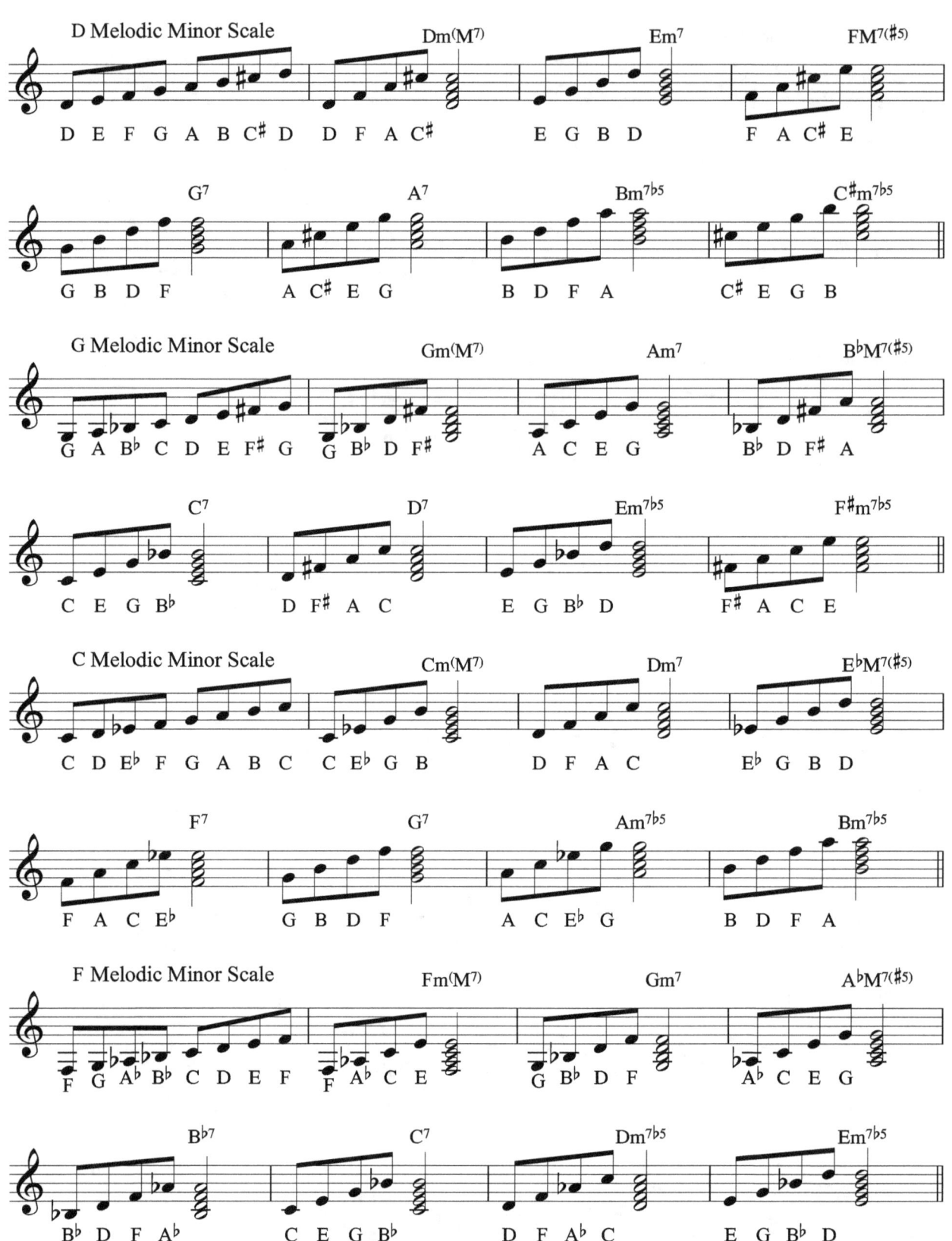

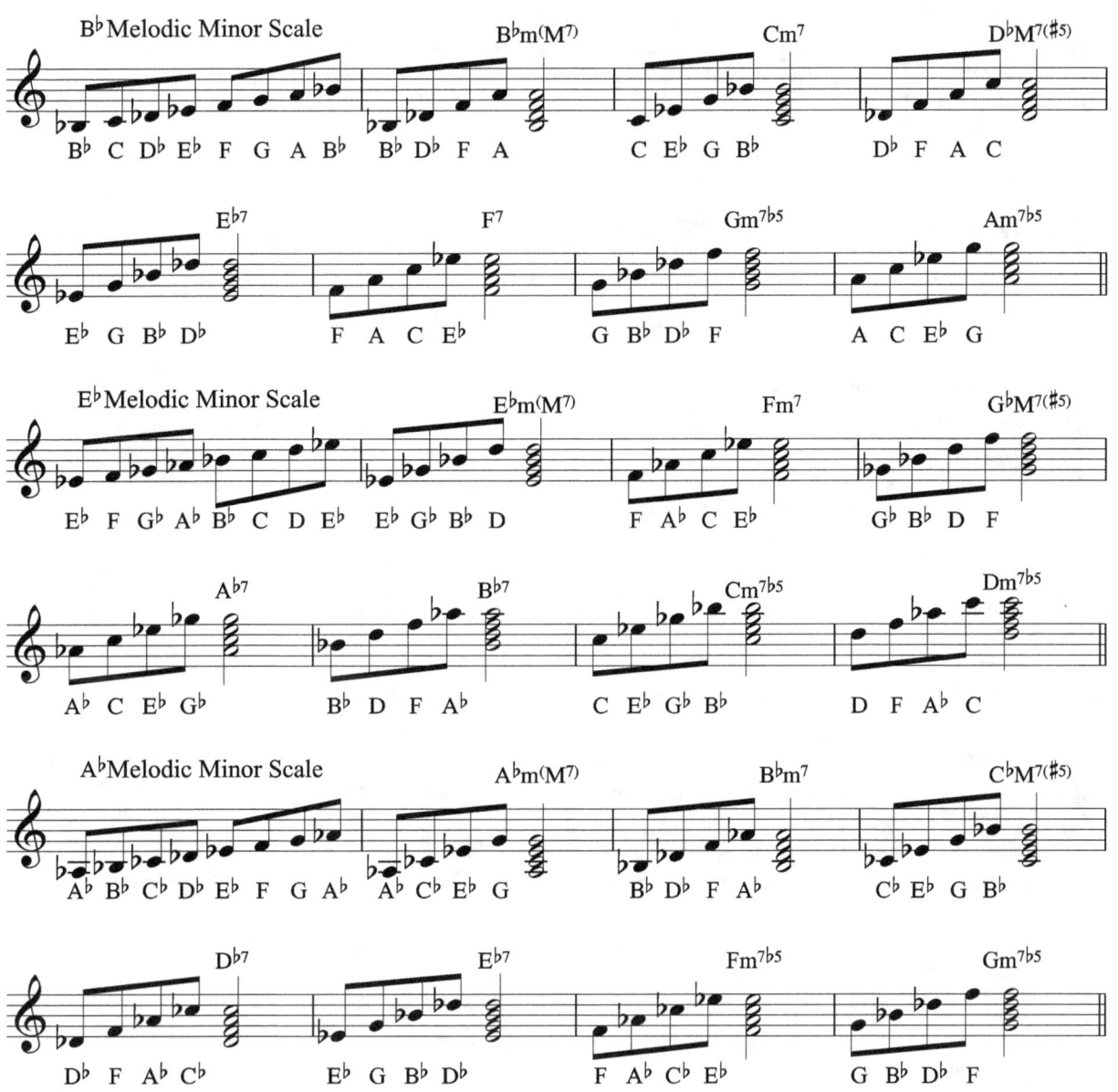

Diatonic 7th Chords: Harmonic Minor Scale

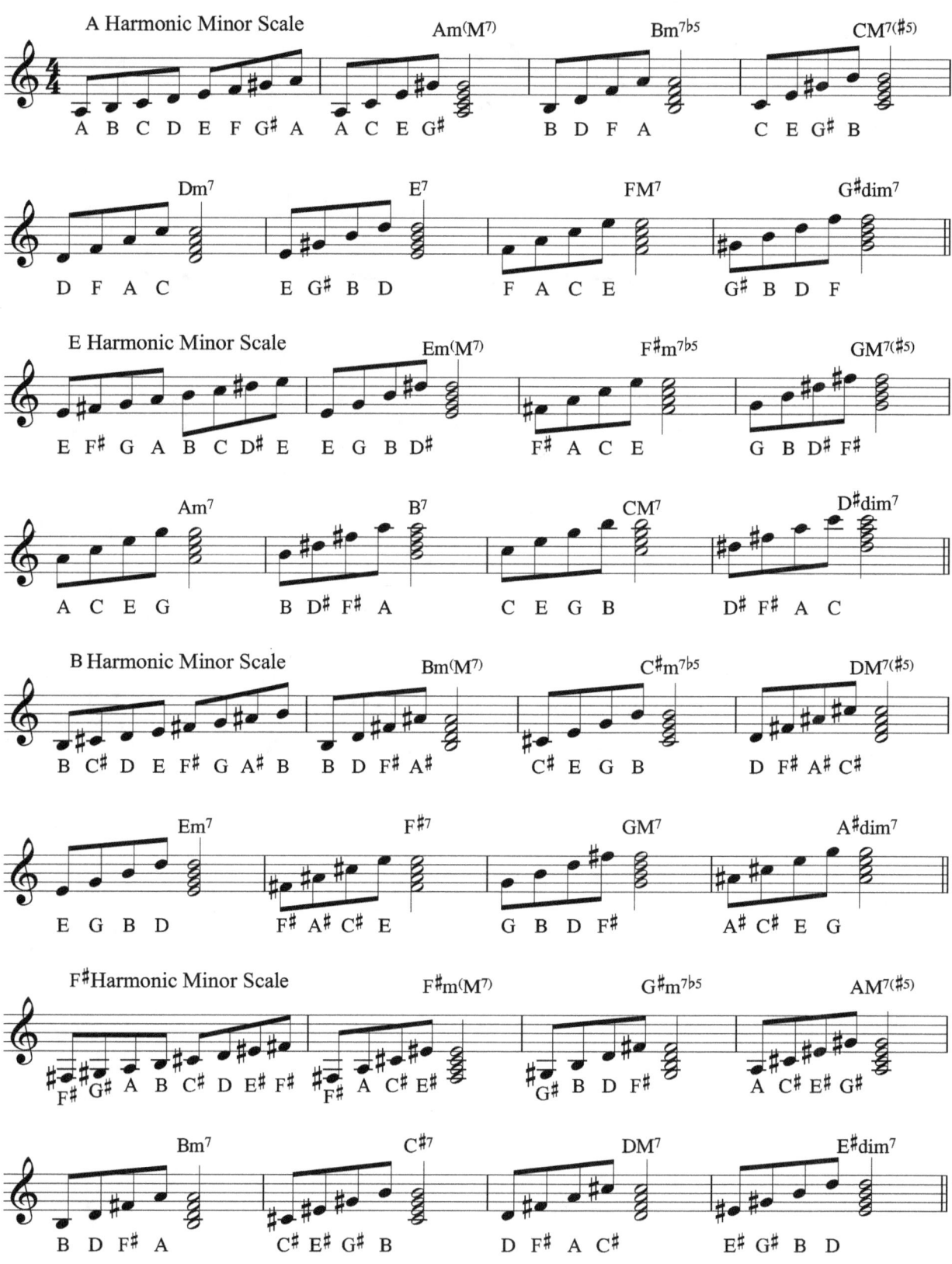

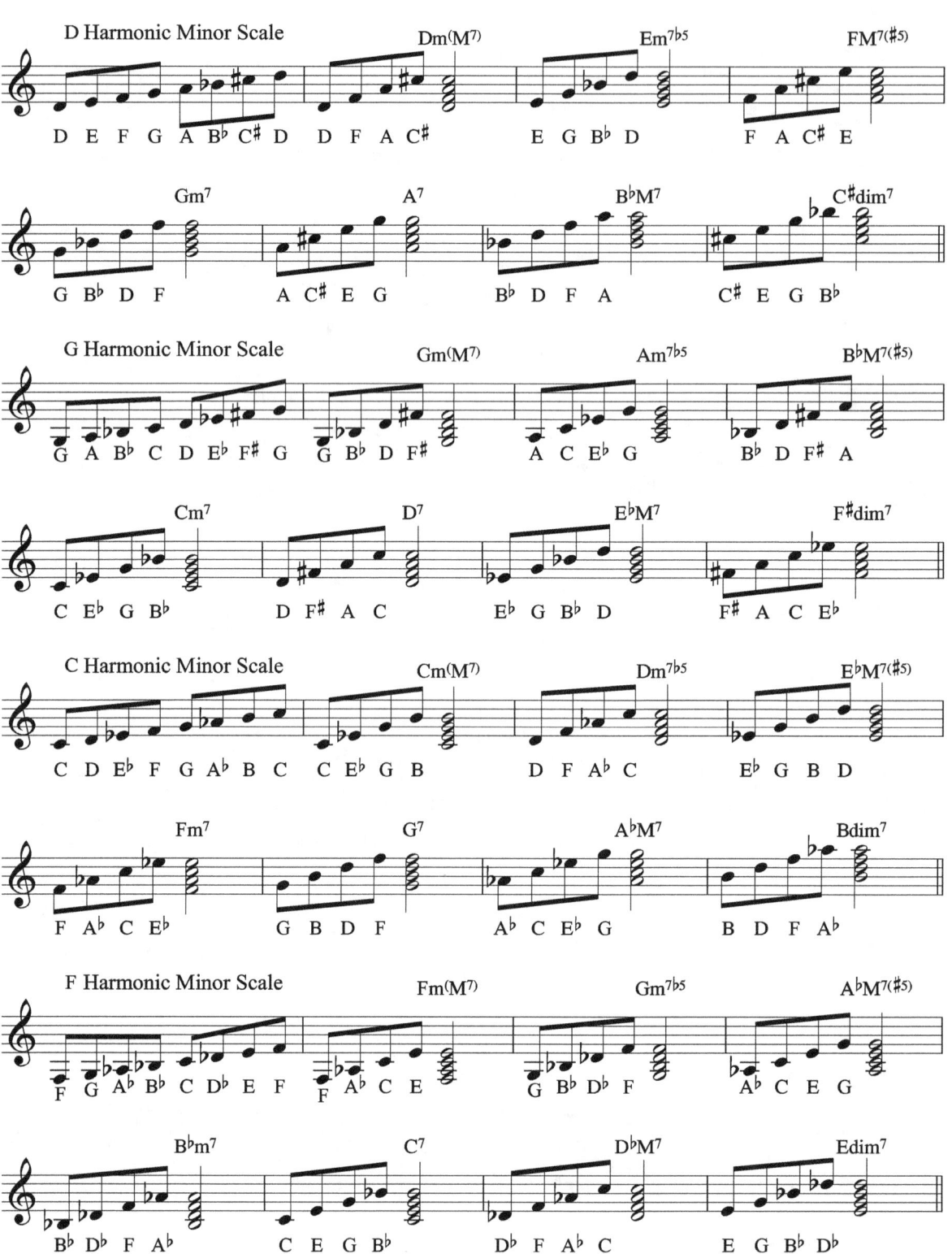

Sit

Think

Memorize

Learn

Practice

Pray

Play

For additional instructional material by David DeLoach, check out

www.MasterGuitarists.com

PSALM 33:3

www.ingramcontent.com/pod-product-compliance
Lightning Source LLC
Chambersburg PA
CBHW082316230426
43666CB00036B/2734